RECORDING A VANISHING LEGACY

NEW MEXICO ARCHITECTURAL
FOUNDATION

& THE
AMERICAN INSTITUTE OF ARCHITECTS,
ALBUQUERQUE CHAPTER

IN ASSOCIATION WITH THE
NEW MEXICO HISTORIC
PRESERVATION DIVISION

MUSEUM OF NEW MEXICO PRESS
SANTA FE

RECORDING A VANISHING LEGACY

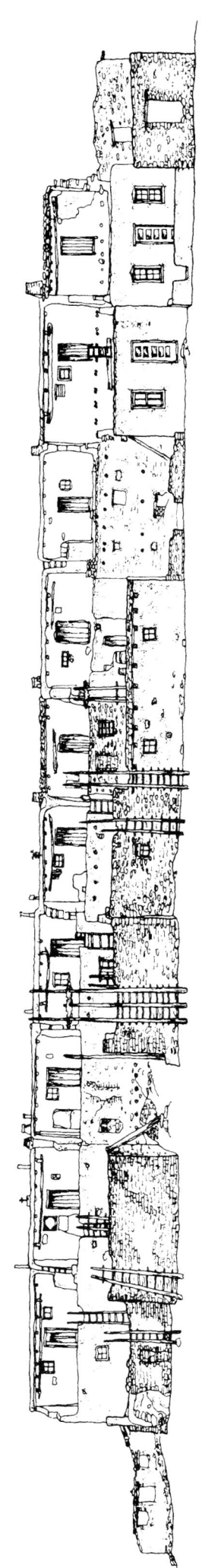

THE HISTORIC AMERICAN BUILDINGS SURVEY IN NEW MEXICO
1933 – TODAY

This publication has been financed in part by a grant from the New Mexico Historic Preservation Division with funds from the National Park Service, U.S. Department of the Interior. However, the contents and opinions expressed do not necessarily reflect the views or policies of the Historic Preservation Division or the Department of the Interior.

This program received Federal financial assistance for identification and protection of historic properties. Under Title VI of the Civil Rights Act of 1964, Section 504 of the Rehabilitation Act of 1973, and the Age Discrimination Act of 1975, as amended, the U.S. Department of the Interior prohibits discrimination on the basis of race, color, national origin, disability or age in its federally assisted programs. If you believe you have been discriminated against in any program, activity, or facility as described above, or if you desire further information, please write to:

Office of Equal Opportunity
National Park Service
1849 C Street, N.W.
Washington, D.C. 20240

Additional financial support has been provided by the New Mexico Architectural Foundation.

Copyright © 2001 New Mexico Historic Preservation Division, Office of Cultural Affairs. All rights reserved. No part of the book may be reproduced in any form or by any means whatsoever without the permission of the copyright holder and publisher.

All HABS drawings and photographs courtesy U.S. Dept. of the Interior, National Park Service.

Published by Museum of New Mexico Press, a unit of the Museum of New Mexico, Office of Cultural Affairs.

Library of Congress Cataloging-in-Production Data
Recording a vanishing legacy : the historic American buildings survey in New Mexico, 1933–today / New Mexico Architectural Foundation & the American Institute of Architects, in association with New Mexico Historic Preservation Division.
    p. cm.
Includes bibliographical references.
    ISBN 0-89013-379-4 (cloth) -
    ISBN 0-89013-386-8 (pbk.)
1. Historic buildings–Conservation and restoration–New Mexico. 2. Architecture–Conservation and restoration–New Mexico. 3. Historic American Buildings Survey–History. 4. History–Methodology. 5. Historic preservation–New Mexico. I. New Mexico Architectural Foundation. II. American Institute of Architects. III. New Mexico. Historic Preservation Division.

F797.R43 2001
720′.0789–dc21
                        00–48943

Project Editor:	Mary Wachs
Volume Editor:	Sally Hyer
Design:	Bruce Taylor Hamilton
Production Supervision:	David Skolkin

Set in Goudy Oldstyle with Charlemagne Display
Manufactured in Hong Kong

10 9 8 7 6 5 4 3 2 1

MUSEUM OF NEW MEXICO PRESS
Post Office Box 2087
Santa Fe, New Mexico 87504

CONTENTS

FOREWORD IX
CHARLES E. PETERSON

ACKNOWLEDGMENTS X

EDITOR'S
ACKNOWLEDGMENTS XI

SPONSORS XII

THE HISTORIC AMERICAN
BUILDINGS SURVEY XIII

PART ONE:
BACKGROUND

CHAPTER 1
THE HISTORY OF HABS
NATIONWIDE 1
JAMES C. MASSEY

CHAPTER 2
HABS RECORDING IN
NEW MEXICO 9
SALLY HYER

PART TWO:
FIRST-PERSON ACCOUNTS

CHAPTER 3
THE 1934
HABS PROJECT 23
VICTOR HORNBEIN

CHAPTER 4
THE BAINBRIDGE
BUNTING YEARS 39
AGNESA REEVE AND
RICHARD SCHALK

CHAPTER 5
PHOTOGRAMMETRIC
RECORDING OF
COMMUNAL
ARCHITECTURE 47
PERRY E. BORCHERS

CHAPTER 6
HABS
RECORDING TODAY 57
MORGAN RIEDER

PART THREE: NEW MEXICO ARCHITECTURE

CHAPTER 7
PUEBLO STRUCTURES AND WORLDVIEW 69
RINA SWENTZELL

CHAPTER 8
RESIDENTIAL RECORDING 75
GEORGE CLAYTON PEARL

CHAPTER 9
RELIGIOUS ARCHITECTURE AND SITES 83
CHRIS WILSON

CHAPTER 10
CIVIC BUILDINGS 93
CHARLES D. BIEBEL

CONCLUSION 101
SALLY HYER

PART FOUR: HABS INVENTORY FOR NEW MEXICO

HOW TO USE THE INVENTORY 103

NEW MEXICO INVENTORY 105
SALLY HYER

APPENDIXES

APPENDIX A
ADDITIONAL RESOURCES FOR HABS RESEARCH 126

APPENDIX B
HABS COLLECTIONS IN NEW MEXICO 129
JAN DODSON BARNHART AND CAROL JOINER

NOTES 135

GLOSSARY OF ARCHITECTURAL TERMS 139
CARLEEN LAZZELL AND BOYD C. PRATT

SELECTED BIBLIOGRAPHY 143

RECORDING A VANISHING LEGACY

CHARLES E. PETERSON

Charles E. Peterson (b. 1906) is an emeritus fellow of the American Institute of Architects, a recipient of many awards, including the Thomas Jefferson Award for Public Architecture, 2000, and an architect of many historic building restorations. He began his career with the National Park Service in 1929 as a landscape architect with a degree from the University of Minnesota; he retired in 1962 but to this day is active in preservation activities. As the creator of HABS and the person who almost single-handedly helped secure its continuation after World War II, Peterson is one of the most influential figures in the field of architectural preservation in the twentieth century.

FOREWORD

CHARLES E. PETERSON

It is a pleasure to look back — if only on paper — to a truly wonderful part of this great country.

My introduction to the American Southwest came early. In 1914, out of a Minnesota winter, my mother took me to visit California. I remember sight-seeing the imagined haunts of Helen Hunt Jackson's 1884 novel, heroine of Ramona, and the colonial San Gabriel Mission. Both were duly recorded for the family snap-shot album. We also collected postcards in color to be shown by a sheet-metal Radiopticon and shared with neighbors back home.

Much later, in 1930 when I began to work with the National Park Service, engineer Kenneth McCarter took me from our headquarters in San Francisco to Arizona to inspect the problems at the prehistoric Casa Grande and to Jesuit Father Kino's Tumacácori Mission. Later that year I was with Department of the Interior archaeologist Jesse L. Nusbaum in Santa Fe. On that occasion he dug the first ceremonial steam-shovelful of earth, making ready for the new anthropological laboratory. Soon after, his wife and son Derek climbed with me to a flat roof in Santo Domingo to watch the Great Corn Dance. Moonlight at Taos Pueblo is vividly remembered.

Although I had hoped to stay outdoors in the western parks, I ended up indoors in the East. But the memories never faded. And when in Washington I outlined the program for the Historic American Buildings Survey — it was in November of 1933 — I specifically recommended that the pueblos of New Mexico be considered for study, measurement, and drawing up. Subsequently, it was cheering to learn that a contingent of Denver architects went down to work on those picturesque villages.

Much later Professor Perry E. Borchers of Ohio State University began exercising his talent in the arcane field of architectural photogrammetry. The first HABS record we commissioned was of the intricate design of the Plum Street Temple in Cincinnati — drawn on a plotting machine. We reported that apparatus as "The Magic Scaffold," publishing in 1958 an elevation in the *Journal of the Society of Architectural Historians*. Later it proved to be just the right technique for recording ancient Pueblo complexes where there are few right angles — a tough problem for draftsmen with T-squares. I am glad to hear that Mr. Borchers has now completed his work.

I hope that HABS continues to make progress in New Mexico as more and more of the American past comes under appreciation and study.

Society Hill, Philadelphia
July 4, 2000

ACKNOWLEDGMENTS

Recording a Vanishing Legacy: The Historic American Buildings Survey in New Mexico, 1933 – Today, was produced under the auspices of the New Mexico Architectural Foundation.

The Historic Resources Committee of the American Institute of Architects (AIA), Albuquerque Chapter, with the assistance of Thomas W. Merlan, former New Mexico State Historic Preservation Officer, conceptualized and compiled this publication. Without the enthusiasm of this committee for New Mexico architectural history, and the financial support of HPD, this project would never have reached fruition.

The members of the Albuquerque Chapter of the American Institute of Architecture, Historic Resources Committee were:

Terrance Brown, FAIA, Steven Kells, AIA, Virginia Kupferman, AIA, Andrew Acoya, AIA, Jan Dodson Barnhart, Edgar Boles, Concepción Lopez-Cherry, Sally Hyer, Barbara Daniels, Carleen Lazzell, and George Pearl, FAIA.

Special recognition is due to Concepción Lopez-Cherry for sharing her design skills with the committee.

The New Mexico Historic Preservation Division enlisted Sally Hyer to organize and edit the manuscript. After editing, the AIA Historic Resources Committee entrusted the manuscript to The New Mexico Architectural Foundation to facilitate publication.

The New Mexico Architectural Foundation Publication Committee was formed to publish books and articles focusing on New Mexico architecture. We are very pleased that Recording a Vanishing Legacy is our initial volume. The HABS projects in New Mexico records our unique architectural history, and they continue to educate our architectural students and involve people with the New Mexico landscape.

The New Mexico Architectural Foundation is grateful to the members of their Publication Committee for their energy, and hard work. Their dedication and professionalism have kept this project on course.

The members of the Publication Committee of the New Mexico Architectural Fundation are:

Virginia Kupferman, AIA, Chair; Jan Dodson Barnhart; Edgar Boles; Terrance Brown, FAIA; Andrew Acoya, AIA; and George Pearl, FAIA.

The New Mexico Architectural Foundation Publications Committee extends a special thank you to George Pearl for his enthusiasm, time and support. Sally Hyer's patience and encouragement has been invaluable to the Chair of the Publication Committee during this process.

Special thanks to the Intermountain Support Office-Santa Fe, of the United States Department of the Interior, National Park Service and to Bob Spude, Program Manager Cultural Resources and National Register Program Services, for their support and encouragement.

Virginia S. Kupferman, President
New Mexico Architectural Foundation
Albuquerque, New Mexico

EDITOR'S ACKNOWLEDGMENTS

The editor wishes to acknowledge the help of the following organizations and individuals in the preparation of this publication:

Eileen Bolger, National Archives-Rocky Mountain Region; Perry E. Borchers, Professor Emeritus of Architecture, Ohio State University; Barbara Daniels, of Owl Editing, manuscript review of an early draft; Amalin Ferguson, Librarian, National Park Service; Monroe Freeman, Textual Projects Division, National Archives; Alison K. Hoagland, Senior Historian, Historic American Buildings Survey; Victor Hornbein, FAIA (Emeritus); Marilyn Ibach, Reference Specialist, Prints and Photographs Division, Library of Congress; Mary M. Ison, Head, Reference Section, Prints and Photographs Division, Library of Congress; Min Kantrowitz, Manuscript Review; Dr. Robert J. Kapsch, Chief, Historic American Buildings Survey/Historic American Engineering Record; Richard Z. Kristin, Assistant Professor of Spanish, College of Santa Fe; Thomas W. Merlan, Former New Mexico State Preservation Office; Donna Quasthoff, Manuscript Review; Richard West Sellars, Historian, National Park Service; Mr. and Mrs. Dudley T. Smith; Ginger Tate, Architects Board of Examiners, Denver, Colorado; Jerry I. Wallace, National Archives; and Tony Wrenn, American Institute of Architects Archives.

Sally Hyer
Santa Fe, New Mexico

SPONSORS

The Publication Committee of the New Mexico Architectural Foundation and the Historic Resources Committee of the Albuquerque Chapter of the AIA wish to thank the following individuals and groups who made this publication possible:

MAJOR SPONSORS
New Mexico Architectural Foundation
George Clayton Pearl
David F. Myrick
John D. and Nancy Meem Wirth
Ruth Hollister Smith and Dudley Tyler Smith, Jr.
Holm O. and Earle Powell Bursum III
College of Fellows Fund of the American Institute of Architects, American Architectural Foundation
Historic Resources Committee, American Institute of Architects, Albuquerque Chapter

SPONSORS
BPLW Architects & Engineers, Inc.
Bradbury & Stamm Construction

CONTRIBUTORS
Kells + Craig Architects
Stuart and Virginia Kupferman
Terrance Brown, FAIA, and Sandra Brown
Van and Sandy Gilbert; Van H. Gilbert, Architects
In Memory of Mrs. Art (Marcella) Dekker by Bradbury & Stamm
Jan Dodson Barnhart

SUPPORTERS
Michael and Linda K. Ogilvie Beltran
Christine Moe and William A. Tuttle
Robert J. Torrez
Raymond A. Trujillo
Robert Slattery Construction, Inc.
Jim and Ann Carson
Weller Architects
R.W. Reisscher
Hal Dean
Octavia Fellin
Gary Embler

Concha Ortiz y Pino de Kleven
Edgar Boles
Dale Zinn
Cherry/See Architects
Sanders Rogers, Architects
John Briscoe, Architect
Beverly Spears
Roger Schluntz, FAIA
Glenn Fellows & Patricia Hancock
Tyler Mason
Albuquerque Reprographics, Inc.

FRIENDS
Joel C. Wooldridge and Duffy Wooldridge
RJ Dean and Assoc.
Britton Construction
Donna Quasthoff

THE HISTORIC AMERICAN BUILDINGS SURVEY IN NEW MEXICO

Unlike many other states' HABS catalogs, *Recording a Vanishing Legacy* is neither an architectural history nor a descriptive update of sites and structures. Instead, it is an overview of HABS recording projects in New Mexico as seen through the eyes of the original New Mexican architects and scholars, and field crews, New Mexican architects and scholars, and a former national chief of HABS. The resulting spectrum illuminates the history of architectural recording in this century in New Mexico. The book also shows how HABS, the depression-era creation of a federal employee, has lent a seventy-year administrative framework for the documentation of New Mexico's architecture. The survey has made it possible for architects and historians to record and study New Mexico's ancient Pueblo communities, plaza-centered Hispanic villages of the eighteenth and nineteenth centuries, and railroad-era main streets of commerce and tourism.

Part one of this unique study provides historical background on HABS nationwide and in New Mexico. The survey was initiated by the Works Progress Administration in 1933 as a short-term relief project. HABS activities were suspended with the advent of World War II but renewed in 1957, when Congress funded the Mission 66 Program to bring National Park Service properties up to proper standards within a decade. HABS was reorganized and centralized in 1966, when it was placed under the Office of Archaeology and Historic Preservation of the National Park Service. Between 1978 and 1981, a short-lived restructuring effort merged HABS and the Historic American Engineering Record (HAER) with the National Architectural and Engineering Record, which joined other Department of the Interior programs to form a new agency, the Heritage Conservation and Recreation Service. Since 1981, HABS/HAER has been a division of the NPS headquarters located in Washington, DC.

Part two is a collection of first-person accounts by HABS supervising architects and team members from 1934 on that illustrate changing concepts of historic preservation, developing recording standards and techniques, and differing notions about what is worth recording and why. In part three, prominent New Mexican architects and scholars evaluate the survey and make use of HABS records in chapters on the state's residential, religious, and civic architecture and on Pueblo attitudes towards architectural documentation. Part four is an annotated listing of HABS sites, projects, and personnel.

The most recent HABS inventory lists New Mexico holdings of approximately 1,200 measured drawings and photographs of nearly 150 sites. However, the impact of the concept of HABS in New Mexico goes beyond the Library of Congress collections. It has been the motivating force behind the majority of architectural documentation in the state. This influence has resulted in some confusion. For example, the term "HABS drawing" has been applied to projects regardless of whether the

HABS format was strictly followed or the drawings were ever submitted to — let alone accepted by — HABS.

This publication includes discussions of two important sets of measured drawings that were inspired by the HABS concept: the Bainbridge Bunting student drawings and Perry E. Borchers's measured drawings prepared by means of photogrammetry. A portion of each collection has been acquired by HABS and processed by the Library of Congress. However, other drawings were not officially part of the survey and are now in New Mexican archives. These collections are documented in Appendix B, "HABS Collections in New Mexico," and referred to throughout the book.

The following pages summarize HABS terminology and abbreviations used and give a brief chronological listing of HABS dates.

HISTORIC AMERICAN BUILDINGS SURVEY SITES, NEW MEXICO

Counties in dark gray are shown in enlarged map at right. Counties in white have no survey sites. The figure in parentheses indicates the number of sites documented in that location or its vicinity.

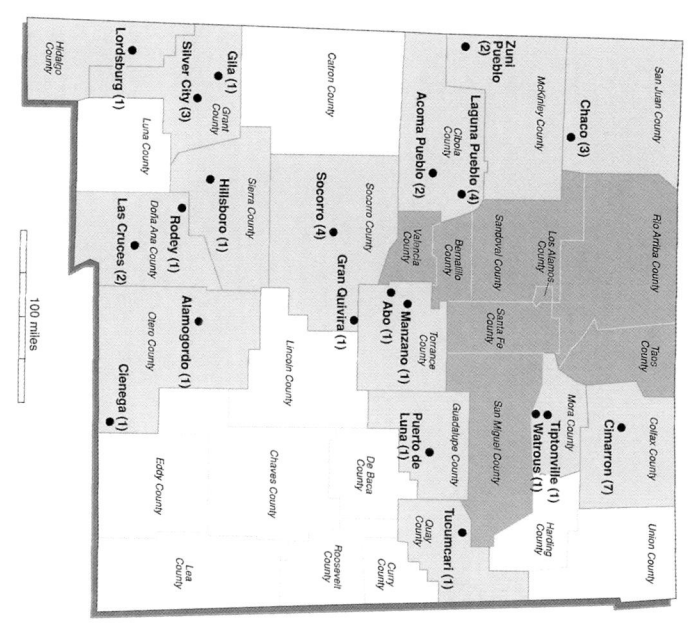

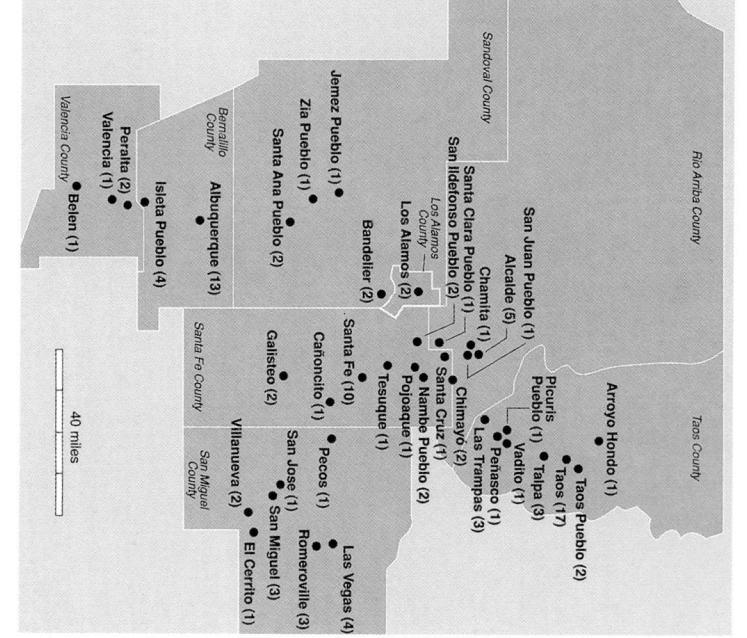

Detail of counties with greatest number of sites documented.

(MAPS: Carol Cooper Rider)

RECORDING A VANISHING LEGACY

ABBREVIATIONS AND TERMS

AIA	American Institute of Architects	
HABS	Historic American Buildings Survey	
HAER	Historic American Engineering Record	
NMHPD	New Mexico Historic Preservation Division	
NPS	National Park Service	
OSU	Ohio State University	
UNM	University of New Mexico	
USDOI	United States Department of the Interior	
data pages	Data pages include information on the structure, such as its physical history and a technical architectural description. Many of the data pages on New Mexican structures and sites are inventories of photogrammetric images.	
(NM-18)	HABS number assigned by the Washington office of HABS to all structures recorded by the survey.	
sheets	Sheets of measured drawings recorded for each entry in the inventory and available at the Library of Congress for study and reproduction. The number of sheets and kinds of drawings (plans, elevations, sections, details, color sheets, restoration drawings) are listed in the inventory, together with their date.	
photos	Photographs in the files of HABS. HABS negatives normally are 5 by 7 inches but are sometimes smaller (4 by 5 inches) or larger (8 by 10 inches).	

ABBREVIATIONS USED IN NOTES AND CAPTIONS

AIA	American Institute of Architects Library and Archives, Washington, DC
BBC	Bainbridge Bunting Collection, UNM
HABS	Courtesy of U.S. Dept. of the Interior, National Park Service.
JGMA	John Gaw Meem Archive of Southwestern Architecture, Center for Southwest Research, University of New Mexico (UNM), Albuquerque, NM
JGMC	John Gaw Meem Collection, HABS Correspondence, UNM
NA	National Archives, Record Group 515, Historic American Buildings Survey, Washington, DC
NMHPD	New Mexico Historic Preservation Division, Correspondence Files, Santa Fe, NM

HABS DATES

1933　HABS proposal submitted by Charles E. Peterson and approved by Secretary of the Interior Harold L. Ickes and Federal Relief Administrator Harry L. Hopkins

1934　Tripartite Agreement between the National Park Service, American Institute of Architects, and Library of Congress

1935　Historic Sites, Buildings, and Antiquities Act, granting HABS permanent authorization to record historic architecture

1941　World War II and suspension of HABS activities

1957　Mission 66 Program funded by Congress

1962　First projects involving photogrammetry

1966　National Historic Preservation Act, directing the U.S. Department of the Interior to set standards for archaeology and historic preservation

　　　Reaffirmation of Tripartite Agreement

　　　Establishment of National Register of Historic Places

　　　HABS reorganized as part of NPS Office of Archaeology and Historic Preservation in Washington, DC

1969　Historic American Engineering Record (HAER) established

1978–79　HABS National Advisory Board dissolved

　　　HABS placed under administration of Heritage Conservation and Recreation Service (HCRS), merged with HAER, and renamed National Architectural and Engineering Record

1980　National Historic Preservation Act Amendments, restating presidential Executive Order 11593 requiring federal agencies to record any historic property under their control that is to be altered or demolished and to use HABS / HAER standards and deposit records in the Library of Congress

1981　HABS / HAER transferred back to NPS

1993　Sixtieth anniversary of HABS

HABS ADMINISTRATION

1934–41	HABS directed by Thomas C. Vint, Chief of Plans and Design, National Park Service.	1972	John C. Poppeliers, Chief of HABS
		1980	Robert J. Kapsch, Chief of HABS
1954–62	HABS organized into two national offices under the National Park Service. Charles E. Peterson directed the Philadelphia-based Eastern Office of Design and Construction, Charles St. George Pope the Western Office in San Francisco.	1985	Kenneth L. Anderson, Jr., Chief of HABS
		1988–Present	Paul D. Dolinski, Chief of HABS
1966	James C. Massey, Chief of HABS	Source:	Carol C. Smith, *Fifty Years of the Historic American Buildings Survey, 1933–1983* (Alexandria, VA: HABS Foundation, 1983).

PART ONE
BACKGROUND

JAMES C. MASSEY

This chapter is an introduction to the history of the Historic American Buildings Survey (HABS) by one of the field's leading practitioners. James C. Massey, the chief of HABS from 1966 to 1972, places the survey within the history of the historic preservation movement in the United States. He outlines HABS' administration and organization at the national level from the original proposal of November 1933 to the surveys of the 1990s.

Massey worked with HABS as a college student in the mid-1950s on a summer project supervised by Charles E. Peterson. He began a fourteen-year career with the NPS as an historian. As chief of the newly formed national office of HABS, he developed the Historic American Engineering Record (HAER), which documents the nation's technological heritage, and promoted cooperation between architects, the private sector, and government. He was an advocate of "preservation through documentation" in an era of relentless demolition of historic sites.

Throughout his career, James Massey has had a particular interest in disseminating HABS documentation to the widest possible audience. As HABS chief, he encouraged many states, including New Mexico, to publish survey catalogs. His consulting firm, Massey Maxwell Associates, prepared the definitive bibliography of HABS / HAER publications (1994), a significant contribution to the historiography of HABS.

CHAPTER 1
THE HISTORY OF HABS NATIONWIDE

JAMES C. MASSEY

The Historic American Buildings Survey (HABS to its friends) is one of the more remarkable products of the Great Depression of the 1930s. At its inception in 1933, it was but one of innumerable federal assistance projects, but unlike the many that disappeared as fast as federal emergency funding ended, HABS survived and has continued to grow to the present time. This may be due to the thoughtful structure of the initial program, which was sponsored jointly by the National Park Service (NPS) of the Department of the Interior, the American Institute of Architects (AIA), and the Library of Congress. The success of the program also represents the widely perceived need in the United States to identify and document surviving architectural masterpieces of the past, particularly those that might be threatened with demolition or development. It was fortuitous that these concerns coalesced at a moment when emergency funding was available and a substantial number of under- or unemployed architects and drafters[1] were at hand to do the work.

HABS' work continues under the aegis of the National Park Service, which is today the lead federal agency for historic preservation. Since 1969, HABS has operated jointly with its offshoot, the Historic American Engineering Record (HAER), in the HABS/HAER Division of the Cultural Resources Program of the park service. As initially, the recording continues to be based on accurate, scale, measured drawings supplemented by professional large-format photographs and written historical documentation and architectural descriptions. The partnership of the NPS, the Library of Congress, and the AIA continues: the NPS prepares the documentation; the Library of Congress maintains the collection, making it available for public use and reproduction; and the AIA, the architects' professional society, continues to provide assistance and counsel. Despite much concern within the profession, the former coordinating body, the HABS Advisory Board, is currently inactive, dormant since an administrative determination in 1978, although HABS supporters hope for its early reactivation.

With 28,226 buildings documented by HABS/HAER up to 1993, resulting in 48,075 measured drawings and 150,262 photographs, the survey today represents a major resource for the student of American architecture. It is, moreover, one of the largest national surveys of its kind in the world. Now over sixty years old, HABS enjoys levels of public support, healthy growth, and public usefulness that make it a valued cultural resources program in the United States.

BACKGROUND

Given the relative youth of our country, there has been a surprisingly long history of concern for preservation

·DEPARTMENT·OF·THE·INTERIOR·
·WASHINGTON·D·C·
·THIS·IS·TO·CERTIFY·THAT·THE·
·HISTORIC·BUILDING·
·KNOWN·AS·

·IN·THE·COUNTY·OF·
·AND·THE·STATE·OF·

·HAS·BEEN·SELECTED·BY·THE·
·ADVISORY·COMMITTEE·OF·THE·
·HISTORIC·AMERICAN·
·BUILDINGS·SURVEY·
·AS·POSSESSING·EXCEPTIONAL·
·HISTORIC·OR·ARCHITECTURAL·
·INTEREST·AND·AS·BEING·WORTHY·
·OF·MOST·CAREFUL·PRESERVATION·
·FOR·THE·BENEFIT·OF·FUTURE·
·GENERATIONS·AND·THAT·TO·THIS·
·END·A·RECORD·OF·ITS·PRESENT·
·APPEARANCE·AND·CONDITION·
·HAS·BEEN·MADE·AND·DEPOSITED·
·FOR·PERMANENT·REFERENCE·IN·THE·
·LIBRARY·OF·CONGRESS·

·ATTEST·
District Officer

Secretary of the Interior

HABS survey certificate,
U.S. Department of the Interior, 1936.
John Gaw Meem Archive of Southwestern Architecture.

ing that the long-missing tower and the assembly room were restored soon afterward. In the same years in Philadelphia, William Strickland, the architect of the restored tower of Independence Hall, engraved an elevation drawing of the "ancient" Anthony Benezet House in Philadelphia just before its demolition for new development — perhaps the first conscious documentation by an architect's scale drawing of a threatened landmark.

By 1850, Washington's headquarters at Newburgh, New York, a fine Dutch house, was restored and opened to the public as a historic monument. In 1857, Carpenter's Hall in Philadelphia, the site of the first meeting of the Continental Congress, was restored and opened to the public as a historical monument by the Carpenters' Company of the County and City of Philadelphia as a public service that continues to this day. In 1863, what may have been the first full set of measured architectural drawings of a historic house were prepared by architect John Sturgis of the Hancock House in Boston before its demolition.

These early instances of preservation were primarily patriotic in inspiration, rather than motivated by the architectural consequence of the buildings, although that was surely also a concern. However, by the time of the Philadelphia Centennial Exhibition of 1876 celebrating our nation's 100th birthday, the pioneer buildings of the eighteenth century had reached a respectable age, and some colonial buildings were displayed. From New England saltboxes to pioneer log cabins, these now-venerable buildings took on a new fascination for Americans. The last quarter of the nineteenth century produced an increasing number of books on historic monuments and houses and, importantly, an increasing number of architects who made measured drawings of selected, often threatened monuments. These drawings appeared regularly in books, folios, and journals by the end of the century. The colonial past had caught on in the public eye, and architects began to produce colonial revival buildings that recalled the now-picturesque memory of the nation's beginnings.

By 1890, the AIA had established its first committee concerned with the preservation of historic buildings, the Committee on Conservation of Public Architecture. It was formed in response to concern over the loss of significant architecture from the early days of the Republic, for with the rapid population growth in our nation, and particularly in our cities, that characterized the dawn of the twentieth century, the preservation of these tangible reminders of the country's past became a more widely felt concern. Now named the Committee on Historic Resources, it continues to be an active and vital part of the nation's preservation activities. At the turn of the century, the AIA and its individual members periodically called for programs to identify and document historic sites. In 1898, the extensive publication of measured drawings and sketches from the weekly *American Architect and Building News* were published as *The Georgian Period*, a six-volume work that remains one of the major monuments of documentary publication of historic buildings in the United States. From this period on, there was frequent publication of measured drawings of historic buildings and houses.

In 1914, the AIA itself sponsored unusually fine measured drawings of the Octagon by Glenn Brown, a pioneering restoration architect. Built about 1800, this historic home had been acquired in 1902 for the AIA's headquarters in Washington, DC. Around the United States, there were found not only restoration projects of seventeenth- and eighteenth-century buildings but pro-

of physical reminders of the nation's origins. Less than fifty years after independence prevailed, Philadelphia's Independence Hall, that primary shrine of America's freedom, was freshly painted for Lafayette's triumphant return to the United States in 1824, and the French general's visit stirred such public interest in the build-

grams to document and make measured drawings of them, often sponsored by architects and AIA chapters. With the organization of Colonial Williamsburg in 1926, architects moved from the study and restoration of isolated buildings to an entire town, and whole staffs set about studying not just the buildings in Williamsburg but those of Tidewater, Virginia, looking for collateral evidence. In New York and Philadelphia at the beginning of the depression, city-organized projects were set up to make measured drawings of significant early buildings, reflecting concern for the underemployment of architects and drafters. Coupled with a sophisticated perception of the importance of identifying and documenting significant historic properties, such programs set the stage for the development of a national program.

FORMATION OF HABS

Not only was interest and activity in the identification and documentation of historic buildings growing throughout the country on a local and individual basis, but the AIA Committee on Historic Resources (as it is now called) continued to press for the establishment of a national program to identify and document these reminders of our past in a systematic and uniform way, as had been done since the nineteenth century in many European nations, such as France, which embarked on a documentation program as early as the 1840s. It was at this moment in 1933, at the bottom of the depression, that Charles E. Peterson, a young architect from the NPS, proposed such a national, systematic program in a memorandum to his superiors. Peterson's proposal for a Civil Works Administration project for unemployed architects and drafters met with strong support from the AIA under the leadership of Leicester B. Holland, who was also chief of the Fine Arts Division at the Library of Congress. It was quickly approved by the director of the NPS, Arno Cammerer, and by the secretary of the interior, Harold L. Ickes. And, in the fortunate way that things could happen in this time of national crisis, it was funded and in operation in the field within two months.

The program received the full cooperation of the AIA. It was guided by an advisory committee of seven distinguished architects and citizens, including John Gaw Meem of Santa Fe, under the leadership of Leicester B. Holland. Calling on the nationwide structure of the AIA, the NPS appointed district officers in thirty-nine sections of the country, generally architects prominent in historic preservation, with instructions to hire architects and drafters and to begin immediately to produce measured drawings. During this initial ten-week phase, with 772 architects and drafters at work, several thousand drawings of buildings were produced. The program met with such success that the NPS and the AIA sought funds from a series of federal relief programs to keep it going throughout the 1930s.

In 1934, this informal partnership — with the NPS making the records, the AIA providing the personnel and local management through district officers, and the Library of Congress receiving the records and making them available for publication and public use — was formalized in a tripartite agreement that, with periodic amendments, still constitutes the institutional charter of HABS. The advisory committee was formalized into the HABS Advisory Board, appointed by the secretary of the interior. The board continued as a coordinating body until 1978, when the Carter administration placed restrictions on outside advisory bodies.

Under the immediate direction of Thomas C. Vint,

Charles E. Peterson.
Photograph courtesy of Charles E. Peterson.

then chief architect of the plans and design branch of the NPS, the survey proceeded so effectively that a national exhibit of HABS.work was held at the National Museum in Washington in 1934. The first catalog of the survey's work was produced in 1935, and in 1938 a

THE HISTORY OF HABS NATIONWIDE

RECORDING A VANISHING LEGACY

John Gaw Meem, 1964. Museum of New Mexico, neg. no. 19646.

national hardcover catalog was made widely available by the government.[2]

The survey gave employment to many who later became prominent historical architects and preservationists, including Frederick D. Nichols, Thomas T. Waterman, and John P. O'Neill, all of whom worked in the Washington headquarters at various times, as well as to noted architects such as Samuel Lapham of Charleston, Richard Koch and Samuel Wilson, Jr., of New Orleans, Earl H. Reed, Jr., of Chicago, Henry F. Withey of Los Angeles, and Marvin Eickenroht of San Antonio, among many. During the 1930s, architectural students and universities were used by the HABS program, with special relief funds available for students. Although this was not a major part of the depression program, the use of students would later become a major aspect of HABS recording teams.

The work focused on the study of buildings in the earlier periods of American architecture with a cutoff date of 1860. It also included the Spanish Colonial culture, with "special attention" to early work in New Orleans and Santa Fe. Under what must have been the influence of John Gaw Meem, HABS Circular No. 1, dated December 12, 1933, goes on to say:

> An important though largely untouched field for exact architectural reporting is the Indian territory of the Southwest. Graphic records should be made of such communal constructions as in Taos and Acoma Pueblos, and the Zuni villages farther west where mutations are fast encroaching upon the flavor of the native aboriginal style. Recording of some of the highly perishable prehistoric remains such as the Pueblo Bonita [sic] (New Mexico) should be included.

Buildings to be recorded were to represent the complete range of the builder's art; in addition to the usual houses, churches, and courthouses, there were to be studies of barns, mills, outbuildings, and bridges. Also specified in HABS Circular No. 1 was the recording of old mining settlements, such as Columbia in the Sierra Nevadas and Central City in the Colorado highlands. Thus, in spite of the 1860 limit, the survey recognized early the special importance of pioneer structures in the West. Recording priorities were focused on threatened major buildings. It remained for the post–World War II HABS to undertake the documentation of the Victorian age and industrial monuments.

One little-known activity of HABS in the 1930s was the recording of historic gardens, and at one point a separate branch of HABS was devoted to landscape documentation. Although there has recently been a renewed interest in landscape recording by HABS, the early efforts represent a scale of activity and concern that has yet to be realized again.

The survey is still without its own formal federal legislation, unusual for a program now sixty years in operation. It was confirmed, however, in the 1935 Historic Sites Act, which established a national policy for the preservation of cultural resources and which specifically authorized the secretary of the interior to undertake cooperative agreements, such as that which forms the basis of HABS.

Through support from one or another of President Roosevelt's New Deal programs — Public Works Administration, Civil Works Administration, Works Progress Administration — HABS continued, sometimes surviving by a hair's breadth, through the 1930s until the advent of World War II, when the survey was terminated as a record-producing activity. HABS had the good fortune to complete and publish a new national catalog, prepared by Frederick D. Nichols, just in advance of the war. (Indeed, it required a temporary draft deferment to allow Nichols to complete the work.) This 1941 publication, listing in detail the records of 6,389 buildings, became the widely known symbol of HABS for many years.[3] In 1942, a strong effort was made to continue federal support, in light of the possibility of wartime damage to historic structures, but the effort, regrettably, failed.

However, because of the good fortune of its tripartite nature, with district offices in place in each area as part of the partnership with the AIA, the survey did not end in oblivion but was able to continue through and after the war years with donations from private architects, often supported by local grants or individual interests. Most importantly, the Library of Congress continued to maintain the records and to make them available for public use and reproduction. With growing public interest, the survey has become the most frequently consulted and reproduced collection in the Prints and Photographs Division of the library.

HABS RENEWED: THE POSTWAR PERIOD
The years following World War II were critical ones for historic preservation in the United States. The nation embarked on a massive rebuilding to make up for the years of depression and war. The situation was further

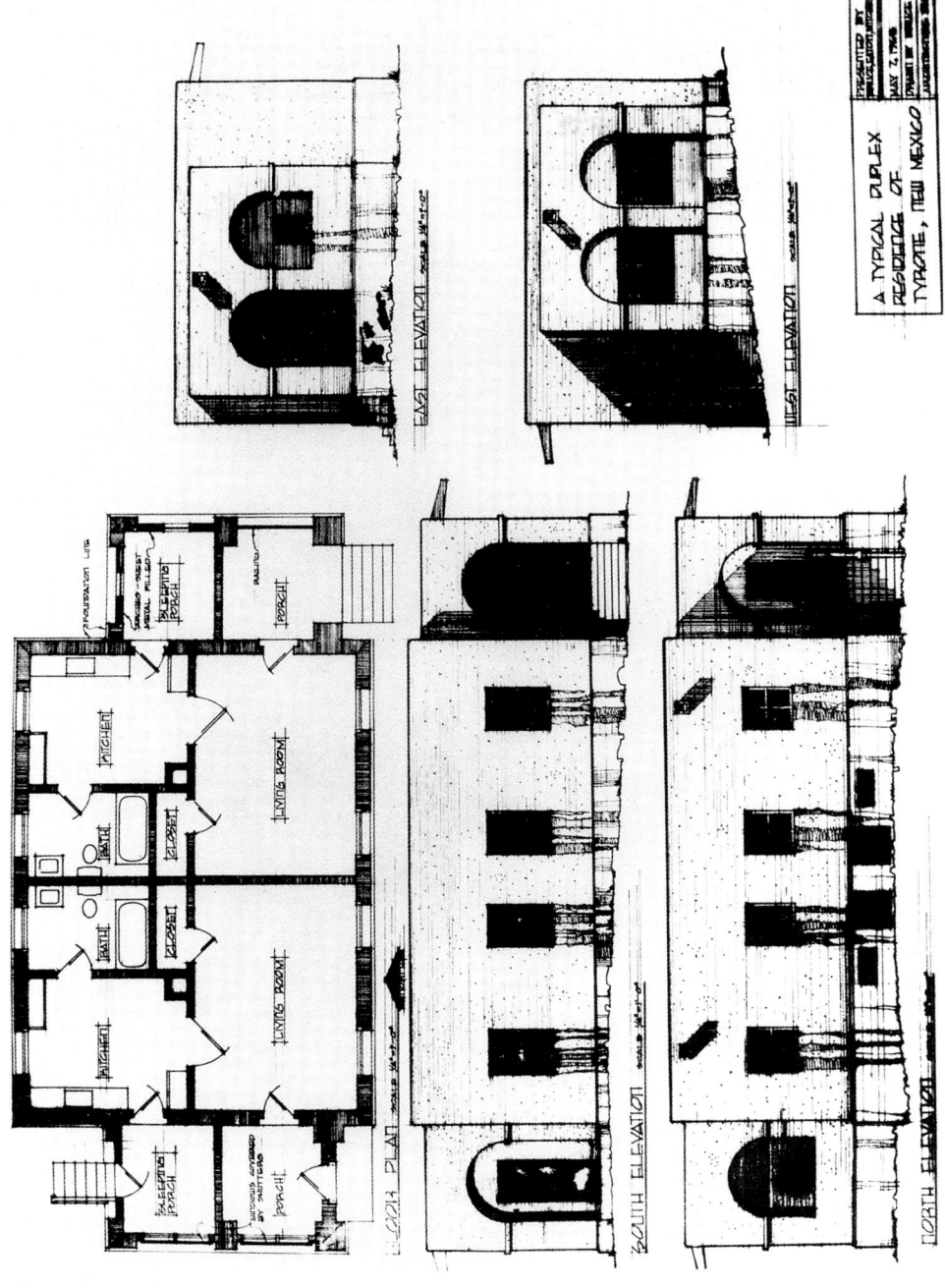

Typical duplex residence, miners' housing, Phelps Dodge Corporation, Tyrone. Caton, Mitchell, and Bruce, dels. (Architecture 261–62) 1965. Bainbridge Bunting student drawings, John Gaw Meem Archive of Southwestern Architecture, University of New Mexico.

THE HISTORY OF HABS NATIONWIDE

aggravated by huge urban renewal projects that tore at the historical cores of the nation's old cities, as well as by much-needed new highway construction that was frequently designed to pass through historic areas. Without the emergency funding programs of the depression, the NPS was unable to resume the funded activities of HABS, although the program continued on a voluntary basis, with donations from architects.

With great determination, Thomas C. Vint, then chief of design and construction for the NPS, finally secured funding in the 1958 fiscal year to resume a formal HABS program as part of a broad NPS construction program known as "Mission 66," intended to catch up on years of slack in the national parks. HABS offices were set up as part of the NPS Design and Construction Office with branches in Washington, Philadelphia, and San Francisco. With architects now in short and expensive supply, the program quickly turned to the expedient of employing architecture students working in summer teams under the direction of experienced professors of architecture. Following on the 1930s precedent, this practice had been pioneered in the early 1950s at Independence National Historical Park in Philadelphia. Under the direction of Charles E. Peterson, who was then resident architect at the park, summer measuring teams studied its numerous historic buildings, using HABS as both the medium and the eventual repository for the work. This practice spread to other national parks and provided the basis of experience for the new HABS program, starting at the end of 1957. It also became the major training program for architectural students in historic architecture; from the early 1950s on, many of today's leaders received their first professional experience with historic buildings as part of these annual park service summer programs.

The mission facing the renewed HABS was immense. In the few decades since the 1930s program, approximately a quarter of the recorded buildings had been demolished, with the number rising in some areas such as Mobile, Alabama, to as many as 50 percent of the recorded buildings. Warnings and pleas were received daily about new threats to historic buildings as development, highways, and urban renewal marched forward. In these years, before the passage of the 1966 Historic Preservation Act, HABS was almost the only federal presence that could be brought to the aid of local preservationists working to save historic buildings. Much recording was done in response to threats to important buildings, and in many cases such attention from a respected federal agency was successful in turning the tide in favor of preservation.

To carry out this effort, the survey developed and soon came to depend on cooperative agreements with local historical societies, preservation groups, and architects to record buildings, sometimes only with photographs and written data and on a matching-fund basis. The new HABS program attempted to record areas previously neglected, as well as those under threat of demolition. There were many gaps in national coverage from the 1930s program, as it had been based on district officers from the AIA coming forth and organizing local programs. This had not been possible in many areas and had resulted in spotty coverage. Moving HABS to the status of primarily a matching-fund program greatly expanded the amount of work that could be accomplished within a modest federal budget.

European programs similar to HABS had long used architectural photogrammetry, a photographic process that permits detailed, accurate measurements from stereo photographs, much in the manner of aerial mapmaking but applied to buildings. HABS undertook a series of experimental projects in the late 1950s in cooperation with Professor Perry Borchers of Ohio State University, who was the first to bring this technique into productive use in the United States. Photogrammetry was particularly useful for large, complex buildings such as Gothic Revival churches that defy hand measurement; it also permitted the relatively inexpensive preparation of the photo stereopairs, leaving the substantial expense of plotting them into the actual measured drawings for a later time as needed.

In the 1960s, the national concern for historic preservation spread to a wide public and, with the spectacle of ever-rising losses of historic resources, resulted in the Office of Archaeology and Historic Preservation Act of 1966. The act established the Office of Archaeology and Historic Preservation within the NPS and made the new coordinated office responsible for the park service's many historic preservation programs under the direction of Dr. Ernest A. Connally, formerly a professor at the University of Illinois and a HABS summer supervisor. The survey and its former field offices were centralized in the new office in Washington, and this writer was appointed as the first national chief of the survey.

HABS faced a broad mandate from the preservation community to revitalize the old program as part of the new national preservation movement. Because the prewar work generally had not documented buildings erected after 1860, substantial attention was given to recording buildings of the Victorian period and new building types developed in the era, such as railroad stations and office buildings. Soon afterward, recording was expanded to include early works of modern architecture, especially in Chicago and southern Illinois, and Frank Lloyd Wright buildings generally. Previously

RECORDING A VANISHING LEGACY

neglected areas of the builder's art, such as factories and bridges, were increasingly studied, resulting in 1969 in the establishment of a companion program, the Historic American Engineering Record (HAER), under a separate agreement involving the NPS, the American Society of Civil Engineers, and the Library of Congress, with other engineering societies later co-opted to participate.

In the early 1960s, Professor Harley McKee of Syracuse University started work on revising the survey's specifications for recording buildings. His efforts culminated in 1968 in the first publication of *Recording Historic Buildings*, which was intended not for those doing work for HABS but as a national guide and standard for the documentation of historic buildings. During the same years, it was apparent that the 1941 catalog and 1959 supplement needed to be revised and expanded with broader catalog entries. Because of the immensity of the task, it was decided to proceed with state and city catalogs. The first of these, prepared in the new format for New Hampshire and Massachusetts by John C. Poppeliers, HABS historian and later chief of the survey, appeared in 1963 and 1965.[4] During the same period, the survey began the series *Selections from the Historic American Buildings Survey*, published by HABS and cooperating organizations to make portions of the records more easily available to the public. A national checklist of HABS records held by the Library of Congress, *Historic America: Buildings, Structures, and Sites*, was published in 1983 on the fiftieth anniversary of the survey, the first national catalog since 1941. A history of HABS, *Fifty Years of the Historic American Buildings Survey*, written by Carol Smith and published by the HABS Foundation, also appeared that year.

In the 1980s, the HABS/HAER Division, as part of the cultural resources program of the NPS, continued to grow substantially under the direction of Dr. Robert J. Kapsch and work effectively as an integral part of the overall historic preservation program in the United States. Cooperative ventures with HABS continued, and much recording was done in fulfillment of the requirement that federal agencies inventory their historic resources and document (at their own expense) federal historic buildings that are to be demolished.

HABS and HAER now field more than thirty teams each year and include interns from abroad as part of a cooperative venture with the United States Committee of the International Council on Monuments and Sites (US/ICOMOS). Today the survey is larger and more effective than ever before, and the impressive series of state and local catalogs, now numbering eighteen, continues. HABS and HAER remain the most frequently reproduced collections at the Library of Congress.

SALLY HYER

This historical overview compares the New Deal relief program planned in Washington in 1933 with the survey as it took place in New Mexico over the past six decades. It draws on records at the National Archives and American Institute of Architects' Library and Archives, as well as the personal papers of John Gaw Meem and Bainbridge Bunting. The chapter also examines the changing concept of what is significant to record and evaluates the measured drawings, photographs, and historical data that have been produced.

Sally Hyer is an independent historian and curator who has worked for southwestern tribal organizations and museums since the mid-1970s. She received her Ph.D. with distinction from the University of New Mexico in 1994 and is a former Fulbright Fellow at the Museum of Anthropology in Lima, Peru. With Governor Frank Tenorio of San Felipe Pueblo, she was awarded the State of New Mexico Heritage Preservation Award for oral history in 1991. Hyer is the author of the book One House, One Voice, One Heart: Native American Education at the Santa Fe Indian School and is preparing an article on Indian boarding school architecture. Her great-uncle, Dudley T. Smith, was part of the HABS crew at Acoma Pueblo in 1934.

CHAPTER 2

HABS RECORDING IN NEW MEXICO

SALLY HYER

In early January of 1934, a HABS crew of Colorado men began to draw the chapel of Nuestra Señora de Talpa near Taos. Less than two months had passed since the November day when Charles E. Peterson drafted his proposal for a relief program employing architects to record American buildings. By December, Civil Works Administration (CWA) funds had been set aside for the Historic American Buildings Survey; a month later, men were at work.

Thirty-five years later one of the original crew, Alan B. Fisher of Denver, recalled that winter afternoon and his sense of the impermanency of the chapel, standing ". . . with an almost innate desire within its very perishable self for destruction and with an inclination to return to the adobe floor of land upon which it stood." He rejoiced that his team had created "the record of a sweet, rare building that is now entirely gone; now lost and back as part of Mother Earth of which it had so tenderly been built in honor of Nuestra Señora."[1]

New Mexicans can also rejoice in the existence of HABS measured drawings and photographs of our state's architectural heritage. They are a reference against which change may be measured and, in some cases, the only record of now-disappeared buildings. Since 1933 crews in New Mexico have documented some 147 sites, creating a Library of Congress archive of more than 596 measured drawings and 620 photographs. Hundreds more recordings that have been inspired by HABS or follow its format are in libraries at the University of New Mexico and the New Mexico Historic Preservation Division.

The West was not exactly a priority for HABS. The cutoff date for construction was 1860, before much of the West had attained statehood. Documentation was limited by a policy not to record buildings in remote locations or under the care of local or state governments. Only the District 36 HABS office covered three entire states: New Mexico, Colorado, and Utah. By the end of the 1934 survey no measured drawings at all had been done in the western states of Idaho, Montana, Nevada, and North Dakota, and fewer than fifteen in each of the states of Colorado, Kansas, Minnesota, Oklahoma, Oregon, Iowa, South Dakota, Utah, and Wyoming.[2]

New Mexico's population was a mere 420,000, and the state was home to only nineteen architectural firms, most quite small. The Interior Department warned that employment quotas were to be based on economic need not number of historic buildings. The quota for District 36 was 25 men: 13 from New Mexico, 8 from Colorado, and 4 from Utah, to be hired through CWA offices in Santa Fe, Denver, and Salt Lake City.

New Mexico had influential friends among the survey's national leaders who had experienced the state's architectural heritage firsthand. Charles E. Peterson felt so strongly that the pueblos should be documented that his HABS proposal specified the survey should not be limited to "styles found on the Atlantic seaboard" but should examine "remnants of the Spanish Colonial culture" and "the Indian territory of the Southwest." Because of his personal interest in New Mexico's monuments Chief Architect Thomas C. Vint, supervisor of HABS, waived the district labor quota and hired additional men from Colorado to work in Santa Fe.

Perhaps the most significant force behind the strong HABS program in New Mexico was Santa Fe architect John Gaw Meem (1894–1983), a member of the Colorado chapter of the American Institute of Architects (AIA). Meem had been deeply involved in New Mexican architecture since opening his first firm in Santa Fe in 1924. He had come to Santa Fe in 1920 not as an architect but as a twenty-six-year-old patient at the city's Sunmount Sanatorium. Like other patients encouraged by Sunmount's director and owner, Dr. Frank E. Mera, Meem developed an interest in New Mexican history and culture. Trained as a civil engineer, he began to sketch and practice architectural drafting.[3]

Meem's professional skills had been shaped by a 1922–23 apprenticeship in Denver with Arthur Fisher, Alan B. Fisher's father, at the family firm of Fisher and Fisher. At night he practiced at the Atelier Denver, associated with New York's Beaux-Arts Institute of Design. At the atelier he worked on individual design problems and received critical guidance from prominent Denver architect Burnham Hoyt. This system, modeled after the program of instruction of the nineteenth-century École des Beaux-Arts in Paris, dominated the training of architects in the U.S. from 1850 until the 1930s and later. At the atelier Meem gained familiarity with classical styles of design and planning and became an expert drafter. In 1924 he returned to Sunmount to embark on an architectural career in partnership with another patient.

According to biographer Bainbridge Bunting, the briefness of this formal education, considerably less than that required for a professional degree in architecture, gave Meem the freedom to be receptive to New Mexican architecture. In the early 1920s he, Dr. Mera, and other Santa Feans helped the socially prominent Anne Evans of Denver organize the Committee for the Preservation and Restoration of New Mexico Mission Churches, which sponsored church renovation projects supported by local communities. In 1924 he replaced Burnham Hoyt as technical advisor to the committee and was involved in church repair work at the pueblos of Acoma, Laguna, Zia, and Santa Ana and in the villages of Las Trampas and Chimayó.

In late November of 1933, Meem, not yet forty years old, was named to the HABS National Advisory Committee by Secretary of the Interior Harold L. Ickes. The committee accepted an honorarium of $12 a year in order to attain federal employee status. The committee head was Dr. Leicester B. Holland, director of the Fine Arts Division of the Library of Congress and chairman of the AIA's Committee on the Preservation of Historic Buildings. When the AIA Colorado Chapter subsequently nominated Meem as district officer for New Mexico, Colorado, and Utah, he declined, citing a conflict with his federal advisory role. At Meem's recommendation, however, Nebraska-born A. Leicester Hyde (1902–76), a 1928 graduate of Columbia University who had worked in Meem's firm since 1931, was named to the position. By late December Hyde was at work in a donated office at Santa Fe's Laboratory of Anthropology.[4]

December 1933 the Colorado chapter of the AIA appointed a local advisory committee for District 36. From Santa Fe, they named Meem; from Salt Lake City, Lewis T. Cannon; and from Denver, Arthur Fisher. Other members appointed by Meem were colleagues who had been active in cultural preservation in Santa Fe since the early 1920s. There was sanatorium director Dr. Frank E. Mera; his brother Harry P. Mera, curator at the Laboratory of Anthropology; archaeologist Jesse L. Nusbaum, director of the laboratory; and Carlos Vierra, a painter and photographer employed by the National Park Service.

Job inquiries began to arrive around the holiday season. Only a few came from New Mexico. One was from John J. Windsor, who registered as an architect in Santa Fe in 1931. At least one woman asked about job opportunities. Some professionals who had come to New Mexico from the Midwest applied, such as Albuquerquean Edwin B. Clarke, an 1891 graduate of the University of Illinois who had practiced in Chicago and Omaha. Charles A. Dieman was born in Milwaukee, Wisconsin, in 1872; William H. Kraemer (1874–1964) was a native New Yorker with training at Columbia University and thirty years' experience in New York and Los Angeles. Urie McCleary hailed from Los Angeles.

Many of the younger architects were from Denver. Bradley P. Kidder (1901–73) had seven years' experience as a junior drafter, an art degree from Colorado College, and some graduate work at the University of Pennsylvania — his current job was selling vacuums. The depression had forced Stanley H. Kent to drop out of architecture school at the Carnegie Institute of Technology. Alan B. Fisher (1905–78) had attended the University of Pennsylvania and M.I.T. and spent the summer at the American Beaux-Arts School at Fountainbleu, France. Dudley T. Smith (1902–94) was an unemployed graduate of Dartmouth College and Yale University. Like Meem, at least five had studied at the Atelier Denver: Arthur V. Hoyer (1909–83), Victor Hornbein (1913–95), O. G. Stromquist, Stanley H. Kent, and H. Paul Atchison. Also from Colorado were Arthur E. Jack, Byron M. Kaufman, M. James Slack, Neal W. Cash, and A. B. Willison, all unemployed drafters. The team leaders were Charles A. Dieman, Bradley P. Kidder, Urie McCleary, Arthur V. Hoyer, C. Truman St. Clair, and Elbert S. Mosher. M. James Slack signed on as photographer.[5]

Charles E. Peterson's proposal stressed that jobless architects and drafters who enrolled in the employment program were to be "trained and experienced men who would be capable of earning much more in normal times," but in recalling the survey in 1969 Alan Fisher jokingly characterized it as "boondoggling." It provided "the bountiful sum — or so it seemed then — of twenty-nine dollars for a week of work for otherwise idle architects' hands," more than $300 a week in today's terms. For a 30-hour week, salaries ranged from $1.10 an hour for squad leaders, to $1 for photographers and 90 cents for architects. The men used their own drafting equipment, and each received $3 for two months of supplies.

While Meem and Hyde selected architects and drafters locally, Meem was involved in setting standards at the national level. The selection criteria were that buildings have historical, archaeological, or architectural importance; be constructed by 1860; and be easily accessible from the district office. Importance was judged by a site's uniqueness, representativeness of a general class, or distinctly local or unusual features.

The instructions were informal, but architects were asked to record plans, elevations, and sections, followed by structural features, and interesting or exceptional decorative details. The drawings were to be on 19-inch by 24-inch rag paper in India ink.[6]

Architects predominated on the national committee and in Santa Fe, although the district advisors did include two anthropologists and an artist. From headquarters HABS Circular No. 1 (1933) proclaimed that architects should record only names and dates, not historical data, because "long accounts of genealogical and sentimental mythology have no place in this program." As Charles E. Peterson's memorandum informed them, "Only the briefest resume of facts is necessary in each case and it does not seem necessary to build up an overhead for the purpose of getting data which is normally obtainable gratis" from local and state historical societies.

Late in 1933 Meem drew up a preliminary list of sites to be recorded by HABS. The pueblos of Acoma, Taos, and Santa Ana were of utmost significance. "It is my opinion," he advised Hyde, "that the Pueblos of New Mexico will be classed by the National Advisory Board as among the worthiest of all buildings to be measured in the United States and if such measurements are obtained will form a unique and important contribution to the whole survey." The largest number of projects on the first list were religious buildings, not surprising given Meem's more than ten years' experience on the churches committee. There were mission churches at Acoma, Laguna, Picurís, Santo Domingo, San Felipe, Santa Ana, Zía, and Zuni, and kivas at Nambé, San Ildefonso, and Santo Domingo. Meem also recognized the significance of military architecture such as the *terreón* at Manzano,[7] a rare example of a defensive tower,

and the American army outpost of Fort Union near Watrous. He advised preliminary surveys be done to select the finest examples of residential architecture in villages such as Galisteo, Abiquiu, Córdova, and Ranchos de Taos, and mentioned his interest in Spanish Colonial, Spanish-Pueblo, Territorial, and "Spanish-Pueblo/Victorian" styles.

Two weeks later, Leicester Hyde created a revised list of over 100 worthwhile measuring projects. It conveys a growing sense of the overwhelming quantity of deserving sites and the lack of basic information needed to evaluate priorities. There were 14 "old towns and villages that so far I have been unable to obtain more definite information as to specific buildings," as well as more than 30 ruins and 28 forts. There are pueblos, mission churches, houses, entire villages that are "veritable museums of Spanish Colonial buildings, . . . literally alive with charming old buildings," stagecoach stations, and archaeological sites. Meem and Hyde began to survey "old-timers" such as Fred Lambert of Cimarron, who recommended recording that town's hotel, mill, county jail, courthouse, government trading store, and gambling hall.[8]

The unique political status of Pueblo governments required a much different approach to gaining approval than that used in rural Hispanic villages or Santa Fe and Taos. Meem's considerable experience gave him insight into the protocol necessary to obtain the formal consent of each pueblo's governor and council as well as the Indian Service. He warned Hyde that work in the pueblos would be impossible without a letter to the Pueblo governors from Commissioner John Collier. Meem wired Collier, who the same day sent letters to each pueblo asking their cooperation. Indian Service administrator Chester Faris, in charge of the Northern

HABS squad climbing mesa to Acoma, 1934. Photograph courtesy of Dudley T. Smith.

Pueblos Agency in Santa Fe, told Hyde he felt the Pueblos would cooperate and specifically that a young governor at Acoma was certain that pueblo could be measured.[9]

When CWA funding ran out and the survey ended on April 26, 1934, Hyde reported to Washington: "Project too short-lived to accomplish but a fraction of work to be done in this area."[10] In barely four months architects had documented nine sites in 231 measured drawings and taken 193 photographs to accompany them. Six religious buildings were recorded: the kiva at Nambé Pueblo, San José de Laguna mission church at Laguna Pueblo, San Esteban del Rey mission church at Acoma Pueblo, San Miguel Church in Santa Fe, La Capilla de Talpa, and El Santuario del Señor Esquípula [sic] in Chimayó.[11] Two civic buildings were drawn, El Palacio Real in Santa Fe and Laguna Pueblo's tribal council meeting house. Following national guidelines the majority of sites recorded had been in the vicinity of Santa Fe and Taos, the area of Meem's greatest interest and expertise. However, Acoma and Laguna, over 100 miles southwest of Santa Fe, were exceptions.

The work at Acoma was not yet finished. The urgent need to thoroughly document the pueblo was recognized even at the national level. NPS director Arno Cammerer wrote Secretary of the Interior Harold L. Ickes asking for help: "This project is the most important one undertaken in New Mexico by the HABS. Pueblo of Acoma is unquestionably the longest continuously inhabited structure included in the survey."[12] Ickes agreed and made a special appropriation of $4,900 in public works funds to complete the documentation. The recording of Acoma in 83 sheets of drawings and 75 photos was completed by summer.

In Washington, Dr. Leicester Holland "spoke of New Mexico's drawings with the greatest of pride and stated that they were among the very finest that had been produced in the U.S." Six watercolor studies of *retablos* in churches at Laguna and Acoma, Talpa, Ranchos de Taos, and Chimayó are extremely rare examples of the use of color in the survey. In elegance of presentation, the work of the 1934 survey has not been equaled in subsequent New Mexico HABS projects. In fact, these virtuoso works are recognized today as among the most outstanding produced in the history of HABS.[13]

The skilled crew members shared drawing skills learned in architectural ateliers and university programs in the U.S. and abroad. Their training in the Beaux-Arts tradition emphasized excellence in drafting and design, clearly evident in the finely designed measured drawings they produced. They believed, in Victor Hornbein's words, that "drawing style, like handwriting, is distinctive. All the drawings for every project were done freehand. The only lines drawn with a straightedge were control lines. This made the work of different men unique." Their measured drawings are exquisite compositions using graceful lines of varying weights, shaded with delicate stippling and adorned

RECORDING A VANISHING LEGACY

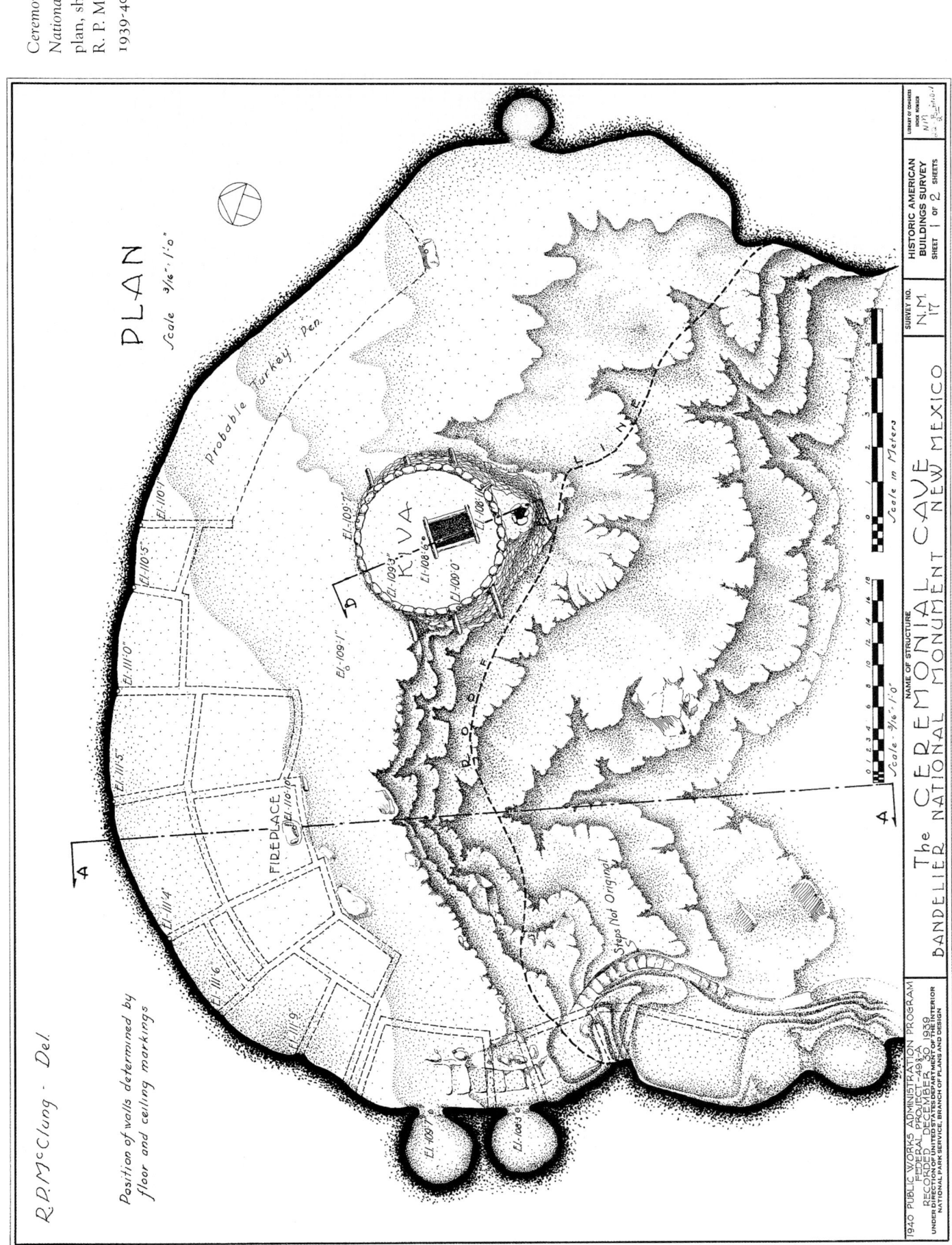

Ceremonial Cave, Bandelier National Monument, plan, sheet 1 of 2, HABS. R. P. McClung, del. 1939–40 (NM-17).

with decorative borders and descriptive notes in ornamental lettering.

As the programs of the New Deal were realigned after CWA funding came to an end, states were allocated federal relief funds through the Public Works Administration (PWA) and Federal Emergency Relief Administration (FERA). About the same time, the survey also came under a new administrative arrangement. The National Park Service was to administer the survey, the Library of Congress was to be the repository for all records, and the AIA was to be responsible for the survey at the local level, according to an agreement forged by Charles E. Peterson, Leicester B. Holland, and Thomas C. Vint. The 39 district offices were reorganized under the AIA's 67 chapters. Meem, as a member of the AIA Committee on the Preservation of Historic Buildings, was notified that he had been named district officer and instructed to promptly negotiate with local FERA officials to resume the survey.[14]

Again, New Mexico's shortage of out-of-work architects made the state ineligible, and the survey could not continue without federal funds. Meem wrote to John P. O'Neill, associate architect with HABS' Washington office, "We are faced with the same old difficulty in renewing the HABS work as we had originally and that is a multitude of ruins and wonderful buildings and almost no unemployed architects or draftsmen available." O'Neill sympathized, lamenting that "We [at HABS] are literally forced to sit and watch destruction and decay of important, early American structures . . . because there do not happen to be indigent architectural draftsmen nearby." FERA officials were unwilling to increase the New Mexico labor quota, insisting that new work be organized through local sponsors such as museums, historical societies, and universities.

In the fall of 1939 after five years of inactivity, a PWA allotment sufficient for eleven months revived the survey. The PWA nonrelief funds were for Federal Project 498-A from September 1939 until July 1940. Fortunately for New Mexico, funds were not tied to the number of jobless professionals. Although many of the key figures were the same, their roles had shifted slightly. Meem was now district officer for New Mexico and Colorado, having been appointed in January 1938 by the executive secretary of the AIA. The district advisory committee included Dr. Frank Mera and Jesse L. Nusbaum as before, and three new members, all architects in Meem's Santa Fe firm: former district officer A. Leicester Hyde, Acoma squad leader Bradley P. Kidder, and architect Truman Mathews.

Fewer architects were involved than in 1934. R. P. McClung and Raymond T. Lovelady measured and recorded buildings. Donald W. Dickensheets produced detailed photographic records to complement their drawings. Trent Thomas, who registered as an architect in 1934 in Santa Fe, and Lyle E. Bennett were with the NPS Southwest Unit in charge of HABS. HABS architect Herbert K. Boone worked with archaeologist R. Gordon Vivian to document archaeological sites at Chaco Canyon in conjunction with a park service Civilian Conservation Corps project.

Under Meem's guidance, the committee drew up a short list of priorities on November 23, 1939. Northern New Mexico was still the focus, but the criterion for selection was no longer historical or architectural importance, a building's uniqueness or representativeness, but simply its imminent danger of destruction. Already buildings on previous lists had collapsed or been torn down, and others were threatened. New Mexico's population had increased 48 percent since 1920, bringing pressure for development. "The survey has no power to arrest this destruction," wrote John P. O'Neill, "but by making full and accurate records, it can make possible a mental or material reconstruction for present and future generations."[15]

Meem narrowed down the most important Pueblo sites to Taos Pueblo and the San Felipe Pueblo Church. Park service officials in Washington preferred small projects to large, so Taos Pueblo was removed from the list. San Felipe's tribal council rejected a survey of their church. Padre Antonio José Martínez's House in Taos was demolished shortly after the list had been drawn up. The torreón at Manzano was a priority to Meem, who observed that because of nearby highway construction, the roof had begun to collapse, and the tower would only last a few weeks. The structure was documented shortly before his prediction came true.

Spanish Colonial, Mexican, and Territorial period houses in Santa Fe and Taos reflected Meem's growing interest in these historic styles. HABS crews recorded the García, Rael, and Borrego houses in Santa Fe; the Don José Albino Baca house in Las Vegas; and the Tipton house and barn and the Watrous house in Mora County. Four archaeological sites were documented, including the ceremonial cave and kiva at Bandelier National Monument and Pueblo Bonito and Kin Klizhin at Chaco Canyon National Monument.

Fewer than 10 sites account for almost 90 percent of the drawings between the beginning of HABS and 1941. As funds dwindled and fewer architects worked on projects, HABS crews relied increasingly on photography. Photographs were better than nothing, and certainly less expensive and simpler to complete than measured drawings. By 1938, 12 sites had been documented, 3 of them exclusively with photographs. Within the next three years, 30 of the 51 sites documented were recorded only with photographs. Thus, although 39 sites were recorded between 1938 and 1941, there were only 75 new drawings, compared to 233 photographs.

The first HABS photographic documentation was done by M. James Slack in 1934. Subsequently three visiting architects from the Washington office of HABS photographed New Mexico. Their somewhat haphazard work, often consisting of a few snapshots of each building, was unlike Slack's earlier, more methodical efforts. More background information exists about other early HABS figures, perhaps because they were from the central office. Frederick D. Nichols from Trinidad, Colorado, was a 1935 architecture graduate from Yale University who joined the Washington office in 1933. In the summers of 1936 and 1937, he took about forty-five photos of structures in the northern counties of Santa Fe, Taos, Rio Arriba, San Miguel, and Colfax, as well as to the far south in Doña Ana and Otero counties. Assistant architect John P. O'Neill was a Notre Dame graduate with fieldwork experience in Central American archaeology who took five photos at Isleta and Laguna pueblos in 1937. A consulting architect with HABS, Delos H. Smith (1884–1963), from Willcox, Arizona, had a graduate degree in architecture from George Washington University. He photographed five buildings in the Albuquerque area in 1940.

Although fewer measured drawings were completed in this era of HABS than in earlier years, many are superb. These drafters shared a sense of personal style and a pride in skillful execution of drawings that showcased their individual talents. They valued creativity and fine draftsmanship over objectivity. Each sheet was an opportunity for an artist to express his talent and high standards of design. This is evident, for example, in R.

Isleta Pueblo, row of houses and sod wall, photograph 4-1, HABS. John P. O'Neill, photographer. 1937 (NM-120).

P. McClung's dramatic plan of the large kiva at Bandelier National Monument.

Historical data proved not nearly as convenient to obtain as Charles Peterson originally assumed. As the final drawings were finished in 1940, Vint wrote to Hester Jones of the Historical Society of New Mexico asking for construction dates and names of architects. He was interested in finding out more about "The City of San Ildefonso Pueblo." According to Dr. Edgar Lee Hewett, librarian Helen Dorman replied, San Ildefonso Pueblo was prehistoric in origin and therefore impossible to date. She included a few facts about other buildings, citing Bradford Prince's 1915 *Spanish Mission Churches of New Mexico* but apologized that dates were difficult to verify.[17] In the Library of Congress collections brief historical backgrounds from secondary sources are provided for fewer than half of the sites recorded between 1934 and 1940 in a total of sixty-five pages.

HABS recording in New Mexico ended when federal funds ran out in the fall of 1940. John Gaw Meem telegrammed Thomas C. Vint October 28 to ask if it was not possible to continue the New Mexico program,

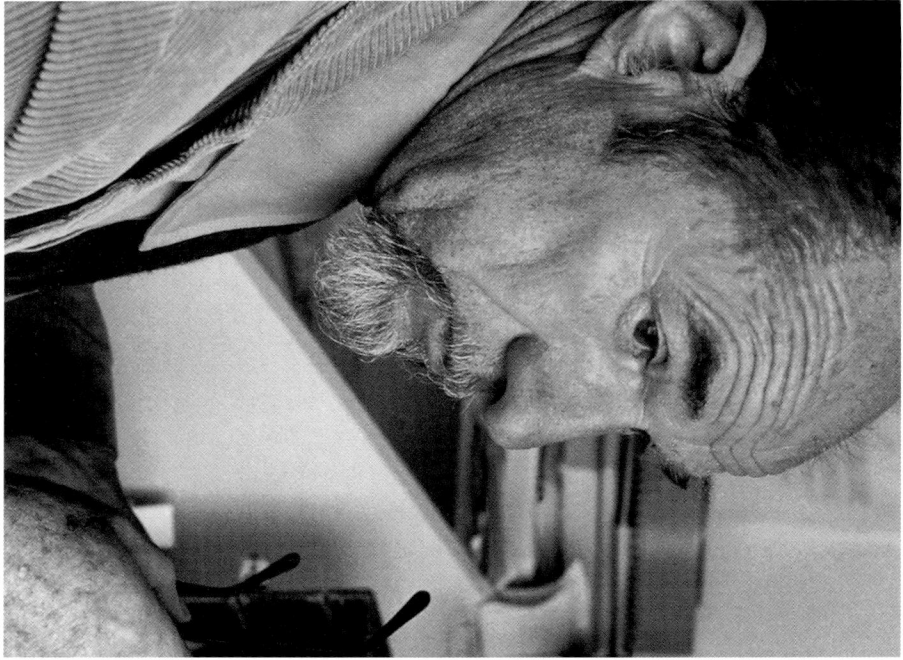

Bainbridge Bunting, ca. 1977.
Photograph courtesy of Mrs. Bainbridge Bunting.

sional architects due to the postwar building boom and the alternative of using college students to record buildings. Nationally, students had participated in HABS fieldwork as early as 1934. Another topic was the potential of architectural photogrammetry; Young architect Perry E. Borchers, recently returned from studies in Sweden, had introduced the technique in this country. He began working on contract with HABS in 1957.

The National Park Service decided to emphasize partnership with local preservation efforts rather than federal support. "It is much easier to help those who help themselves," said Charles E. Peterson at the Washington meeting. "Collaborative effort with the local people is the best method to accomplish the aims of HABS." In New Mexico it was a challenge to muster local action without federal funds. Private wealth was scarce, state support was not forthcoming, and few architects were able to volunteer their time.

New Mexico, however, was blessed with human resources. Meem was joined by two colleagues profoundly interested in the state's architecture, Bainbridge Bunting and George Clayton Pearl. Bunting (1913–83), an architectural historian with a doctorate from Harvard University, came to New Mexico in 1948 as the first art historian on the faculty at the University of New Mexico. As a conscientious objector in World War II, he had spent six years working with the American Friends Service Committee. Pearl (b. 1923) was a 1950 graduate in architecture from the University of Texas at Austin who was beginning his career in the Albuquerque firm of Stevens, Mallory, Pearl & Campbell.

New Mexico's AIA chapter was formed in 1947, and its preservation committee was made up of Meem, Pearl, Bunting, and architectural historian David Gebhard, director of the Roswell Museum. The state's architecture had a champion in Earl Reed, national chairman of the AIA Committee on the Preservation of Historic Buildings, who was also a HABS Advisory Board member and former district officer for northern Illinois. Reed told Pearl and Bunting in 1959 that he believed HABS should place greater emphasis on the West than on the East. After a visit to Albuquerque, he remarked to architect Richard Milner that Albuquerque's San Felipe de Neri Church was of such high quality compared to buildings included on surveys elsewhere that it highlighted the incomplete state of the New Mexico survey.

As HABS revived, the National Park Service formalized its selection criteria and documentation procedures. Eligibility was now based on a minimum age of fifty years. Recording techniques became increasingly standardized, and instructions were spelled out in government publications, not brief outlines. Drafters used uniform mechanical lettering, not hand-done captions and notes. Drawings were to be done in ink on polyester film rather than on rag paper sheets. Accuracy and uniformity were emphasized over elegance and individual expression.[18]

The revised standards did not have an immediate impact on New Mexico. The preservation committee, assisted by E. Boyd, curator of Spanish Colonial art at the Museum of New Mexico, compiled an updated list of priorities in June 1959 comprised of 15 pueblos, 19 churches, 22 houses, 4 villages, a jail, and a hotel. Taos Pueblo, mentioned as a priority in 1933, 1934, and 1939, headed the 1959 list. Three pueblos had been listed in 1933: Acoma, Taos, and Santa Ana; in 1959, 16 were deemed significant. San Ildefonso, Santa Clara, San Juan, Tesuque, Cochiti, and Sandia, judged low pri-

given the number of structures and their fragility. Indomitable and always a volunteer, he offered to assist in any way necessary. Meem continued to be involved in the National Advisory Board until 1961.

World War II brought a definitive end to HABS. It was not until 1958, well after the war, that limited federal funds were allocated to formally renew the survey. At a meeting early that year in Washington, DC, the National Advisory Board discussed the scarcity of profes-

ority in 1933, were now considered important. Pueblo missions had predominated in Meem's earlier lists, and churches at Isleta, Picurís, Santo Domingo, San Felipe, Zía, and Santa Ana pueblos were still included in 1959. Twelve Hispanic village churches and the *morada* at Abiquiu were listed. Las Trampas, Truchas, and Córdova had been on the original 1933 list, to which the Chimayó plaza was now added. Twenty houses in diverse styles from "late Territorial" to "ranch house" and "army period" were listed. Nine were in Santa Fe.

The 1959 list highlighted the same region and types of sites that had been identified in 1933, 1934, and 1939. As in previous HABS lists, portions of the state were virtually ignored. Pueblos, churches, and residences, primarily in Rio Arriba, Taos, Santa Fe, and San Miguel counties, were ranked as most significant. The later cutoff date had little effect on entries.

Because of the influence of George Pearl, however, eight important buildings south of Albuquerque and two ranches west of the city in northern Cibola County were included, expanding the list's scope slightly.

The first architectural documentation projects after World War II were initiated by Bainbridge Bunting, who assigned University of New Mexico students in his Architecture 261-62 class between 1958 and 1975 to measure and record historic buildings as term projects. Importantly, for the first time young Native American and Hispanic students brought their own cultural perspectives to the process. By documenting buildings according to HABS standards, they learned basic recording techniques and contributed to the emerging field of New Mexican architectural history. This work was accomplished with occasional praise or advice — but no formal support — from HABS. Lacking the funding and transportation enjoyed by earlier projects, Bunting and his students overcame daunting obstacles to produce a unique body of work.

Just as Meem had used his judgment as an architect to determine which buildings were important in the 1930s, so did Bunting use his knowledge as a historian to broaden the geographic scope and selection of buildings and locations. Under his guidance, students recorded a provocative variety of sites ranging from domestic and religious architecture to housing for copper miners, a mining town's assay office, a farming community's schoolhouse, a brewery, and a cemetery.

The meticulousness, accuracy, and completeness put into the drawings varied according to each student's background and ability. Several sheets out of the nearly one thousand that were produced met HABS standards. Bunting and students Jean Lee Booth and William R. Sims, Jr., documented sites in the Taos area according to the HABS format between 1960 and 1961 under the auspices of the Fort Burgwin Research Center in Ranchos de Taos. In 1964 HABS acquired 69 of these original drawings of the Upper Penitente Morada in Arroyo Hondo and ten residences in the villages of Ranchos de Taos, Ranchito, Arroyo Hondo, Llano Quemado, Peñasco, Talpa, and Vadito in the Taos Valley and Las Trampas to the south. Later, between 1966 and 1972, HABS acquired 59 sheets of drawings recording ten structures: five houses, three churches, a morada, and a Catholic grade school. The houses were in Taos, Puerto de Luna in eastern New Mexico, and Los Luceros near Alcalde. The religious buildings included San José de Gracia Church at Las Trampas — on the priority list since 1933 — a morada at Talpa, a small chapel at Los Luceros, and a church at Peralta south of Albuquerque.

During the nearly two decades that Bainbridge Bunting encouraged his students to record buildings according to HABS standards, the field of architectural history was in its infancy in New Mexico. Few studies of towns or individual buildings existed. Aside from primary documents, potential sources of information were limited to nineteenth-century Bureau of American Ethnology reports, highly specialized archaeological studies, and a few popular overviews. In architectural schools nationally, this was an era of modernism in which there was little interest in historic styles or preservation. The University of New Mexico was an exception because of Bunting, a gifted historian. His research and publications, followed by those of his students, laid the groundwork for the study of architectural history in the state. Nevertheless, the records at the Library of Congress include less than ten pages of historical data gathered by his students.[19]

Five years after Pope's visit to New Mexico another administrative shift centralized HABS in Washington, DC. Its new national chief, James C. Massey, traveled west in 1970 and met with Bunting and John Gaw Meem, who, at nearly eighty years old, was still active in architectural preservation. Massey wrote Bunting that he found the students' drawings an impressive and unique collection. He recommended that a HABS catalog for New Mexico be published, as had been in other states in the 1960s. He urged both Meem and Bunting to reactivate HABS, inquiring as to priorities for recording, urgent preservation problems such as urban renewal, and sources of financial support.

Although the drawings by Bunting's students seldom comply with the survey's rigorous specifications, they show the influence of changed standards of architectural education after World War II. Unlike the members of 1934 HABS teams who had been educated at eastern

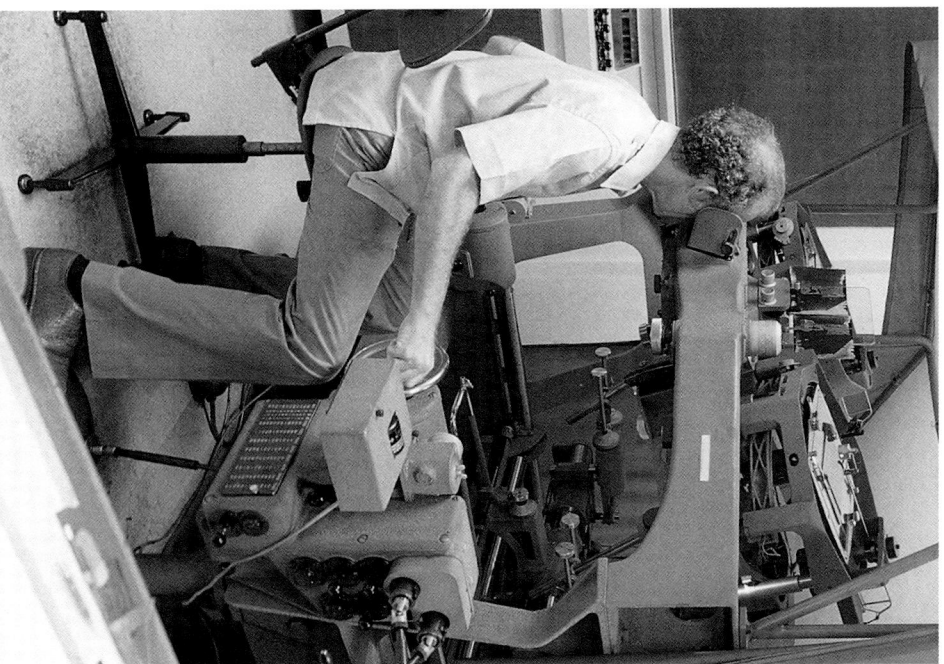

Perry E. Borchers at the Wild A7 Autograph plotting machine at OSU. Photograph courtesy of Perry E. Borchers.

quality of the work done in the 1930s and early 1940s, they convey invaluable information about a wide variety of structures, many of which have been destroyed.

In the postwar period HABS at the national level accorded photography growing importance as a documentation technique. Jack E. Boucher, a professional photographer, was hired by the National Park Service in the late 1950s. Boucher's technically superb black-and-white photographs record architectural details of buildings in an artistically sensitive manner and make dramatic use of interior lighting. When the photographer prepared to visit New Mexico in 1961, Bunting was asked to prepare a summary of architectural details and to assist in manipulating lighting for interior shots. Boucher's photographs are works of art, more sophisticated than the record shots taken by the architect-photographers of the 1930s.

Boucher took 66 photographs in New Mexico, 12 of which are part of the Library of Congress inventory and depict the Upper Penitente Morada Chapel and San José de Gracia Church at Las Trampas. Other Boucher photographs of Northern New Mexico, many of which are only partially catalogued, are part of the Bainbridge Bunting Collection in the John Gaw Meem Archive of Southwestern Architecture at the University of New Mexico, along with work by M. James Slack, Frederick Nichols, John O'Neill, Delos Smith, and Donald Dickensheets.

As early as 1920 John Gaw Meem had realized the architectural importance of the New Mexico pueblos. A half century later, James C. Massey, Bainbridge Bunting, and Professor Perry E. Borchers of Ohio State University began planning how to accomplish these measured drawings are simple and unadorned and rarely use subtle lines, dramatic shading, or artistic lettering. Although the drawings lack the style and expressive

universities and abroad, most students had no prior training in the fine art of drafting. Exquisite Beaux-Arts renderings were replaced by straightforward black-line records of company housing and schoolhouses. The measured drawings are simple and unadorned and rarely use subtle lines, dramatic shading, or artistic lettering. Although the drawings lack the style and expressive

Art in Stockholm, uses paired photographs and survey control to record and measure buildings in three dimensions and a photogrammetric plotting machine to convert the pairs to accurate scale drawings. In his *Early Architecture in New Mexico* (1976), Bunting observed that because present-day Pueblo people are reluctant to permit photography or examination of their communities, information on historic architecture must be limited to the study of ruins. Massey and Borchers, however, believed that Pueblo people would not have the same objections to aerial photogrammetry that they had to the intrusive presence of measuring teams in the villages.

Meem pointed out to Bunting the need for tribal approval and state and federal governmental support. The Bureau of Indian Affairs, the state Historic Preservation Office, and tribal governments all cooperated on this recording effort. Diplomatic skills were called for, and Borchers notes that he only worked with the consent of each Pueblo governor and tribal council, apparently with oral agreements. Between 1972 and 1993 he completed the remarkable task of documenting 16 of New Mexico's 19 pueblo communities. Taos Pueblo, a priority on every HABS list since 1933, was finally recorded in 1973; by 1993 drawings were completed for San Juan and Sandia pueblos. Santo Domingo, San Felipe, and Pojoaque remain undocumented, the last of which Borchers considers to have an essentially obliterated traditional core. In spite of repeated requests, the tribal councils of Santo Domingo and San Felipe pueblos continue to deny Borchers permission to measure and record these villages.

Only a portion of the drawings prepared by means of photogrammetry are at the Library of Congress, consisting of 39 sheets of drawings of the pueblos of Zuni,

San José del Vado, plan, sheet 2 of 3, HABS. Jack Schafer and Michelle F. Lewis, dels. 1975 (1NM-126).

Casita Martinez, Vadito.
Roy Boyd, photographer, n.d.
Bainbridge Bunting Collection,
John Gaw Meem Archive
of Southwestern Architecture,
University of New Mexico.

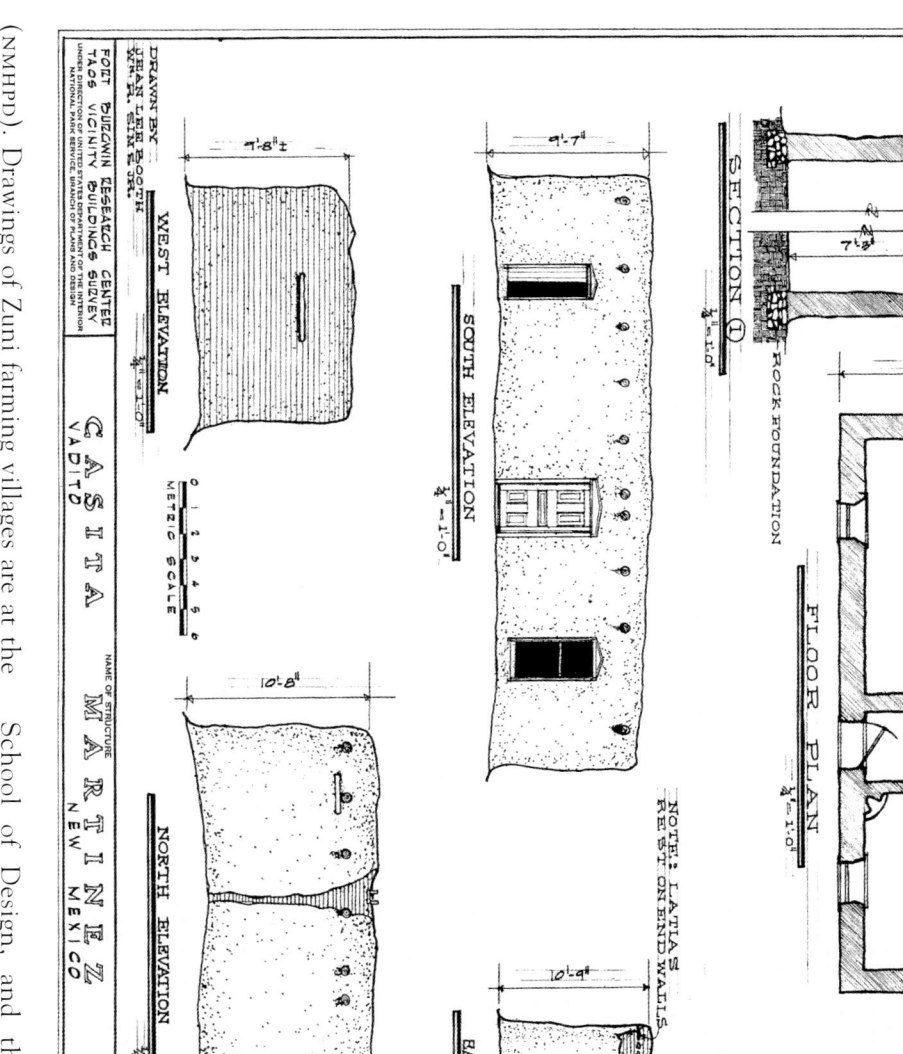

Casita Martinez, Vadito,
floor plan, sheet 2 of 3, HABS.
Jean Lee Booth and William R. Sims, Jr.,
dels. 1963 (NM-72).

Santa Clara, Tesuque, Taos, Acoma, San Ildefonso, Santa Ana, and Nambé. Unfortunately, an additional 14 sheets of the pueblos of Cochiti, Isleta, Sandia, Jémez, Laguna, Zía, San Juan, and Picurís are not part of the HABS collections and are only available at the New Mexico State Historic Preservation Division (NMHPD). Drawings of Zuni farming villages are at the School of Design, and the University of Chicago pueblo in the collections of the Zuni Archaeological Project.

In the 1970s, with the support of HABS and NMHPD, Perry Borchers and summer teams of students from Ohio State University, the Rhode Island School of Design, and the University of Chicago recorded Spanish American villages on the Pecos River and mining towns in the southwestern part of the state. The Library of Congress collections include 16 drawings of El Cerrito, San Miguel del Vado, San José del Vado, Chimayó, and La Luz. Again, a portion of the

RECORDING A VANISHING LEGACY

style, with which I was more than a little familiar. It was what we now call a bed and breakfast, although I was the only guest.

After breakfast the next morning, I telephoned Leicester Hyde, who instructed me to go to the Palace of the Governors on the north side of the plaza and report to the squad leader, who would put me to work. I was given a six-foot, folding carpenter's rule and a field notebook and assigned to measure a number of interior details. I was to continue working with the squad on the Governor's Palace until a new group was assembled.

During the lunch break, Hyde took me to John Gaw Meem's office, which was used as the headquarters of the New Mexico projects. He introduced me to Meem and several of his employees, Hugo Zehner and Gene Evans among them. Meem was a quiet person, almost shy. In my first meeting with him, I was struck by his manner in welcoming me to New Mexico and the HABS project; he made me feel that I had something to give to the project and was not just another drafting hand. As I learned in the ensuing years, he was sincerely interested in the developing careers of the younger men around him and did as much as he could to foster their ambitions. After the war I saw him infrequently, but whenever I visited Santa Fe, he always took time to spend a few hours with me, to talk of architecture, of what it meant to him and how he saw its development over the forthcoming years. I have regretted that I allowed so much time to elapse between visits.

Most, if not all, of the men working on the project at its start were New Mexico residents, but there were not enough New Mexico architects, with or without jobs, to do all the work that John Meem hoped to do; for this reason, he had been authorized to recruit unemployed architects from other states — Colorado, Arizona, and California, primarily. I was one of the earliest arrivals from out of state and an eager recipient of New Mexico lore, which the first generation native and the adoptive residents were equally eager to pass on.

Almost the first of the many bits of history that came my way was the fact that General Lew Wallace, when governor of the Territory of New Mexico (1878–81), and, consequently, a resident in the building we were now measuring, had written most of his famous novel, *Ben Hur*, sitting under the great cottonwood tree in the *placita*, the enclosed court within the building. There was more to come: a steady stream of miscellaneous history and legend about the oldest continuously occupied capital city in the United States.

In the week that followed, I measured both interior and exterior details and came to know the building and its history quite well, both from taking measurements and from the legends and oral history that came my way. The building is officially called the Palace of the Governors, but the word *palace* is misleading to those for whom the word calls to mind the Louvre, Versailles, or Buckingham.

It is a single-story adobe building occupying the entire length of the block on the north side of Palace Avenue, which bounds the plaza on the north. I would guess that it is about 250 feet long by about 120 feet deep, which depth includes a spacious placita, walled off from the street on the west. The main body of the building, fronting on the plaza, is two rooms deep for its entire length. There is a wing on the east side of the center which extends to the rear and contains the service portion of the palace, including the stables. The facade facing the plaza has a covered walkway, or portal, running the full length of the building. This *portal* is about 15 feet wide and extends to the curb; the roof is supported by peeled log columns with carved and painted wood bracket capitals. The brackets carry a heavy wood beam which, in turn, supports the roof *vigas*, as roof and floor beams are called, and adobe parapet wall. The portal shelters the Indians who, for as long as there have been tourists, have gathered there daily to sell the pottery, jewelry, and other articles they make.

One of the interesting facts about the building is that the Spanish conquistadors had erected the palace on the foundations of an earlier Indian structure, which was built of a very stiff adobe molded by hand. In 1934, a portion of the floor fell away, exposing the older, hand-molded adobe of the original building, on top of which the adobe brick had been laid. The building has been renovated many times, but I think that in 1934 it was much as it was in Territorial days.[1]

After six or seven days, Hyde had gathered a new team of four; besides me, there were Stanley Kent, my friend from the atelier; Edwin B. Clarke, an Albuquerque man; and Urie McCleary, from Los Angeles. McCleary, who was our crew leader, was in his early thirties, married, and, I think, had two small children. He often spoke of his aim, when back in Los Angeles, to give up architecture and start a new career in the film industry as a set designer and art director, which he ultimately did. He described the advantages of such a career mostly in terms of not having to worry about waterproofing foundations.

Hyde briefed us on the two projects assigned to us, told us that he had made arrangements for us to stay at a small hotel, the only one in Española, a town of a few hundred people situated on the Rio Grande, about 25 miles north of Santa Fe on the Taos road. We piled into

THE 1934 HABS PROJECT

Kiva, Nambé Pueblo, northwest elevation, photograph 1-3, HABS. M. James Slack, photographer. 1934 (NM-8).

Mac's [McCleary's] car with all our luggage, drove to Española, and settled into the hotel.

Española was a pleasant village located on the west bank of the river, across which is the highway, its main street running west from the bridge over the river. In addition to the hotel, there were a number of small businesses: grocery stores, a drugstore, several souvenir shops, a dry goods or general merchandise store, two or three cantinas, and a cantinita that sold bottled liquor only. A fairly large dance hall was located on the river's bank, with a railroad station nearby.

The railroad station served a narrow-gauge line popularly known as "the Chile Pepper Line," which ran between Alamosa, in south-central Colorado, and Santa Fe. The train left Alamosa in the morning, spent the night in Santa Fe, and returned to Alamosa in the late afternoon. The station in Española was open for three-quarters of an hour only, when the train was due, and, as the stationmaster was also the telegrapher, telegrams could be sent or received only during that period. Urgent messages had to wait, unless one wished to trust his luck to the long-distance telephone service, which could also be somewhat difficult, time-consuming, and frustrating. Once I tried calling Denver: the operator could not get through to Raton in order to relay the call on to Pueblo, Colorado Springs, and finally to Denver. She did manage, after some little time, to put the call through via Albuquerque, Phoenix, Salt Lake City, and on to Denver. It probably would have made more sense to wait for the train.

The next day, Leicester Hyde took us to Nambé Pueblo, introduced Mac to the governor of the pueblo, produced all the credentials necessary, and left us to start work. It was not as simple as I make it seem; a large amount of paperwork was necessary to secure the permission of the governor and his people, and that had been under way well before we drove there that first day.

The kiva at Nambé Pueblo, which was our first project and which John Gaw Meem had selected for recording, was chosen for two reasons: it was certainly the most dramatic and handsome of the kivas in the Rio Grande Valley, and of equal, if not greater importance, it was the only one, at that time, that had lost its religious significance and now served as a sort of men's club and, consequently, was accessible for recording.

Nambé Pueblo is located about five miles east of Tesuque Pueblo, which is, in turn, about five or six miles north of Santa Fe. Both pueblos are at the foot of the Sangre de Cristo Mountains, on rivers that drain into the Rio Grande to the west. Access to the pueblo was on an unpaved road, more or less following the arroyo.

The Nambé kiva is circular in plan, with a grand, sweeping stairway to the roof, in which there is an open hatch on the east-west axis and just off center of the skyward, north-south axis. A ladder, with its two long

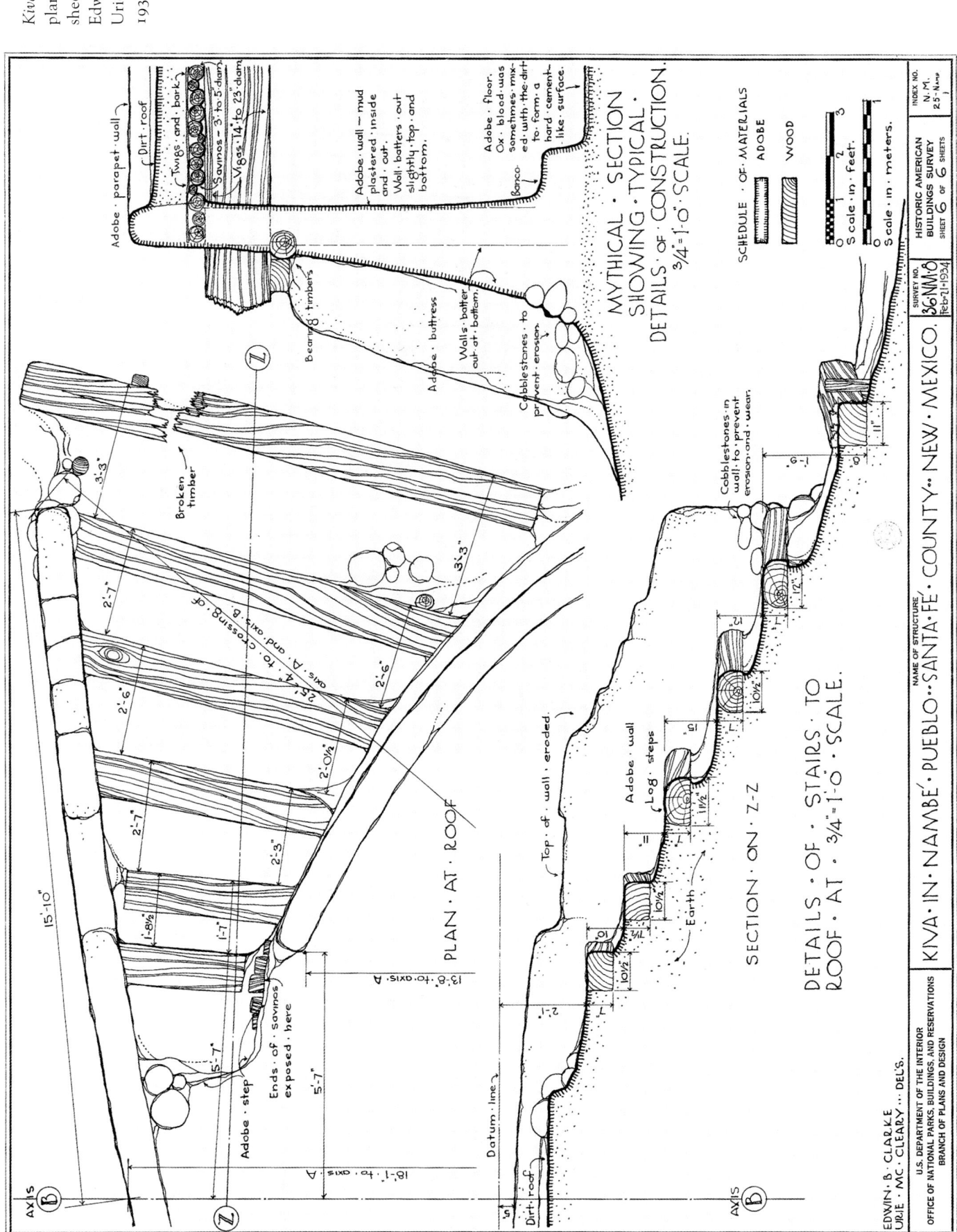

Kiva, Nambé Pueblo, plan of stairs at roof, sheet 6 of 6, HABS. Edwin B. Clarke and Urie McCleary, dels. 1934 (NM-8).

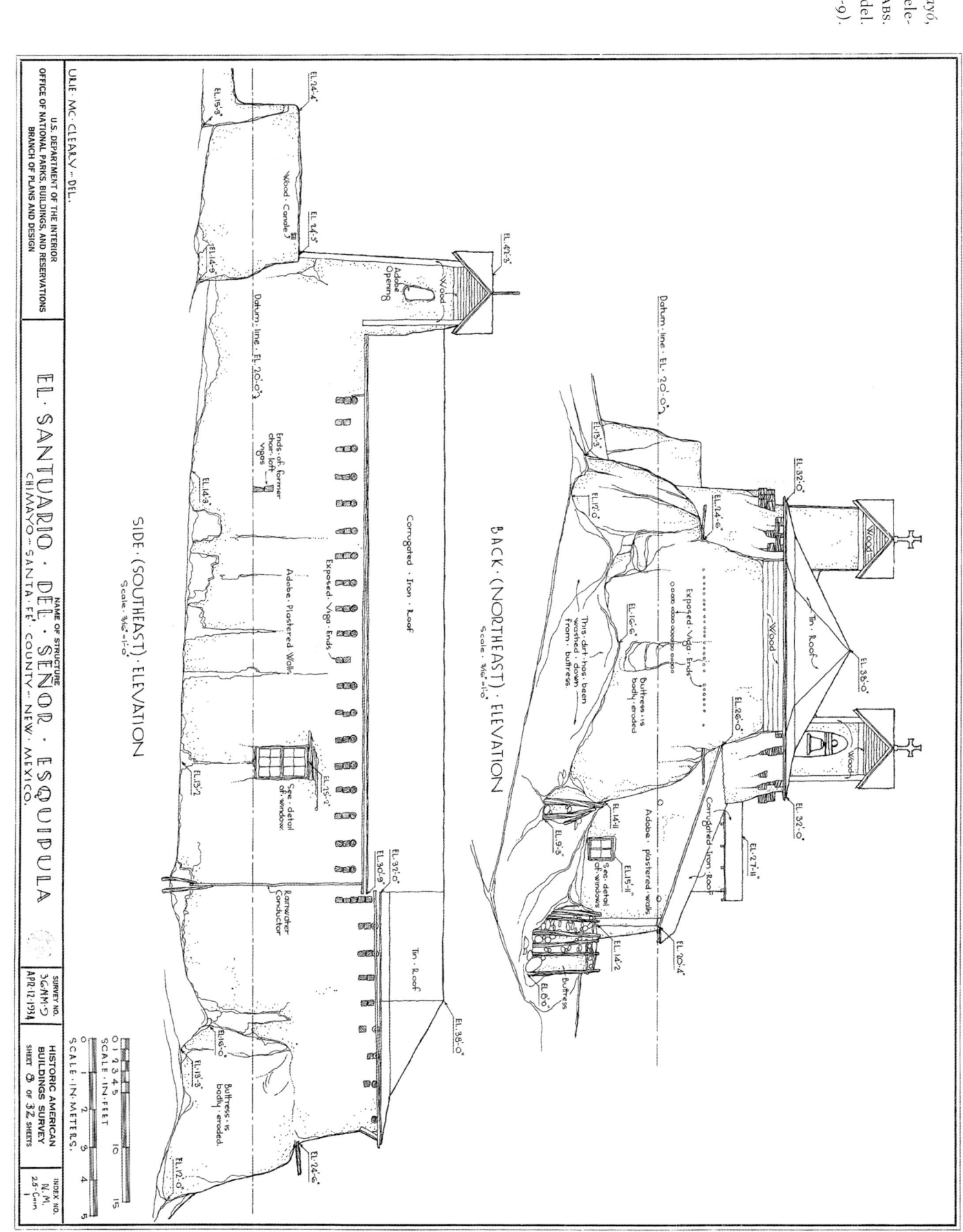

El Santuario, Chimayó, northeast and southeast elevations, sheet 8 of 32, HABS. Urie McCleary, del. 1934 (NM-9).

the absence of a surveyor's rod, and the simple transit that HABS furnished could only turn horizontal angles. Against one of the bell towers was a long ladder for the use of the sexton whenever it was necessary to toll the single bell, and it was this ladder that gave us the most help in measuring elevations.

Exterior details were left for the time being, and we moved indoors, where it was several degrees colder than outside. It was early March, and signs of spring were beginning to show; the cloudy-rainy-snowy days were behind us, although winter could and did return from time to time. The sun felt good when we were protected from the wind, but there was no sun in the church, or not enough to create warmth; shelter from the wind helped some, but it was still cold and the small woodburning stove in the middle of the nave, reserved for the Sunday service, was icy.

There were indications that a choir loft had once existed, and it was obvious that the pitched, gable roof covered with corrugated, galvanized iron had been added at a later time. Other curious details led us to see the need to learn more about the history of the building. Mac consulted the padres in Santa Cruz, and, either from them or from sources they referred him to, he acquired a magazine or journal article that gave us a great amount of helpful information. Included were photographs of the building before the pitched roof had been erected in the very early 1920s. A parapet was revealed on the front facade, a wavelike form with the crest on the centerline, dropping away at each side, then rising to engage the two bell towers. We explored the attic space between the original roof and the new and found the parapet intact, then we measured it for the restoration drawing that was included in the set.

Originally a choir loft had, indeed, been built at the narthex end of the nave, but we were unable to learn when or why it had been removed. Perhaps the structure had failed.

The apse end of the building is quite dramatic: at the rear of the church the land drops away some 15 to 20 feet to the floor of a wide, cultivated valley. The heavy adobe buttresses that support the apse wall, at an angle steeper than the slope, continue down until the two intersect. Adobe, eroded from the buttresses, flows down the slope and becomes, like the talus of a mesa, part of the earth from which it had come. That most dramatic facade is never seen by the pilgrims or the tourists, only by the farmers working in the fields below.

On each of the sidewalls of the nave are two large *retablos*, or *reredos*, each almost as high as the bottom of the carved, painted brackets that support the roof vigas. The retablos are divided into nine panels, three high and three wide; some are recessed as niches to display hand-carved and painted *bultos*, statuettes of saints, most of which are clad in lacy robes made by the women parishioners. The remaining panels are painted representations of other saints, one of the Guadalupe Madonna and one of Jesus. The paint was locally made of various colored earth and berries, all with a water vehicle.

A fifth retablo, larger than the others, entirely covers the apse end wall. It contains a recessed, proscenium-like structure, which, in turn, contains *el sagrario*, the tabernacle. It, too, is covered with paintings, religious symbols, and decorative motifs. The altar in front of the retablo is also painted but in a completely different style, that is, delicate, well composed, and the subject matter is floral. At the time of our visit, all of the retablos were partially covered with lace curtains, and the altar front was entirely covered.

We finished measuring the structure itself and then concentrated on details: the carved, panelled doors; a carved and painted confessional; *viga* brackets; the altar rail; cupboards; the retablos; the altar and sagrario; and the hand-wrought hardware, including locks with their keys and hasps and staples.

The panelled doors are all quite beautiful, and the pair between the narthex and nave, most particularly so. Each door is a little over eight feet high and about three and a half feet wide. The right-hand door has a small door within it. The upper third of each door is panelled in a geometric pattern with a floral design carved in high relief in the center. The panels surrounding the center piece have a carved, raised inscription, with the bottom of the lettering toward the center, so that the inscriptions on the lower panels are upside down. We were able to translate most of the individual words, but they did not make sense so, again, we consulted the padres. It seems that the inscribed panels had been installed out of order; when arranged as intended, the meaning of the whole was clear, although we were baffled by one word: *selago*. Our consultants, who were accustomed to the question, explained that it was three words telescoped, with the third word corrupted: *se le [h]ago*.

The inscription, properly ordered, reads: *Esta puerta, hiso Pedro José Corea el año de mil ocho cientos diciséis por solicitud del selago del Señor Domingues por de boción del R. P. F.* (Our translation: These doors were made by Pedro José Corea in the year one thousand eight hundred and sixteen by solicitation of Señor Domingues (*selago* — I made them) in his devotion to the Reverend Franciscan Fathers.) The doors were beautifully designed and the hand-run moldings refined, in good scale, and carefully executed.

THE 1934 HABS PROJECT

Governor and tribal officials from Acoma Pueblo with HABS squad members and others, Acoma Pueblo, 1934. Photograph and identifications courtesy of Dudley T. Smith.

polished English riding boots protected by a pair of unbuckled galoshes.

The plaza was still in a sad condition after the disastrous fire of the previous year that had razed most of the buildings on its three sides. Some of the structures had been rebuilt, but most were still untouched and the charred timbers and caved-in walls were depressing.

The rain having let up, at least temporarily, we drove to the pueblo and spent some time wandering around. Even then it was necessary to visit the pueblo's governor for permission to photograph the pueblo and its dwellers. The fee required depended on the size of the camera; motion picture photography was more expensive than still. Happily, there was no charge for drawing or painting, and I did do a few sketches.

We knew that John Gaw Meem had wanted very much to include the Taos Pueblo in the HABS projects, and being there, seeing the pueblo, we understood perfectly why he so much desired to have it recorded. Taos Pueblo is unique among the Rio Grande Valley pueblos and, with few exceptions, among all the others in New Mexico. The massing is beautiful, particularly of the Winter, or North, House, which, when seen against the mountain background and under dark and lowering cloud formations, was the most dramatic architectural work I had ever seen. It was probably then that I discovered the mix of cobalt blue and burnt sienna to represent that wonderful, deep blue-gray of thunderheads. The Summer, or South, House, lower and more spread out, is not quite as dramatic, but no matter, it too was beautiful.

When we were close to finishing the drawings of the Santuario de Chimayó, we suggested to Leicester Hyde that it would be desirable to do color drawings of the retablos. He agreed and sent us a half dozen sheets of

One weekend we drove to Taos, where we met some of the members of the team working there. They showed us around the mission church of Ranchos de Taos, the subject of many photographers and painters, including Margaret Bourke-White and Georgia O'Keeffe. We then drove to the little settlement of Talpa, where the team had measured a very small, but beautiful, private chapel with the lovely, euphonic name of La Capilla de Nuestra Señora de Talpa.

Arthur Hoyer, another atelier man, was the only member of the team known to me, but it was at Taos that I first met Alan B. Fisher, Paul Atchison, and Bradley P. Kidder. Brad Kidder interested me because his late father, a practicing architect, had written what was then the bible of architectural practice, the *Architects' and Builders' Handbook*, my primary source when cramming for the state board exams during the coming four years.

It was a rainy weekend, and the Taos Plaza was a sea of mud. I still have the mental image of a dignified Taos Indian, wrapped in his store-bought, gaudy blanket, picking his way carefully across the muddy street, his

RECORDING A VANISHING LEGACY

CHAPTER 4

THE BAINBRIDGE BUNTING YEARS

AGNESA REEVE

AND

RICHARD SCHALK

Any enterprise as extended in time and area as the Historic American Buildings Survey is like a circus tent — it must have a number of supports or it will collapse. During the 1960s and 1970s, HABS in New Mexico would have sagged to the ground without the support of Dr. Bainbridge Bunting, architectural historian and professor of art history at the University of New Mexico. Bunting had two motivations that drove him to keep the project alive for two decades: First, he was aware of both the importance and the fragility of the native New Mexican architecture; second, he was devoted to inspiring his students with this awareness while teaching them the basics of recording structures.[1]

To Bunting, understanding architecture required as much study of a society as of its structures. The adobe buildings of New Mexico could be read not only in terms of mass and material but as evidence of their owners' lives and values. Fortunately for social historians, he was particularly interested in domestic architecture. Although in this impoverished area domestic styles differed less from ecclesiastical than they did elsewhere, homes still offered a more individual look at their occupants. There are as many modest houses represented in the Bunting collection of drawings as there are public buildings.

An intense teacher, he inspired his students with such an enduring interest that decades later one cannot drive through the countryside without fingers itching to grab the camera and capture every appealing building—the beautiful, the analogous, the marvelously typical. Bunting himself said his family refused to accompany him on motor trips because he so frequently stopped to record an imposing Georgian facade or an odd oriel.

The multitude of images he photographed himself or collected from other sources was the beginning, and forms the nucleus, of the 350,000-item slide library at the University of New Mexico, appropriately named the Bainbridge Bunting Slide Library. Used frequently and augmented continually, it is now housed for the most part in ranks of neat, catalogued drawers. However, Bunting preferred slide storage consisting of vertical racks of large frames about three feet square, each of which could display dozens of images, thus enabling him to look at the big picture, made up of many distinct elements — hundreds of facades, plans, roofs, chimneys, windows — and details down to the grain of the wood in a carved corbel.

The scope of Bunting's training and experience provides a logical background for the range of his interests. His undergraduate degree was in architectural engineering at the University of Illinois (B.A. 1937); a specialization in architectural history took him to Harvard University (Ph.D. 1952). As a Quaker and conscientious objector during World War II, he was assigned to forestry and firefighting in Coalville, Nevada, a period that introduced him to the West.

39

RECORDING A VANISHING LEGACY

Leandro Martinez House, Ranchito, main facade, 1901. Photograph courtesy of Mr. Leandro Martinez. Bainbridge Bunting Collection, John Gaw Meem Archive of Southwestern Architecture, University of New Mexico.

These opportunities to experience the various areas of the United States, coupled with extensive travel abroad, ensured that Bunting's focus on the architecture of any region would be enriched by a broad perspective. His view would always include not just the present site or structure but what existed before and what was contemporary in other localities.

With his bride Dorie, Bunting came to New Mexico in 1948 never having seen the state but hoping to find it like Nevada. It proved a happy choice, both for the Buntings and for New Mexico. For the next thirty-five years he would make valuable contributions to the preservation of the region's cultural roots and distinctive style. In addition to teaching, he served in a number of organizations devoted to conservation of the environment, both natural and man-made.

His professional affiliations were integral to furthering his efforts. Although not a practicing architect, he was awarded honorary membership in the Albuquerque chapter of the American Institute of Architects in 1970. He served two terms, 1969–72 and 1977–81, on the national Board of Directors of the Society of Architectural Historians. In the latter position he was instrumental in attracting a national convention for architectural preservation to New Mexico, realizing that the best, probably the only, way to convince architects from the rest of the country of the significance of southwestern building history was to show them.

In this connection, his "Take a Trip with NMA: An Architectural Guide to Northern New Mexico," was published in the Fall 1970 issue of *New Mexico Architecture*,[2] the official publication of the New Mexico Society of Architects. The article remains, more than two decades later, the definitive tour guide for that area. The periodical itself owes much to Bunting, as he worked for its establishment and subsequently as associate editor.

His other publications also remain seminal in the study of architectural history. For the region, *Early Architecture in New Mexico* (1976) is the most comprehensive account, with further description in *Taos Adobes* ([1964] 1990) and *Of Earth and Timbers Made* ([1974] 1990).[3] His other publications include numerous articles and a biography of prominent Southwest architect John Gaw Meem, published posthumously in 1983.

As a teacher, Bunting always emphasized awareness of context, rather than rote memorization. He believed that names and dates of specific structures were useful tools in acquiring an understanding of larger cultural movements; he expected students to be able to examine a slide of an unfamiliar building and place it in its proper historical setting. It was not uncommon in one of his exams for the class to be shown a structure displaying a peculiar amalgam of quoins and towers, dormers and balustrades, to be unraveled coherently. If a structure was correctly identified in type and period, an approximate date within a decade was acceptable.

He taught developments in architecture as part of the development of other aspects of culture: economics, art, politics, religion. His time lines related changes in New Mexico culture and building customs to parallel changes in other parts of the world. At the same time, he fostered an appreciation of the Southwest's indigenous architecture, knowing it was essential to document the techniques and details of the past, both as history and as tools to be incorporated into the architecture of the future.

He was able to make such an enormous contribution to the recording of structures in New Mexico because he encouraged his students, as an option to writing a term paper, to record a significant building. He felt strongly the necessity for this documentation:

So, in the use of native materials lies a historical paradox. Despite the strong historical continuity of the region's architecture as a whole, most individual buildings are distressingly short lived. Because adobe also lends itself well to remodeling, old structures can be so easily and drastically changed that little trace of their earlier appearance remains....

This is what is happening in New Mexico today. For this reason, the series of photographed and measured drawings . . . will be of value as a historic record and of unique interest to those who cherish the old traditions.[4]

More than a thousand sheets make up the Bainbridge Bunting student measured drawings collection, now part of the John Gaw Meem Archive of Southwestern Architecture at the University of New Mexico's Zimmerman Library, a component of the Center for Southwest Research.[5]

The selection of sites to be used in the student drawing project was important both for historical preservation and student training. In determining which sites were of historical value and worthy of recording, Bunting consulted colleagues and advanced students. In addition to a site's historic significance, he considered its suitability in such ways as proximity to the university, accessibility granted by the owner, and complexity of the recording required. All of these had to be coordinated with a student's schedule and technical ability. He visited the proposed site himself, often staying overnight or returning for a second visit before making his final decision.

Bunting's idea of a field trip included "roughing it"; if necessary, he was content to sleep on the ground. Even

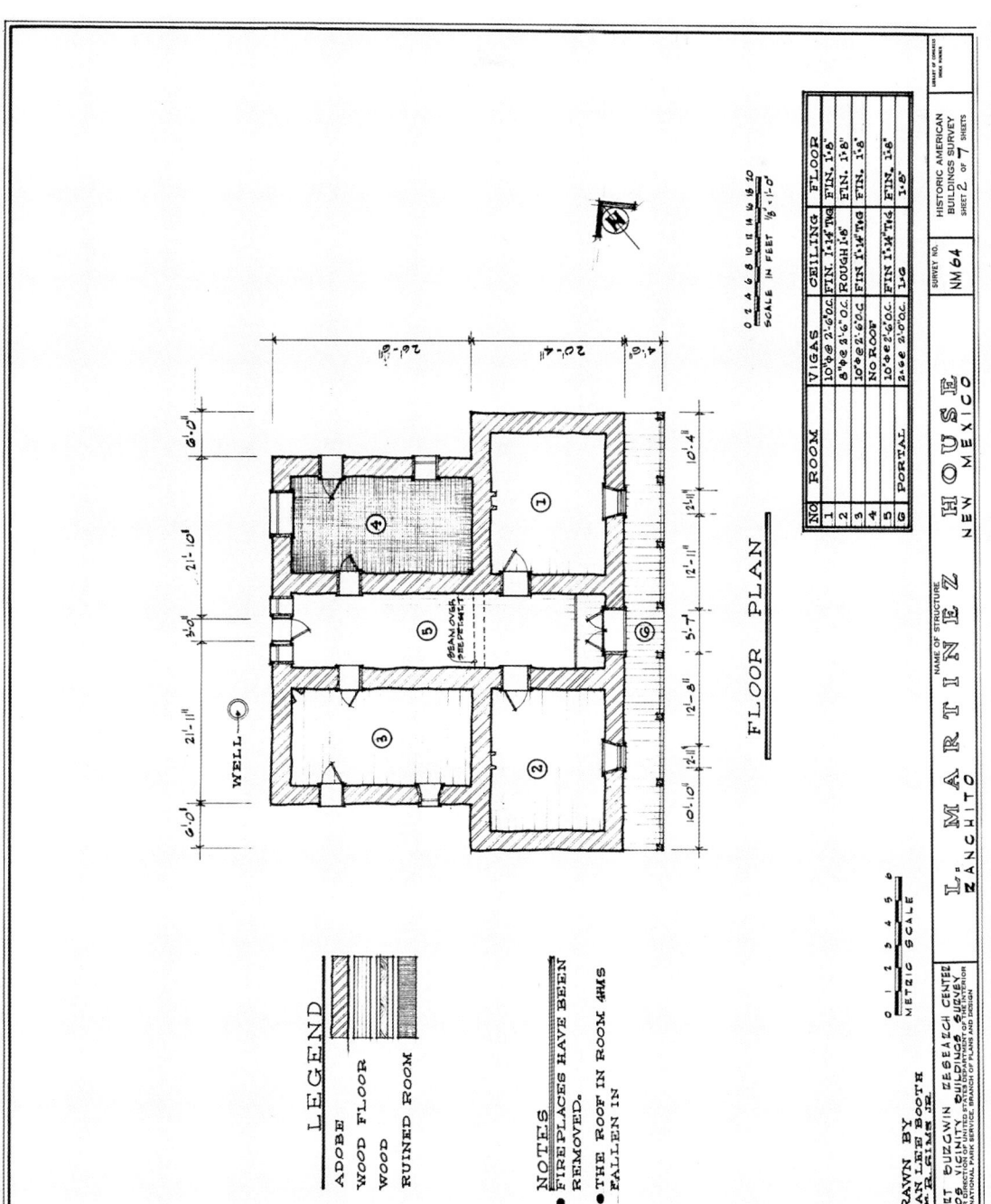

Leandro Martinez House,
floor plan, sheet 2 of 7, HABS.
Jean Lee Booth and William R. Sims, Jr., dels.
1963 (NM-64).

THE BAINBRIDGE BUNTING YEARS

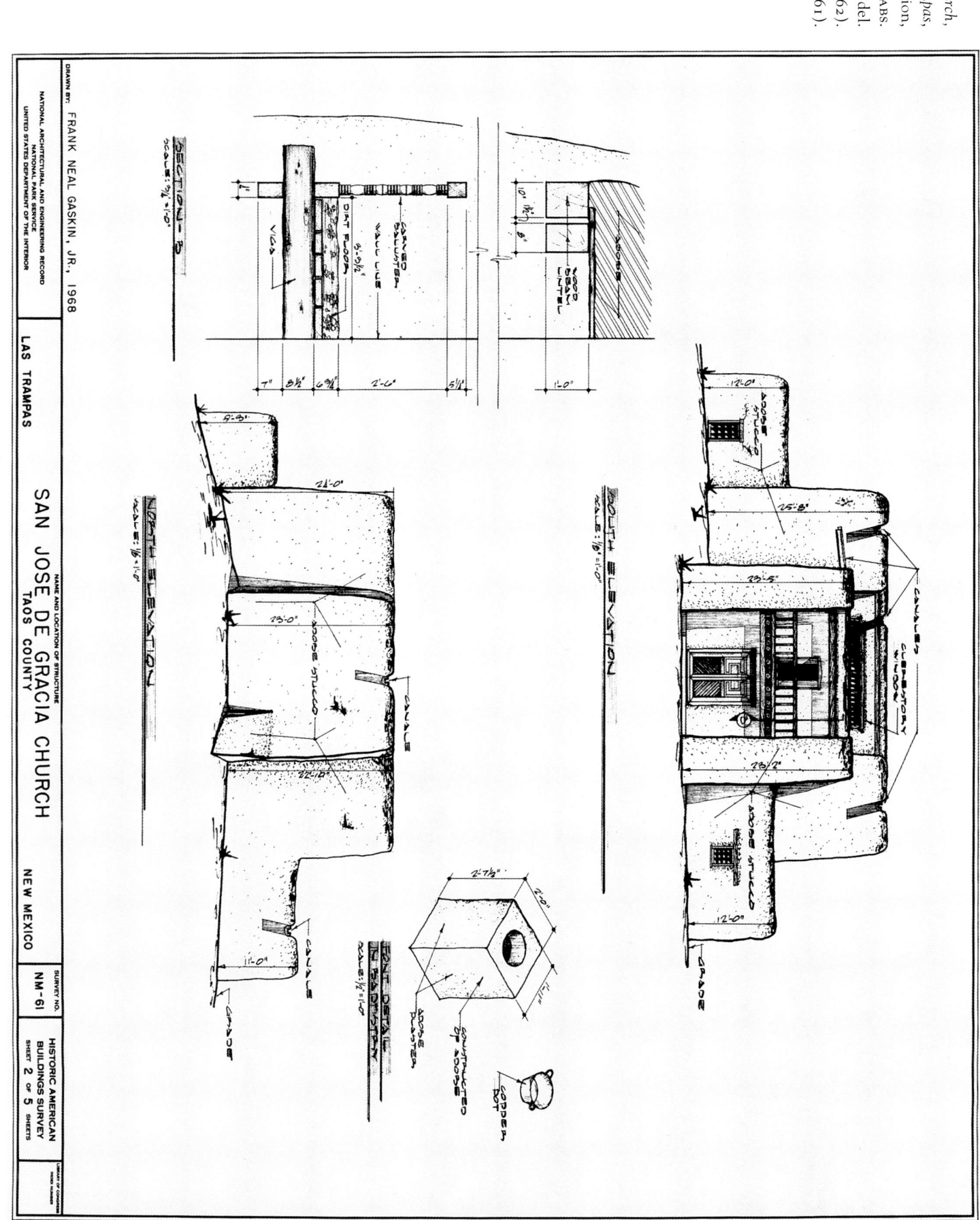

San José de Gracia Church, Las Trampas, north elevation, sheet 2 of 5, HABS. Frank Neal Gaskin, Jr., del. (Architecture 261-62). 1961 (NM-61).

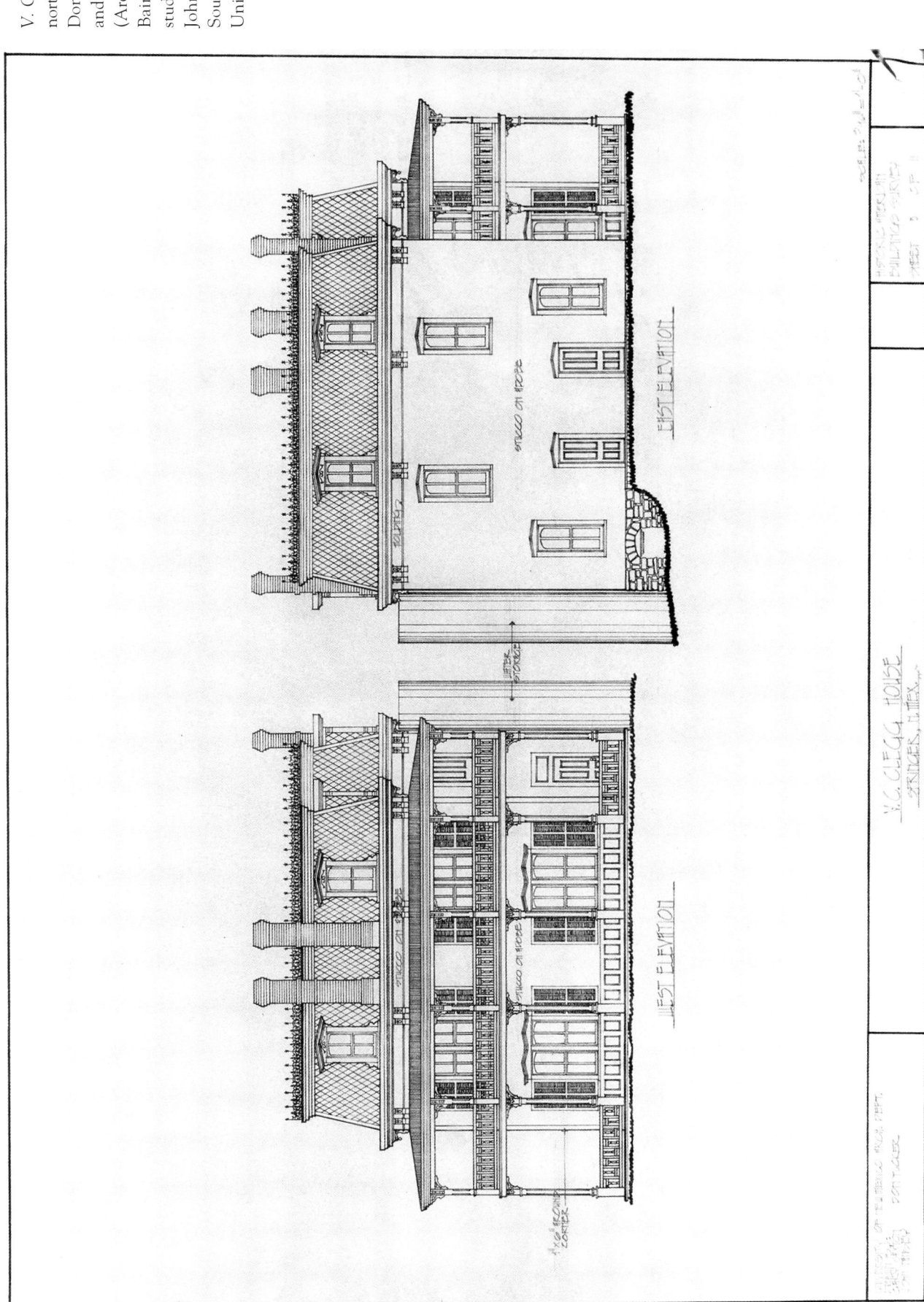

V. C. Clegg House, Springer, north elevation, sheet 5 of 11. Don Tucker, Gary Saxton, and John Tansey, dels. (Architecture 261-262). 1963. Bainbridge Bunting student drawings, John Gaw Meem Archive of Southwestern Architecture, University of New Mexico.

after he suffered a heart attack, he continued enthusiastically, heedless of medical advice. On one occasion he sent his surgeon a postcard depicting an Aztec priest offering to the heavens the heart of a human sacrifice, his message saying that he had been sleeping under the stars, supplied only with a Hershey bar, a bottle of whiskey, and a sleeping bag.

Whether or not his pupils entered into the projects with such dedication, they did learn methods of preparing measured drawings and documenting historic sites with floor plans, elevations, and distinctive details. They were encouraged to take as many photographs as possible, valuable for checking the drawings as well as for a photographic record. Questioned about getting permission to photograph the exterior of an occupied house (and perhaps trespassing), Bunting suggested not asking permission until all the necessary pictures had been taken.

In many instances the site drawings were imprecise in terms of measurements and outline. Some imprecision can be attributed to irregularities in the structure itself — the organic nature of the adobe materials, the unskilled labor, and the crude tools originally used in construction. In other instances, the lack of precision was the result of the students' lack of experience and expertise. As novices, these aspiring architects did not yet understand the critical importance of true measure in documentation and architectural practice. However, in a number of cases the student drawings, though flawed, are the sole surviving record of a particular site. The Venceslao Jaramillo house in El Rito, for example, an important illustration of the Queen Anne style adapted to an adobe, was demolished soon after a student documented it in 1979.

To record the vernacular was an elaborate undertaking even with the best of tools and techniques. To many students it was, to say the least, challenging. When no corner can be assumed to be a right angle, and no floor or roof to duplicate any other, it is an enormously painstaking task to illustrate the subject correctly.

Ultimately, Bunting's students documented buildings in Albuquerque, Taos, Santa Fe, Las Vegas, Belén, Bernalillo, Corrales, Cuba, Deming, and Galisteo, as well as a few isolated examples in Arizona and Colorado. Their prodigious output included homes, churches, stores, plazas, moradas, breweries, railroad depots, barns, mills, and schools. Of the 181 sites covered in the measured drawing collection, 86 (almost half) are houses, and 51 are churches, church-related, or moradas. The percentage of residences in the entire body of work confirms the importance Bunting gave to domestic architecture.

During the summer of 1967, the then chief of HABS, James C. Massey, was in correspondence with Bunting regarding "possible ways of carrying on further HABS work in New Mexico."[6] After a visit with Bunting and John Gaw Meem in April 1970, Massey noted in a letter that five possible projects were promising: the use of University of New Mexico students, both already completed and in the future; the creation of a HABS student summer measuring team, especially to record Indian pueblos; photo-data recording by students; use of aerial photogrammetry to aid in recording pueblo sites; and completion of a plan by John Gaw Meem to publish a collection of HABS drawings and photographs done in New Mexico in the 1930s.[7]

The first of these projects was implemented the following February, when Bunting sent drawings of 37 sites to Washington, DC, no small task in itself. As he commented in a letter to Massey, "Gosh what a job! Getting the piles of sheets and photographs sorted took an entire day to say nothing of the packaging. [I] hope some of them will be acceptable though I am only too aware of [the] amateur quality of some of the drawings."[8]

Money proved to be a bigger hurdle than some amateur drawings, but Massey wrote Bunting in October 1971 that his budget would allow him to buy 16 sheets for $400. The three sets chosen were the Antonio Valdez House in Taos, the stone house in Puerto de Luna, and San José de Gracia Church in Las Trampas. In addition, although they could not afford to purchase them, Massey asked for reproduction rights on five other sets: the morada in Talpa, Our Lady of Guadalupe Church in Peralta, the chapel at Los Luceros, the Romero house in Taos, and the Lucero house in Galisteo.[9]

Other facets of the program proposed by Massey, Meem, and Bunting in 1970 were partially carried out in succeeding years. Unfortunately, ill health prevented Meem from completing his intended publication. There are a number of structures represented in the Bunting collection that should be submitted or resubmitted with new drawings to HABS for possible inclusion: the Melvin W. Mills house in Springer (confusingly termed the "Clegg house" in the file), the Watrous house and trading post, and the Severino Martinez house in Taos, to mention only a few possibilities.

What this teacher brought to his subject was not only an understanding of the physical evidence of structures "of earth and timber made" but an illumination of the beauty inherent in them and the atmosphere they create. Of interior space in an adobe, Bunting said it might be described by plain walls, flat ceiling, and mud floor, but an interior of warmth because of the undulating walls and the textures of the surfaces. These elements in a room with almost no furniture offer great repose.[10]

It is impossible definitively to evaluate the influence of Bainbridge Bunting in the field of architectural history, or preservation, or art history. The material record alone is impressive, in the collections of slides and measured drawings and in his published works. He brought standards of research and scholarship to bear on a critical and new discipline that he helped to establish in New Mexico — the unified study of culture, architecture, and archaeology. Finally, his commitment to HABS generated important documentation. But beyond these, Bainbridge Bunting inspired a generation of architectural, art, and art history students to continue the study of architectural history in the Southwest.

PERRY C. BORCHERS

Recording Pueblo communities has been a priority of HABS since the original 1933 proposal, which identified them as "neglected subjects." The documentation process has required the consensus of both the HABS teams and the Pueblo governments, from Bautisto Pino, Acoma's governor in 1934, to the tribal officials of the 1990s. Today sixteen pueblos in the state have been recorded. In this chapter, Perry E. Borchers discusses aerial and terrestrial photogrammetry, which he has used to document Pueblo communities since 1972.

Photogrammetry is the science of measurement by means of photography. Photogrammetric recordings are based on pairs of glass plate photographic images taken under carefully controlled field conditions. Using plotting machines operators measure and draw architectural and topographic details seen stereoscopically from these plates. Borchers states that photogrammetry may be done from a distance, it is fast and economical, and it produces accurate drawings of complex or inaccessible sites. It is particularly appropriate for documenting communities that find other methods of documentation intrusive, as well as historic sites under threat of immediate destruction.

Aerial photogrammetry is superior to earlier individual aerial photographs of the pueblos, according to Borchers, because it supplies more data, compensates for perspective distortion, and captures the plan relation of buildings to plazas. He gives examples of how photogrammetric analysis of historic photographs of the pueblos in the 1800s can be used to reconstruct sites in measured drawings. Finally, he shares some of the insights that photogrammetric recording has provided during the course of his career.

Perry E. Borchers is an architect, architectural photogrammetrist, and professor emeritus of architecture of Ohio State University. Trained in architecture at Columbia University and the Royal Academy of Art in Stockholm, Sweden, he introduced architectural photogrammetry in the United States in 1956 and began his first HABS contract as a young teacher at Ohio State University in 1957. He is the author of over thirty articles published internationally and is responsible for the preparation of over 200 sheets according to HABS specifications. In 1997 he was elected fellow of the Historic American Building Survey and in 1999 was named a distinguished alumnus of Ohio State University. He often had the assistance of his family as a photogrammetric team and, until her death in 1983, his wife Myra Borchers also carried out her own parallel architectural photography and stereophotography.

CHAPTER 5

PHOTOGRAMMETRIC RECORDING OF COMMUNAL ARCHITECTURE

PERRY E. BORCHERS

The traditional communities and communal architecture of the Pueblo Indians and the Spanish settlers of New Mexico could hardly have been recorded for HABS by any other means than photogrammetry from air and ground.

The first problem of HABS recording — that of gaining permission for it — was reduced because photogrammetry (the geometrical science of measuring by means of photography) is a form of remote sensing. Photogrammetric recording, grasp, and measurement of complex and fluid forms of architecture and terrain can be accomplished with minimum intrusion on privacy and minimum disruption of activities in communal space.

This was certainly in mind when, in the spring of 1970 Bainbridge Bunting conducted James C. Massey, chief of HABS, and me from Albuquerque north along the Rio Grande into the very traditional and reclusive Keres pueblos of San Felipe and Santo Domingo, and thereafter into the Tewa pueblo of Tesuque, to consider these pueblos for photogrammetric recording.

We had the example of Stanley A. Stubbs, who, in his pioneering book *Bird's-Eye View of the Pueblos* had taken individual aerial photographs of the pueblos of New Mexico and Arizona and from them had traced the main clusters of rooms and plaza in small diagrams of each pueblo.[1] These photographs and tracings were too small for detail, contained the perspective distortion normal to single aerial images so they could not be measured directly, lacked the clear recognition and drawing of subsidiary structures, such as *hornos*, outbuildings, corrals and pens, and conveyed none of the major irregularities of the ground. The HABS recordings of twenty years later had to supply the data and accuracy that was lacking.

It was evident to us that aerial photography was ideal for grasping the complete plan arrangements of the pueblos. It was also evident that considerable improvement in accuracy and coverage could result from aerial stereophotogrammetry of the pueblos, which would produce stereoscopic "optical models" — scaled, leveled, and oriented in the three-coordinate system by photogrammetric plotting instruments. Unlike individual aerial photographs, optical models can be measured and drawn without perspective distortion. In them, structures and topography become three-dimensional visual forms that the operator of the plotting instrument can traverse with a measuring mark, touching all visible surfaces and traveling along all visible edges, while the movements of the mark are recorded by a pencil traveling over the plotting table adjacent to the instrument.

PRIOR PHOTOGRAMMETRIC RECORDING

At Ohio State University since 1957 I had carried out a series of contract projects of architectural photogrammetry for which our first sponsors were Charles E.

Plan of Taos Pueblo, sheet 2 of 8, HABS. Julsing J. Lamsam, del. 1973 (NM-102).

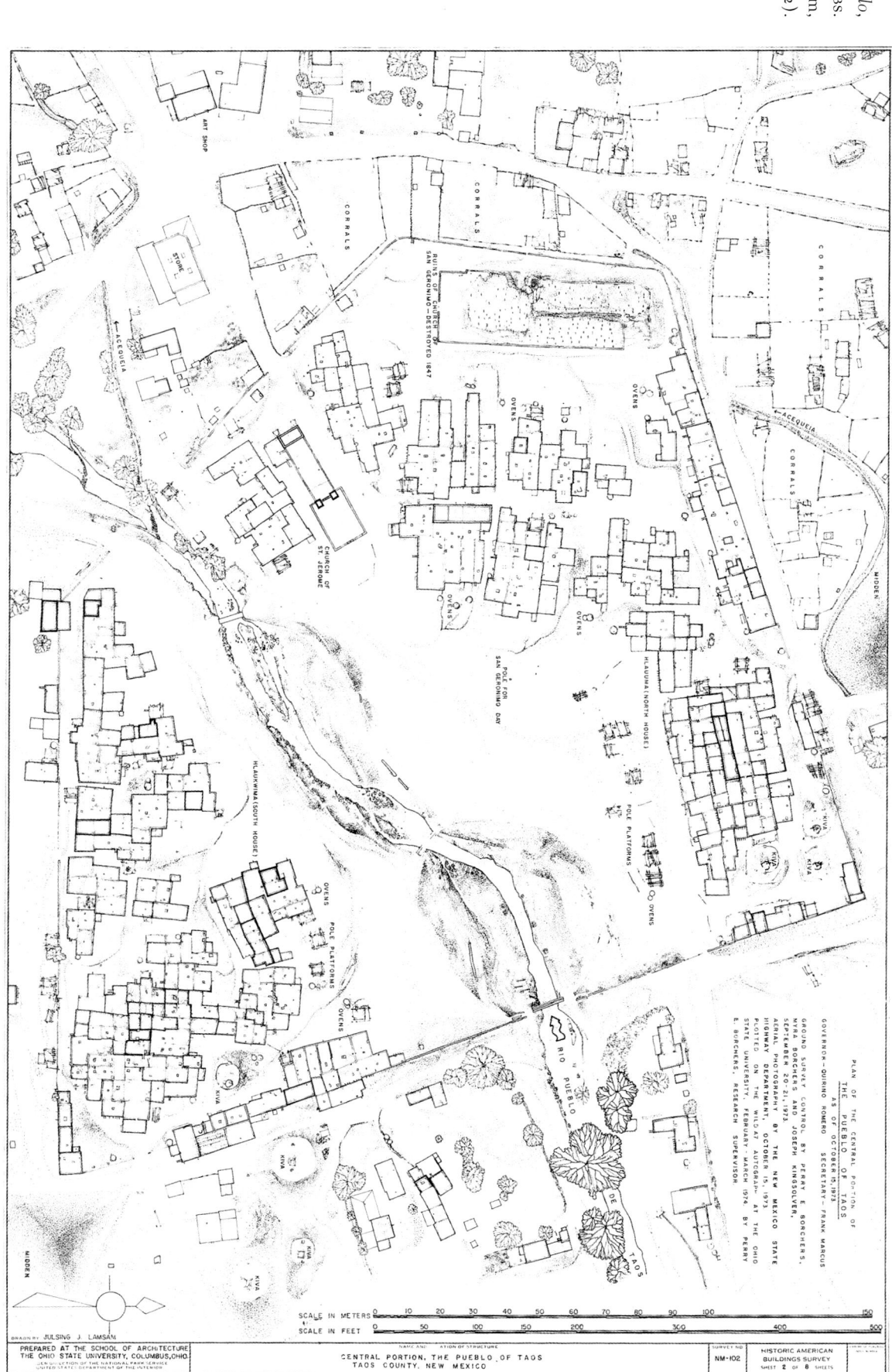

Peterson and Thomas C. Vint of the Eastern Office, Design and Construction, of the National Park Service. These projects — recording historic architecture in Ohio and then historic buildings throughout the eastern United States — were of a type known as terrestrial photogrammetry, which employed phototheodolites in photography from positions on the ground. A phototheodolite is a precisely calibrated camera of rigid geometry mounted upon a surveying instrument that allows choice and determination of camera station locations, camera axes, camera inclinations and stereo base, and also allows determination of survey control at a series of points established in "object space" at the height of the camera horizon. The resulting glass plate negative stereopairs and accompanying survey control data constitute the initial photogrammetric record which can, at any time afterwards, be set into a photogrammetric plotting instrument, such as the Wild A7 Autograph, for orienting, scaling, and plotting the optical model for preparing drawings to HABS standards.

Terrestrial photogrammetry results in detailed elevations of building facades, in partial horizontal sections or exterior plan drawings, and sometimes — when the phototheodolite is aimed vertically upwards — in detailed drawings of the interiors of domes and vaults.

The same Wild A7 Autograph accepts the glass plate diapositive copies of aerial photography for orientation and plotting in plan drawing and also in vertical section or elevation drawing parallel to the flight line of the aerial photography.

SPECIAL PHOTOGRAMMETRIC
PROCEDURES IN NEW MEXICO

It was aerial photogrammetry that predominated in the recording of the Indian pueblos and the Spanish American villages of New Mexico, for the plan relation of buildings to plazas was of major interest. Furthermore, the small-scale facade drawings that also resulted were sufficient for the limited details of adobe walls, projecting vigas, ladders, hornos, and relatively small areas of windows and doors.

The aerial photography was special in several ways. The flying heights were at the allowable minimum of 1,500 feet above populated areas in order to have the largest possible scale of photography. Instead of a single flight line over the center of a community, there were at least four flight lines specified to pass just outside the perimeter of the built-up areas, so that the wide-angle aerial camera reached out sideways, recording not only the rooftops of the buildings but every vertical wall as seen in oblique view from at least one of four different directions. The overlap of successive aerial photographs was 80 percent, instead of the usual 60 percent, to make certain that surfaces would be recorded stereoscopically even into narrow passages between buildings.

This aerial photography was carried out for us by the New Mexico State Highway Department through John Waller, their photogrammetric engineer, in 1972, 1973, and 1974. For the recording of the Spanish American towns along the Pecos in 1975, and for later recordings of Indian pueblos, the aerial photography was flown by John Mansfield of Koogle & Pouls Engineering, Inc., of Albuquerque.

In contrast to the earlier uncontrolled photography by Stubbs, this aerial photogrammetry required survey control on the ground in order to level, scale, and orient the optical models for plotting and drawing. In most cases, survey control came from the manholes of sewer systems in the pueblos built by the Indian Health Service (IHS). The as-built drawings that we obtained from the IHS office in Albuquerque gave manhole cover elevations and the directions and length of sewer run between manholes. In each pueblo roughly one-half of the manholes were clear of dirt and identifiable in the aerial photographs, and this was more than sufficient to establish a horizontal plane and a scale for the drawings. By avoiding intrusion for survey control work on the ground, we simplified the gaining of tribal council approval for the HABS recordings.

Bainbridge Bunting secured the first tribal council approvals for our recordings of Zuni Pueblo and Santa Clara Pueblo in 1972. Approval by the tribal councils or officers of the other pueblos from Tesuque Pueblo north to the pueblo of Taos were secured by Joe Kingsolver of the Santa Fe office of the Bureau of Indian Affairs in 1973 and in following years. My wife Myra and I attended tribal council meetings at Acoma in 1973 and at Santa Ana in 1975 to gain approval for the recording of those two pueblos. Our experiences seemed to indicate that a man and wife together represented, in the eyes of the tribal councils, a less aggressive Anglo-American interference in their affairs,[2] for they treated us much more considerately than they did some contractors who had other business with them at the same meetings.

The handsome, traditional pueblos of Taos, Acoma, and Santa Ana had no sewer systems. In Taos, my wife and I set up our terrestrial photogrammetric equipment — the Galileo Santoni phototheodolite of the School of Architecture, Ohio State University — and with cover and assistance from Joe Kingsolver quickly took terrestrial stereopairs of the North House and the South House (turning 180° from the same camera stations) to establish survey control for later aerial photography of Taos.[5]

El Cerrito, plan drawing, sheet 2 of 3, HABS. Jack W. Schafer, del. 1975 (NM-127).

Montezuma Hotel, south elevation, New Mexico State Planning Office. Kun-Hyuck Ahn, del. 1976. New Mexico Historic Preservation Division.

La Concepción, Quarai, photograph prior to 1934 of the unrestored ruins of the mission church. Aultman Studio, Trinidad, Colorado. Photograph courtesy of Perry E. Borchers.

Acoma Pueblo had been previously photographed from the air by the New Mexico State Highway Department in preparation for planning a new highway to the "Sky City." With the help of Bainbridge Bunting, my wife and I took terrestrial stereopairs within the *camposanto* of the church at Acoma to serve as survey control for the four aerial photographs (this time on a single flight line), on which the pueblo and mesa had been recorded eight years earlier. As a normal photogrammetric team would consist of four or five persons, my wife and I were grateful for Dr. Bunting's assistance.

At the pueblo of Santa Ana, four control points were surveyed on the ground in a large rectangle surrounding the mission church at the north side of the pueblo. These were marked in the standard photogrammetric manner with white plastic panels that recorded clearly in the aerial photography by Koogle & Pouls Engineering. Basil Pouls warned us at the time that range cattle often ate the plastic panels and died from them, resulting in lawsuits filed by the ranchers who lost the cattle. We quickly removed these markers after the plane passed overhead.

The same type of survey was established in the Spanish American villages along the Pecos River, which were the subject of recording by combined photogrammetry and hand measurement carried out by a HABS student team in 1975. This was a summer project jointly planned by John C. Poppeliers, chief of HABS, and Thomas Merlan, New Mexico State historic preservation officer. The team had Jack W. Schafer as student chief, Joseph J. Bilello, Michele F. Lewis, and Zeno A. Yeates as drafters, and Nelson Arroyo-Ortiz as historian. At Ohio State University, Muzzafir El-Ghazali was graduate research associate for the orientation and plotting of the aerial photography taken in New Mexico. This was the first occasion that I had not oriented and plotted the aerial photography myself; it required considerable travel for me to check and coordinate work that was so widely separated in New Mexico and Ohio.

In the remote village of El Cerrito, our preparations in laying out survey control for aerial photography so diverted the attention of a young man driving a tractor along a high embankment that the tractor turned over on the slope and pinned him under it. Only Jack Schafer's quickness in reaching him, turning off the ignition and organizing the others to dig the young man's leg free from under the tractor, saved him from very serious injury.

In the summer of 1976, my wife Myra and I, with a team composed of our children, Christina, Erik, and Charlotte — all students at Ohio State University — carried out a series of projects across New Mexico for the State Historic Preservation Office. We used both terrestrial and aerial photogrammetry, various methods of survey control, and additional stereophotography to record Jemez Pueblo, the Spanish American town of La Luz near Alamogordo, Anglo-American mining towns in southwestern New Mexico, and hotels near the Santa Fe Railroad through Las Vegas.

It is noteworthy that the Anglo-American mining towns showed little of the communal organization of the Indian pueblos and the Spanish American towns. Only the L. C. Ranch Headquarters near Gila represented a truly organized group of buildings.

In the following four years there were isolated projects. Some New Mexico State parks, such as Quarai and the Dorsey Mansion, were recorded for the state, with copies of the drawings going to HABS. Federal funds at the disposal of tribal councils paid for plotting and drawing some pueblos from aerial photography taken years earlier. Tribal councils at Nambé, Picurís, and Zuni pueblos also supported photogrammetric analyses of historic photographs of the pueblos (such as those taken by early photographer John K. Hillers in 1879 and by Adam Clark Vroman in 1889 on glass plate negatives filed in the Anthropological Archives, Smithsonian Institution, Washington, DC) from which to make measured drawings of the pueblos as they were in the nineteenth century. Copies of these drawings also went to HABS.

After 1980, no state funds were available for HABS recording in New Mexico. We did not resume work there until 1991.

PHOTOGRAMMETRIC ANALYSIS OF HISTORIC PHOTOGRAPHS

Photography can be an activity characterized by intrusive and rude curiosity. Even at best, it is a competing form of memory that dilutes the strength of the memory necessary for oral traditions. It is appropriate that some of the strength "stolen" by historic photography be yielded back to the tribes through photogrammetric analysis, which gives them detailed quantitative knowledge of their past structures and environment.

A major reason to record every Indian pueblo in New Mexico, even those most deteriorated and fractured in form, is that every surviving structure that can also be recognized in nineteenth-century historic photographs of the pueblos provides geometric control for photogrammetric analysis of the historic photographs. From this analysis one can make measured drawings of the pueblos as they were and perhaps even restore them to that former condition.

There is, of course, no ideal form in which to perpetuate the pueblos, for the clan clusters that made up the pueblo continually waxed and waned, and the appearance of the pueblo changed. But it is my opinion that many of the pueblos were much more impressive, and expressive of the life in them, than they are now.

A young Catholic priest came to me about 1980 saying he wanted to restore the fine church with a balcony front, existing until 1925 at Tesuque Pueblo, which he had seen illustrated and described in an architectural history of New Mexico. I could tell him the church must have stood in the neighboring village of Tesuque, instead of in the pueblo, for photogrammetric analysis showed that the extant church was the one that appeared in the photographs of Tesuque Pueblo taken by John K. Hillers and Adam Clark Vroman in 1879 and 1889. This old building deserves to be considered remarkable and special because it faces immediately upon the central plaza instead of being shunted to the outer edge of the pueblo as were almost all other pueblo mission churches.

Our most successful measured drawings from photogrammetric analyses of historic photographs were of Tesuque and Nambé pueblos, because of the extent of surviving structure, and of the Zuni farming village of Ojo Caliente, because of the great rocks of the cliff on which some buildings once stood and beneath which other buildings were clustered. These rocks were a major source of geometric control. At Ojo Caliente, many building clusters had disappeared, and smaller rocks on the hillsides in the photographs were gone, probably fractured into building stone.

Two sites we failed to reconstruct in measured drawings from historic photographs were the Zuni farming villages of Upper Nutria and Lower Pescado. The building corners and walls that stood in the photographs and those lying in ruins on the ground could not be matched. The horizons of the nineteenth century could not be matched with the horizons now, because of the growth of trees that must have been restrained earlier by constant cutting for firewood. The photographs of John K. Hillers, like the plan drawings prepared by Victor Mindeleff, the anthropologist for whom Hillers worked, concentrated on individual clusters of rooms to the neglect of the spaces connecting the separate clusters. Extensive work on the ground, in addition to photogrammetric analysis of historic photographs, is necessary to ever recover the historic forms of these villages in measured drawings.

We must mention the tremendous documentary value of original glass plate photographic negatives. They are bulky and heavy as historic archives, but they are dimensionally stable, unaffected by the swelling and shrinking that occurs in most photographic films and paper prints. They do not have additional distortions contributed by the lenses of copy cameras and projectors, and they are exceptionally fine material for precise geometrical work. The plates must be preserved as they are; their special value is lost in microfiche copies.

SPECIAL INSIGHTS RESULTING FROM PHOTOGRAMMETRIC RECORDING

Photogrammetry is unrivaled both for quick recording of complex and irregular structures and spaces on-site and for the later prolonged study and drawing of them in the laboratory, although sometimes a longer direct acquaintance with the site is desirable. For example,

PHOTOGRAMMETRIC RECORDING OF COMMUNAL ARCHITECTURE

DRAWINGS OF STRUCTURES AND SITES IN NEW MEXICO PREPARED BY MEANS OF PHOTOGRAMMETRY

This table lists sheets of measured drawings in the HABS format taken from photogrammetric glass plate stereopairs. These sheets are filed with the Library of Congress and the New Mexico Historic Preservation Division (see HABS Inventory for New Mexico locations). No photogrammetric measurement has been made of Santo Domingo Pueblo, San Felipe Pueblo, or Pojoaque Pueblo.

1972	Pueblo of Zuni (NM-78)
	Pueblo of Santa Clara (NM-98)
1973	Pueblo of Tesuque (NM-103)
	Pueblo of Taos (NM-102)
	Pueblo of Acoma (NM-6)
	Pueblo of San Ildefonso (NM-89)
1974	Pueblo of Laguna (NM-27)
	Pueblo of Zia, aerial photography (NM-104)
	Pueblo of San Juan, aerial photography (NM-101)
	Pueblo of Tesuque (NM-103)
1975	Pueblo of Santa Ana (NM-125, NM-106)
	Spanish American Villages on the Pecos (NM-131)
	Village of El Cerrito (NM-127)
	Village of San Miguel del Vado (NM-139, 139a, 139b)
	Village of San José del Vado (NM-126)
	Village of Chimayó (NM-128)
1976	Pueblo of Jémez (NM-145)
	Village of La Luz (NM-141)
	Town of Hillsboro (NM-142)
	Ghost town of Shakespeare (no HABS number)
	L.C. Ranch Headquarters (no HABS number)
	Montezuma Hotel (no HABS number)
1977	The Castaneda Railroad Hotel (no HABS number)
	Silver City, terrestrial stereopairs (NM-150, NM-151, NM-143)
	Pueblo of Nambé, restoration drawings (NM-107)
	Pueblo of Picurís, restoration drawings (NM-100)
1978	La Purísima Concepción de Quarac (no HABS number)
	Dorsey Mansion, restoration drawing (no HABS number)
1978–79	Zuni farming villages: Upper Nutria, Lower Nutria, Upper Pescado, Lower Pescado, Tepako, Sacred Spring, Ojo Caliente (no HABS number)
1984	Zia Pueblo (NM-104)
1991–92	Pueblo of Cochiti (no HABS number)
	Pueblo of Isleta (no HABS number)
1993	Sandía Pueblo (no HABS number)
	San Juan Pueblo (NM-101)
1994	Truby's Tower and the Citadel
	Three Corn Ruin and Old Fort

when plotting the plan of Taos Pueblo from aerial photogrammetry, a road to the east of the wall surrounding the central pueblo seemed to me to be too straight to be an element of the original pueblo. In the final drawing, I covered part of this road with the main title and legend and later discovered from Joe Kingsolver that I had partly obscured the sacred racetrack of the pueblo.

On the other hand, only by photogrammetry would one discover the remarkable, and evidently intentional, agreement in height between the highest points of the North House and the South House and the highest ladder pole of the eastern kiva. The highest point of the greased pole set up for the annual San Geronimo's Day celebration was only a little short of this same height.

The aerial photography used for plotting and drawing Acoma Pueblo was taken on a single flight in 1965 and did not allow complete drawing of the vertical cliff faces and walls of the pueblo. However, I drew a vertical section through the mesa of Acoma because I was interested in the heights for this mesa, which varied from 350 feet to 375 feet above the desert floor as mentioned in four books describing Acoma. I was shocked when this height scaled at only approximately 225 feet in my drawing, and I went back through all my orientation and plotting without finding any error. Then I consulted the U.S. Geological Survey map of Acoma and found that, interpolating between the contours of 20-foot intervals on that map, 225 feet was a reasonable measure of the height of the mesa of Acoma. Meanwhile, the Enchanted Mesa, within sight and reputed to be the original home of the Acomas before an earthquake made it inaccessible to them, is approximately 360 feet in height above the desert floor. The most recent state highway map of New Mexico still says that Acoma, the Sky City, "perches atop a 357-foot mesa."

The aerial photography of Acoma contained another surprise. Perhaps the flight followed a cloudburst, because, in addition to the Great Cistern and the small pools within the streets of the pueblo, there were dozens of rock basins on the mesa top that brimmed with water.

In drawing the east elevation of the church ruin of La Purísima Concepción de Quarai at the ruins of Quarai — in 1978 a state monument but now a part of the Salinas Pueblos National Monument — I compared it with a historic photograph showing the ruin before its partial restoration in 1934. At that time, "restorers" replaced the door and window lintels and built the stone walls higher. My comparison showed that the workers had also filled in a neat gap in the east wall into which a great wooden truss could have fitted naturally, with its bottom member at the height of the vigas of the nave, its top member at the height of the vigas of the chancel, and between the two a clerestory opening lighting the whole width of the transepts and chancel. Other restorations of historic structures and monuments deserve similar study to correct possible errors of reconstruction.

In 1991, aerial photography of Cochiti and Isleta pueblos and terrestrial photogrammetry of the Church of San Agustín at Isleta were carried out, with three sheets of HABS drawings resulting. Photogrammetry, plotting, and drawing of Sandía Pueblo, drawing of Zía Pueblo from 1984 plottings of 1974 aerial photography, and plotting and drawing of San Juan Pueblo based on 1974 aerial photographs were completed in 1993.

In 1994, four refugee sites of Dinetah — Truby's Tower, the Citadel, Three Corn Ruin, and Old Fort — were recorded and drawn on two HABS sheets from a mixture of aerial photography, terrestrial photogrammetry, and from extensive stereophotography. For structures as irregular and primitive as these, this would be the most efficient data to put in the hands of a restoration craftsman for an immediate sense of how to choose rock and slap mud. Stereophotography in both black and white and color should be part of the HABS archive.

The only color in the national HABS record comes from New Mexico in the 1930s, where watercolorists did renderings of a few church retablos. There are many similar retablos and chapels worth recording, and their color can be recorded with complete archival permanence in the form of black-and-white sheets of color separation such as must be prepared for color printing in publication. The unique murals in the mission church of Zuni Pueblo deserve similar recording in color.

Drawings of New Mexican structures and sites prepared by means of photogrammetry according to the HABS format are listed on the facing page. Still to be documented, besides the now largely obliterated pueblo of Pojoaque, are the conservative pueblos of San Felipe and Santo Domingo, the first pueblos I visited with Bainbridge Bunting and James C. Massey in 1970.

MORGAN RIEDER

Today, recording techniques and methods range from those used by HABS teams in the 1930s to variations on the photogrammetric process introduced to HABS by Perry E. Borchers in the 1950s. As in the past, students of architecture and history are recruited to work on summer projects. The Southwest Regional Office of the NPS sponsored HABS projects in New Mexico in the 1980s. The NPS uses HABS drawings to meet its cultural resource management needs; for example, existing condition drawings are the basis for preservation, maintenance, interpretation, and reconstruction of sites.

This chapter is contributed by Morgan Rieder, who describes three major HABS documentation projects that he supervised between 1986 and 1988. He first outlines the history of the seventeenth-century Franciscan missions at Quarai, Abó, and Las Humanas in the Salinas Basin southeast of Albuquerque, discussing building materials, techniques, and architectural form. Rieder then summarizes the goals and findings of two pilot graphic documentation projects conducted at the Anasazi sites of Chaco Canyon in northwestern New Mexico and Canyon de Chelly on the Navajo Reservation in Arizona. These projects contributed to the NPS regional documentation plan to reach the long-term goal of comprehensively documenting all sites and structures under its administration in the Southwest.

Morgan Rieder has lived much of his life in the Southwest. He earned his B.A. and M.A. in Architecture at the University of New Mexico School of Architecture and Planning and has an extensive background in the study and preservation of prehistoric and historic architecture in the region. He is the recipient of the Historic Commisssion Award for Contributions to Pima County Historic Preservation in Tuscon, Pima County, Arizona. Currently he is an archaeologist based in Tucson, Arizona.

CHAPTER 6
HABS RECORDING TODAY

MORGAN RIEDER

In recent years, HABS seasonal recording projects in New Mexico have been sponsored by the NPS, which has determined priorities and provided funding. In 1985 and 1986, HABS teams completed the documentation of seventeenth-century Franciscan missions at Salinas National Monument. The year 1986 also saw an NPS proposal for a regional graphic documentation plan to establish a systematic procedure for recording *all* prehistoric and historic sites and structures in the Southwest region that are administered by the NPS and lack such documentation. The proposal called for HABS' participation in this comprehensive, long-range effort. HABS teams participated in a pilot project at Canyon de Chelly National Monument in Arizona in 1987 and a follow-up at Chaco Culture National Historic Park in 1988 to determine the most effective methods of graphic documentation for the plan. Today HABS continues to participate in recording projects as part of the regional graphic documentation plan.

SALINAS NATIONAL MONUMENT
The region known in the seventeenth century as Las Salinas, or the salt lakes, lies in the foothills of the Manzano Mountains in central New Mexico, about 25 miles east of Albuquerque. Prehispanic pueblos there maintained economic and cultural contacts with the Rio Grande pueblos to the west and the Plains tribes to the east. Following Spanish colonization in 1598, the Salinas pueblos were incorporated within the Franciscan mission system. Between 1610 and 1630 missions were established at the pueblos of Chililí, Taxique, Quarai, Abó, and Las Humanas, the last named after the Jumanos, a Plains tribe that traded there.

Before 1680, however, the Salinas region was completely abandoned, and resettlement of the region did not take place until the nineteenth century. At that time Las Humanas became known as Gran Quivira, the mythical city of gold sought by Francisco Vásquez de Coronado in the 1540s. Today the area is still sparsely populated and retains a distinctly rural character. In this setting, the ruins of the missions still standing at Quarai, Abó, and Las Humanas are all the more impressive in their scale and isolation.

These remains, now forming Salinas National Monument, were the subject of HABS recording projects. The church and *convento* of Nuestra Señora de la Purísima Concepción at Quarai was recorded by Perry E. Borchers and his team in 1978 as a project funded by the state of New Mexico when it was still a state monument. San Gregorio at Abó was recorded in 1985 and San Buenaventura and San Ysidro at Las Humanas (Gran Quivira) in 1986. The projects, which involved both photogrammetry and conventional recording techniques, illustrate the challenges inherent in recording such sites. The drawings themselves are important contributions to the constantly evolving body of knowledge relating to seventeenth-century New Mexico.

The Franciscans brought with them to this far northern frontier an architectural program based on sixteenth-century missionary experience in Mexico. The program, as used in the missions of the Salinas region and elsewhere in New Mexico, consisted of certain constant elements. The church had a nave without aisles; above the entrance at the east or south end of the church was the choir loft; by the sanctuary at the opposite end, a polygonal or rectilinear apse. Alongside the church was the convento, the administrative core of the mission, built around a central patio. Public access to the convento was through the *portería*, in the front next to the facade of the church. Adjoining the convento was one or more service courts.

The missionaries used the labor, materials, and many of the techniques of the native inhabitants of the Salinas pueblos, although the buildings were constructed on a consistently larger scale. The local building stone (sandstone at Quarai and Abó, limestone at Las Humanas) was used to construct the massive core-and-veneer walls of the missions, but structural timber had to be sought farther afield. Stands of ponderosa pine on the slopes of the Manzanos supplied the beams for the churches at Quarai and Abó; for Las Humanas, the closest source was the Gallinas Mountains to the east. As with materials, the basic structural principles involved were the same as those of the Pueblo building tradition. The difference in scale, particularly in regard to the churches, required that the friar-in-charge have a working knowledge of European building practice.

The building history of the missions at Quarai, Abó, and Las Humanas can be briefly summarized. Construction of the church and convento of La Concepción at Quarai was begun in 1627 under the direction of Fray Juan Gutiérrez and was completed about 1632. The existing structures date from this building episode, except for the addition of the baptistry about 1640 and a remodeling of the convento in the late 1650s.

The sequence of construction at San Gregorio de Abó presents a more complex picture. The first church and convento, built in the 1620s under the direction of Fray Francisco Fonte, were relatively modest. In 1645 Fray Francisco Acevedo, Fonte's successor, began a more ambitious project. The original church was partially dismantled, and the walls of its nave were incorporated into the larger, extant church. By 1658, the convento had also been entirely reconstructed and expanded.

At Las Humanas, the earlier church known as San Isidro, was begun under the direction of Fray Francisco Letrado in 1630; rooms in the pueblo itself served as a convento. Letrado's assignment here was brief, and San Isidro became a *visita*, or adjunct, of the mission at Abó. Acevedo, as *visitador*, oversaw the completion of the church by 1635. Las Humanas remained in this status until 1659, when Fray Diego de Santander was assigned to the pueblo. Construction of the church and convento of San Buenaventura began the following year. After Santander's departure in 1662, the convento was completed, and by 1667 the choir loft was installed in the church. After 1667, work on the church ceased and never resumed.

By this time, crop failure and increasingly frequent Apache raids threatened the very existence of Las Humanas, which soon became the first of the Salinas pueblos to be abandoned. Before the end of the 1670s, the region was deserted and the Pueblo populations relocated to missions along the Rio Grande. In 1680, the Pueblo Revolt saw churches in the insurrectionist pueblos throughout New Mexico razed or at least partially destroyed (with the exception of San Esteban at Acoma). Only after the Spanish *Reconquista*, beginning in 1692, were missions reestablished at many pueblos, and the mission structures were accordingly rebuilt or replaced.

As unaltered survivors of the period before the revolt, the Salinas missions reveal much about church construction in New Mexico in the late seventeenth century. During this formative period — when European architectural conventions were translated into indigenous materials and resulting innovations such as the transverse clerestory became part of the architectural repertory — the Franciscans often aimed at a greater monumentality in form and scale than would be seen in the following century. While their aims were not as grand as those of Fray Andrés Juárez, responsible for the huge seventeenth-century church at Pecos, the friars who designed and supervised the construction of the churches of La Concepción, San Gregorio, and San Buenaventura did have considerable architectural ambitions and, at least in the former two, the ability to realize them. Enough survives of the nave and transept walls at La Concepción and San Gregorio to reconstruct visually their imposing interiors, dramatically illuminated by transverse clerestories. The friars' competence in structural engineering was equal to the requirements of the spaces they envisioned. Recent investigations have shown that the nave and transept beams at these two churches were "very close to the sizes that would be required had the structures been built in accordance with current building codes."[1]

In the early years of the nineteenth century, settlers from the Rio Grande Valley began to establish communities in the Salinas region. Resettlement proceeded slowly, still hindered by Apache raids. The former *tor-*

Misión San Gregorio de Abó, south elevation of the church and convento, ca. 1670, Jean L. Pike, del. NPS Southwest Cultural Resources Center.

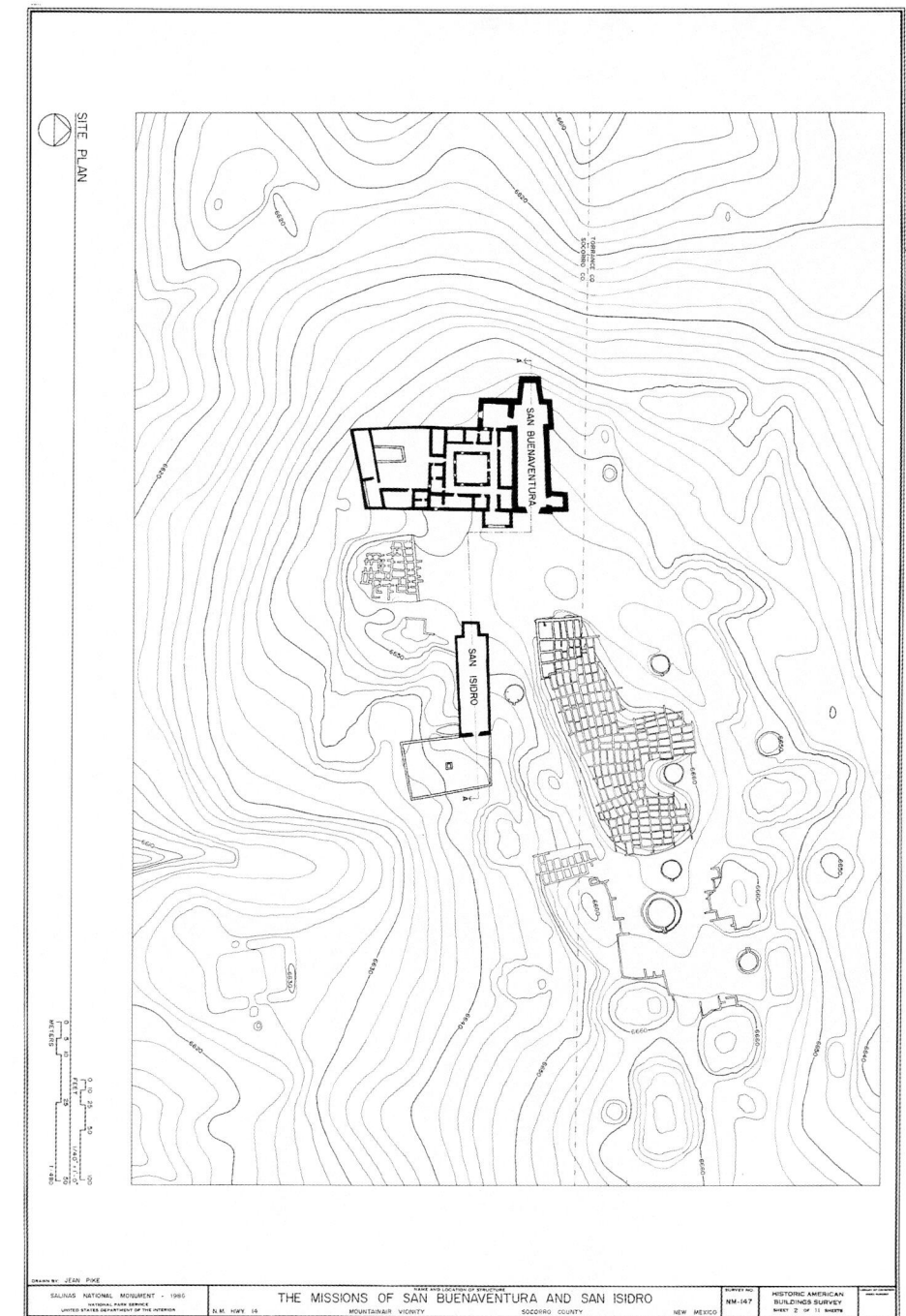

HABS team surveying and measuring San Buenaventura, 1986. Setting interior datum line: (left) Daniel Hernandez, holding rod; (right) Jean L. Pike, taking field notes. Photograph courtesy of Morgan Rieder.

(above right) Missions of San Buenaventura and San Isidro, Gran Quivira, Salinas National Monument, site plan, sheet 2 of 11, HABS. Jean L. Pike, del. 1986 (NM-147). NPS Cultural Resources Center.

reón, or defensive tower, at Manzano, a few miles northeast of Quarai, was typical of the fortified structures built by these settlers and was recorded by HABS in 1939 and 1940. By 1850, Chililí and Taxique were established; there are no standing remains of the Pueblo missions of La Natividad de Chililí or San Miguel de Taxique. Quarai, Abó, and Las Humanas remained relatively isolated, although there were enough settlers in the area to use the missions as a source of scavenged building material. Further depredations resulted from the activities of treasure hunters

who dug holes in floors and dismantled walls, searching for Spanish gold. Fortunately, however, much of the architectural fabric that disappeared during these years was preserved in the sketches, journals, and photographs of visitors, among them Adolph Bandelier.

Official recognition of the significance of the ruins at Las Humanas came as early as 1906 with the establishment of Gran Quivira National Monument; in 1919 the monument was entrusted to the recently created National Park Service. The Museum of New Mexico conducted an initial survey of the pueblo and mission

RECORDING A VANISHING LEGACY

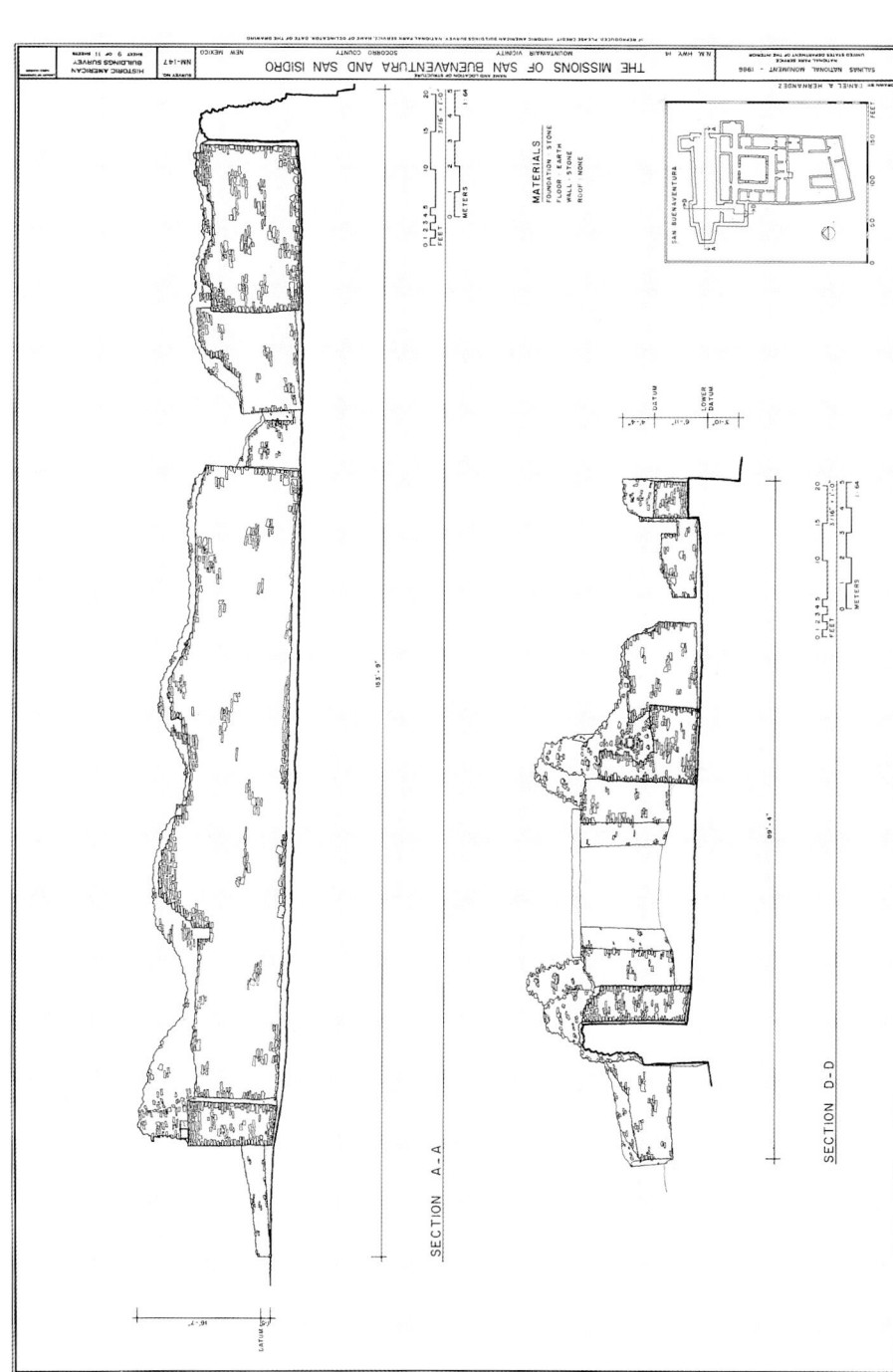

Mission of San Buenaventura, longitudinal section through nave (top), transverse section through nave (bottom), ca. 1670. NPS Southwest Cultural Resources Center.

structures in 1923. Rubble was cleared from the church and convento of San Buenaventura, and in 1925 the site was officially opened to the public. Major excavations were carried out at San Isidro in 1951 and at Mound No. 7 in 1965–68; during the latter excavations, the pueblo rooms serving as the convento for that church were found directly north of San Isidro. Stabilization at Gran Quivira was undertaken on an ad hoc basis until 1976, when a regular program was established.

Quarai became a state monument in 1935, Abó in 1938. Excavation and stabilization began at La Concepción in 1934, and work continued there and at San Gregorio through the end of the decade. Works Progress Administration and Civilian Conservation Corps funds were involved; a HABS team operating on similar funding in 1939 recorded the torreón at Manzano mentioned above. The project was undertaken as mitigative documentation, since the structure stood in the path of the new state highway NM 14.

Further stabilization was undertaken at both state monuments in the 1970s. In conjunction with a major program to document Quarai in 1978, the Museum of New Mexico provided funds necessary to accept the proposal of leading photogrammetrist Perry E. Borchers of Ohio State University to record La Concepción at Quarai. Terrestrial photogrammetry was done that year by the team of Perry, Myra, Christina, and Erik Borchers, using the Galileo-Santoni phototheodolite. Koogle & Pouls, Albuquerque-based engineers, did the low-level aerial photography, and Borchers, with Sootipong Winyoopradist and Muzaffir El-Ghazali of OSU, carried out orientation and plotting on the Wild

HABS RECORDING TODAY

National Park Service and became, with Gran Quivira, the three units of the present monument. The resource management plan of 1982 specified the need for a historic structures report to provide the basis for implementing a comprehensive program of preservation, maintenance, and interpretation for all three units. Since graphic documentation is an integral part of such reports, HABS recording projects are often involved, particularly when the structures under consideration are of major architectural significance.

Funds were therefore allocated for HABS teams to complete the graphic documentation of the Salinas missions, begun by Borchers with the project at Quarai, by carrying out recording projects at Abó and Gran Quivira. HABS fielded teams for two consecutive summers in 1985 and 1986, cosponsored by the Southwest Regional Office of the NPS and the Salinas National Monument. Kenneth L. Anderson, Jr., AIA, then chief of HABS, was project leader for both seasons. Monument Superintendent Thomas O. Carroll provided enthusiastic support, and the School of Architecture at the University of New Mexico furnished drafting tables for the teams. Team members at Abó in 1985 included project supervisor Leonard Kliwinski (University of Chicago) and architecture technicians John Jennings (Texas Tech University) and Rudd Long (University of Texas at Arlington). The team working at Gran Quivira the following summer consisted of project supervisor Morgan Rieder (University of New Mexico) and architecture technicians Daniel Hernandez (University of California at Los Angeles) and Jean Pike (Yale University). Both of these projects used conventional recording techniques, using the same methodology as that employed by the HABS teams working in New Mexico in the 1930s.

A datum is established with a transit or spirit level at an appropriate height on the building that is being recorded. All horizontal measurements are taken along this line; all vertical measurements are taken in reference to it. The procedure is straightforward, but it takes time and patience to deal with fragmentary structures like those at Abó and Gran Quivira. On standing walls, surfaces and corners are warped from settling; elsewhere, large sections of wall are missing. In order to translate the horizontal measurements into a plan, the walls, vertical measurements are taken with a plumb bob at each of the increments along the datum line is divided into increments. Each of these points along the line is then fixed in space by measurements to two other points (in effect, each point is triangulated). Similarly, to plot the irregular profiles of the walls, vertical measurements are taken with a plumb bob at each of the increments along the datum line. Though labor-intensive, this technique is still a reliable method to obtain an accurate architectural plan. Once the measuring points are established, the elevations and sections will fall into place.

The 1985 HABS team at Abó, working in their quarters at the site, produced a 14-sheet set of drawings that comprehensively recorded the church and convento of San Gregorio at a scale of 3/16 of an inch to 1 foot. An isometric rendering of the complex was included. At Gran Quivira in 1986, the team concluded documentation of the missions with 11 sheets of drawings, including the church and convento of San Buenaventura and the church of San Isidro, at the same scale as the drawings of Abó. A site plan at 1 inch to 40 feet shows both structures and the excavated portions of the pueblo, including the first convento.

The HABS drawings of the Salinas missions were put to immediate use. At the monument, they serve as the graphic basis for routine inspection and for planning

A7 Autograph at the university. From the plottings, delineators Varathorn Bookaman and Joseph Trepicone, also of OSU, produced 13 sheets of drawings.

The emphasis in this project — appropriate for terrestrial photogrammetry — was on the thorough documenting of existing vertical surfaces, and in this respect the results were quite successful. Ten sheets at a scale of 1 inch to 5 feet recorded the principal elevations and sections. A detailed architectural plan at the same scale was not developed; however, supplemented with data from additional fieldwork, a horizontal section could be generated from the stereopairs, as were the vertical sections. The site plan, at a scale of 1 inch to 25 feet, shows the tops of the walls of the mission structures and traces of the surrounding pueblo. At the same scale are the site sections and supplementary sections taken through the convento.

As part of this project, additional photography was done in 1978 for the specific purpose of detecting and measuring future structural movement in the walls of the church. Ten photographs of the interior and exterior were taken from surveyed camera stations marked by pairs of pins (rebar driven thirty inches into the ground). Each of these photographs constitutes one-half of a potential stereopair. When the procedure is duplicated after a period of time, each of the photographs in the second set can be viewed together with its pair in the first set. Any movement that has occurred over that interval will be apparent, and stereoscopic measurement can then determine the degree of movement. To date, the second set of photographs has not been taken.

In 1980, Salinas National Monument was created. Quarai and Abó were transferred from the administration of the Museum of New Mexico to that of the

stabilization. NPS historian James E. Ivey, who wrote the historic structures report (1988), used the drawings extensively, first in his fieldwork and then in the report, where they are the bases for graphic reconstructions, in section and elevation, of the churches. On a larger scale, these HABS drawings constitute an invaluable reference for all those interested in the architecture both in its own right and in the larger context of seventeenth-century New Mexico.

CANYON DE CHELLY NATIONAL MONUMENT AND CHACO CULTURE NATIONAL HISTORIC PARK

In 1987 and 1988, HABS activity in the Southwest concentrated on architectural documentation of prehistoric sites as part of an NPS regional graphic documentation plan. A draft plan prepared in 1987 by NPS historical architect Anthony Crosby, working with the Southwest Cultural Resources Center, established priorities. A well-justified emphasis was placed from the outset upon archaeological sites. In particular, the prehistoric Native American sites of the Southwest constitute a unique legacy, long acknowledged for its archaeological value and increasingly recognized for its architectural significance, in terms of both aesthetic qualities and appropriate response to the environment. Although HABS has documented many of the present-day pueblo communities, there are relatively few HABS drawings of Pueblo archaeological sites. Their physical fabric urgently needs thorough architectural documentation.

Canyon de Chelly National Monument, located on the Navajo Reservation near Chinle, Arizona, was selected for the initial phase of the pilot project. The work was undertaken by a HABS team with the purpose of determining the most effective approaches and appropriate methods for graphic documentation.

The site was inhabited by the Anasazi, prehistoric Native Americans who occupied the Four Corners states where New Mexico, Arizona, Utah, and Colorado meet. Their settlement patterns do not correspond to present state lines; however, the research findings from Canyon de Chelly are directly applicable to sites in New Mexico. Within the monument are several hundred sites representing successive stages of Anasazi culture, from Late Basketmaker (A.D. 400–700) through Pueblo III (A.D. 1100–1300). The most extensive architectural remains are those of Pueblo III, situated in the cliffs or on the canyon floors and constructed of local sandstone, timber, and clay.

Over the course of the 1987 season, the HABS team documented nine sites in these canyons: White House, Antelope House, First Room, Tse-ta'a, Bad Trail Ruin, Ledge Ruin, Kokopelli, Big Hand, and Yucca Cave. The team also reconnoitered a number of others. Criteria for selection were based in part upon the current needs of the monument's monitoring and stabilization programs; of equal importance was the need to document sites representing a diversity of conditions. Methods of recording were varied but included the following: surveying (using a theodolite and stadia rod or, to take bearing and distance for less precise work, a Brunton pocket transit); sketching; measuring by hand or with an electronic distance meter; 35mm photography, using a perspective-correcting lens for black-and-white rectified photographs and a conventional wide-angle lens for color transparencies; close-range terrestrial photogrammetry; and videotape.

A five-day training seminar was conducted by photogrammetrist Robert Ryan of the firm of Dennett, Muessig, Ryan and Associates of Iowa City, Iowa, to instruct HABS team members, monument staff, and NPS regional office personnel in the use of the Wild C120 wide-angle stereometric camera. This equipment differs from the single metric cameras used by Perry Borchers for HABS photogrammetric documentation in that the stereopairs are taken simultaneously by two cameras on a fixed base, in this case 1.2 meters apart. The principal advantage of photogrammetry at archaeological sites is that it allows the relatively rapid acquisition of architectural data with minimal impact upon the site. In addition, the low impact advantage permits data to be obtained from the fragmentary walls encountered at many sites not only for exterior elevations but also for sections and plans, although these require taking supplementary measurements by hand.

From the outset, the HABS team realized the vast scope of the task involved in a comprehensive regional documentation effort. The U.S. Forest Service, Bureau of Land Management, and NPS have estimated that almost two million sites may be located in the Four Corners states, of which only 7 percent have been documented.[2] At Canyon de Chelly alone, the number of sites seemed infinite. And, as the fieldwork progressed, the team became acutely aware of how susceptible such sites are to the adverse impacts that can result from even the most carefully conducted operations.

Gradually, however, the basic elements of a systematic approach were developed. The recording techniques employed at a given site were determined by three interrelated variables: the conditions at the site (or portions thereof), the documentation level required, and the time and expense factors involved. After sets of conditions were analyzed and classified, a site typology was developed. Insofar as each site constitutes a unique interaction between the built and natural environment, both architectural and environmental aspects had to be considered. Criteria established for evaluation included base condition of structures, degree of preservation, period of architecture, and disposition of structures. The other critical consideration in terms of site condition involved the constant problem of deterioration and the ongoing process of stabilizing the ruins. Documentation teams had to work in coordination with maintenance and repair schedules so that sites could be recorded prior to impending stabilization. The documentation itself could thus be used to plan and record stabilization procedures.

The HABS team worked with three basic levels of documentation. Level III, intended as the minimum for all sites and structures encompassed by the plan, requires site and floor plans, including sketches of sections and structural details as necessary; 35mm black-and-white photography of exteriors and interiors of structures; 35mm color transparencies of the overall site; and comprehensive videotape coverage. Level II consists of these components, in addition to measured drawings of plans and sections of critical elements and either measured drawings or rectified photographs of principal elevations. Level I builds upon the foregoing and requires measured drawings of all plans, sections, and significant details, as well as measured drawings or rectified photographs of all elevations, exterior and interior.

The decision to conduct Level I or Level II documentation is primarily determined by the significance accorded to a particular site in the priority list. Typically, HABS seasonal projects involve the equivalent of Level I documentation of a single site (often a single structure). At Canyon de Chelly, HABS was able to accomplish Level I documentation at portions of certain sites, but an equally important goal was the development of rapid and effective methods for obtaining Level III data. These methods were then available to be utilized by NPS personnel continuing this type of documentation.

All graphic documentation is, of course, dependent upon the factors of time and expense. Trade-offs must be considered carefully: for instance, a given site can be recorded photogrammetrically in considerably less time than it would take to obtain the same data by conventional recording techniques. This substantially reduces time in the field, but before drawings can be produced, the stereopairs must be plotted, which involves considerably more time and money. Other decisions involve the degree of documentation: e.g., should a given amount of labor be used to record one site thoroughly or to obtain less detailed data for a number of sites?

To deal with the issues involved in implementing a documentation program, a conference was held in November 1987 at Chaco Culture National Historic Park. In addition to the HABS work at Canyon de Chelly, ongoing recording projects at Chaco, Wupatki, and Mesa Verde were reviewed, and participants discussed requirements, appropriate levels, and future directions for graphic documentation. The following summer, a HABS team was assigned to Chaco. This 1988 project, again funded by the Southwest Regional Office, was conceived as a continuation of the pilot Canyon de Chelly project.

A vital consideration at Chaco is the need for documentation that will assist in carrying out the park's resource management plan. The park is responsible for the maintenance and stabilization of more than fifty sites; all require historic structures reports and preservation guidelines, which in part must be based upon architectural documentation. In 1988, the need was even more critical for those sites that were scheduled for a program of repairing and constructing drainage systems and equalizing unexcavated fill and backfill levels.

Like all traditional Pueblo architecture, the structures were originally built to stand indefinitely, given periodic maintenance of exterior walls and roofs. However, exterior plaster and roofing have long since disappeared, and the structures have been substantially excavated. The exposed wall surfaces require constant stabilization. Also, unequal levels of rubble fill between rooms — and between rooms and exterior grade — result in uneven pressure that, when compounded by insufficient drainage, results in wall collapse. According to NPS archaeologist Larry Nordby, "Normal masonry repair techniques are treating the symptoms of the problem without alteration of the source. If the problem is permitted to continue, it is not difficult to envision a ruin constructed of stabilization masonry without a shred of aboriginal workmanship."[3]

Currently, the best way to deal effectively with further deterioration of the Chaco ruins is selective backfilling, thereby ensuring proper drainage. Comprehensive architectural documentation is needed to record sections to be backfilled and to provide the data for designing new drainage systems.

Of the sites included in the program, Pueblo del Arroyo, on the edge of the Chaco Wash some 300 yards

SITES RECORDED BY HABS AT CANYON DE CHELLY, 1987

Note: In the mid-1970s, Perry E. Borchers was involved in HABS photogrammetric projects at White House, Antelope House, and First Ruin. The documentation was complementary because Borchers used a single metric camera for comprehensive long-range coverage (i.e., from the other side of the canyon), while the 1987 team used a stereometric camera for close-range terrestrial photogrammetry.

White House	Cliff alcove and canyon floor site in Canyon de Chelly. Extant room blocks and kivas, PII – PIII. Recording technique: photogrammetry (room block on canyon floor).
Antelope House	Canyon floor site in Cañon del Muerto. Extant room blocks and kivas, PII – PIII. Recording technique: photogrammetry (south room block).
First Room	Cliff alcove site in Canyon de Chelly. Extant rooms and kivas, PIII. Recording techniques: surveying, hand-measuring, EDM, 35mm photography.
Tse-ta'a	Canyon floor site in Canyon de Chelly. Extant (unexcavated) rooms and kiva, PII - PIII. Recording techniques: surveying, 35mm photography, videotape.
Bad Trail Ruin	Cliff alcove site in box canyon off Canyon de Chelly. Extant rooms and kiva, PIII. Recording technique: photogrammetry.
Ledge Ruin	Cliff alcove site in Cañon del Muerto. Extant rooms, PIII. Recording techniques: surveying, hand-measuring, 35mm photography, videotape, photogrammetry.
Kokopelli	Cliff alcove site in Cañon del Muerto. Extant room and kiva, PIII. Recording techniques: surveying, hand-measuring, 35mm photography.
Big Hand	Cliff alcove site in Cañon del Muerto. Extant rooms and kivas, PIII. Recording techniques: surveying, hand-measuring, 35mm photography.
Yucca Cave	Cliff alcove site in Cañon del Muerto. Extant rooms and kiva, BMIII – PI. Recording technique: photogrammetry.

west of Pueblo Bonito, was chosen as the scene of HABS operations in 1988. The scale of the site is commensurate with its status as one of the major Chacoan towns: the pueblo visible today extends about 290 feet (north to south) and 240 feet (east to west) and contains substantial portions of standing walls, some as high as the original fourth story. Since the south wing has the greatest amount of exposed building fabric and is experiencing some of the most dramatic deterioration, the HABS team concentrated on this section. In conjunction with the HABS fieldwork, aerial photogrammetry was undertaken for the entire site by Jim Walker of Brigham Young University, making innovative use of remote-control model aircraft equipped with 35mm cameras, a system previously tested at Pueblo Bonito. The most important point here is that graphic documentation, particularly at a site such as Pueblo del Arroyo, is most effectively accomplished by a combination of recording techniques: whatever methods are appropriate for each different component of the site.

Since 1988, much has been done to implement the goals of the regional documentation plan, and NPS personnel at monuments and parks have recorded a number of sites. Expanding the scope of documentation beyond NPS-administered properties, the NPS Rocky Mountain Regional Office, with the Bureau of Land Management as a co-sponsor, undertook an important HABS project in 1990. A unique group of sites were recorded on BLM land within the area of northwestern New Mexico referred to by the Navajo as *Dinetah*, their old homeland. At the end of the seventeenth century, Pueblo refugees from the Spanish reconquest fled to this area and joined with the Navajo. The small defensive sites, called *pueblitos*, date from this period to the mid-eighteenth century. Architecturally, the pueblitos show influences from Pueblo, Navajo, and Spanish traditions. Constructed of masonry and timber in locations with difficult access, the buildings were challenging to record.

HABS will continue to play a major role in recording our state's architectural heritage. The wide range of prehistoric and historic resources requiring architectural documentation ensure that a variety of recording techniques, coupled with consistently high standards, will likewise continue to characterize HABS work in New Mexico.

Acoma Pueblo, elevations and roof plan, Block 6, sheet 46 of 83, HABS. Howard Speer, Stanley H. Kent, Paul Atchison, and A. G. Longfellow, dels. 1934 (NM-6). (see p.70)

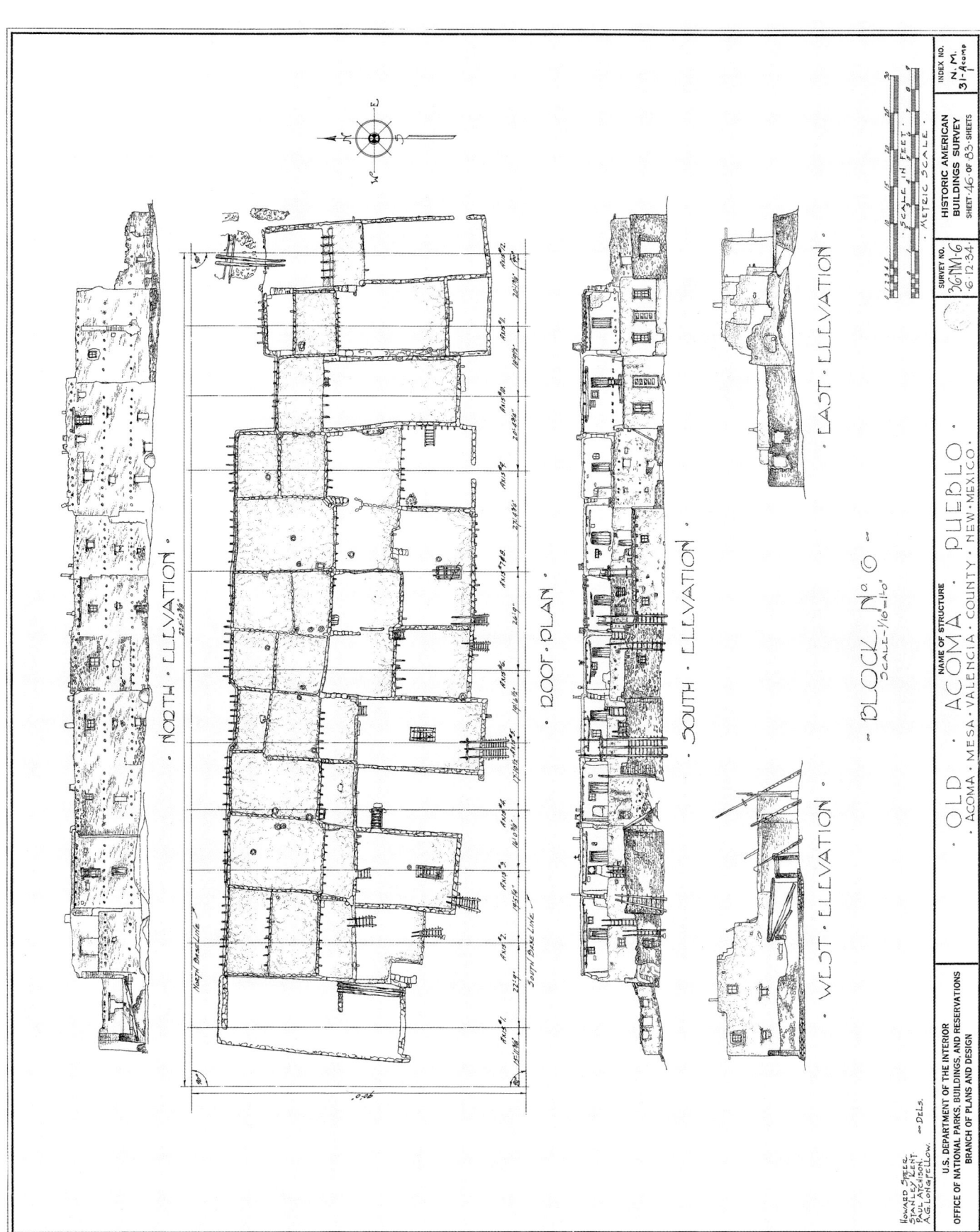

PART THREE
NEW MEXICO ARCHITECTURE

RINA SWENTZELL

In the past sixty years, only one Pueblo Indian has participated in a HABS-related project in New Mexico, a student of Bainbridge Bunting's in the 1960s. As more Native Americans become architects and historians, their insights will surely enrich the process of documentation. The cultural perspectives of the creators and users of the structures being measured are a much-needed contribution to both the methods and goals of HABS.

Paradoxically, while HABS architects and administrators are deeply committed to the concept of historic preservation through documentation, the original architects and their descendants may not share this cultural value. In this personal narrative, Rina Swentzell shows us that there is more to Pueblo buildings than dimensions and drawings. A cultural historian from Santa Clara Pueblo, she looks at structures from the perspective of community culture and tradition. She finds the drawings exquisite but explains that measuring and recording are antithetical to the Pueblo belief system as she has experienced it. Swentzell eloquently articulates the Pueblo concept that buildings and town forms share in the interconnectedness of all life, including cycles of life and death.

Rina Swentzell received her M.A. in Architecture and Ph.D. in American Studies from the University of New Mexico. Her master's thesis, "An Architectural History of Santa Clara Pueblo" (1976), examines change in the pueblo's form over time. Swentzell has written many articles and books, including To Touch the Past (with Jerry Brody, 1996). Her latest book, Younger-Older Ones, is currently in press. She writes and lectures about the philosophical basis of the Pueblo world and its educational, artistic, and architectural expression.

CHAPTER 7
PUEBLO STRUCTURES AND WORLDVIEW

RINA SWENTZELL

The HABS recordings of Pueblo structures and community forms create philosophical problems and issues which do not exist in the recording of other American communities. Those other American communities are of the tradition of measuring, drawing, photographing, and recording, while the traditional worldview of the Pueblo communities is antithetical to measuring and recording even for the sake of preservation. Recording of structures for the benefit of making a "mental or material reconstruction for the present and future generations"[1] is alien to Pueblo thinking, where present-orientedness is predominant and where the organic nature of existence recognizes life and death cycles and the interconnective quality of life expressions.

I grew up in Santa Clara Pueblo, one of the first communities recorded by photogrammetry in a 1972 HABS project. Two important moments from my childhood remain with me and show the extreme differences in worldviews — which determine what and how structures are built — between the recorders of the HABS project and the people of the Pueblo communities. As children growing up in the pueblo, we had the habit of tasting houses and kiva structures. All the structures were, of course, of adobe mud, and they tasted differently depending on the source of the adobe clay. In my daily walks back and forth from the Bureau of Indian Affairs (BIA) school, which was about half a mile from the pueblo, I watched a crack grow in one of my favorite-tasting houses. The crack grew through many weeks until I knew that the house could not stand much longer. I asked my great-grandmother why the people who lived in that house were doing nothing about keeping the house from collapsing. Her response was, "That house has had a good life. It has been fed, blessed, and healed, as it should have been, throughout its years. It is now time for it to go back into the earth."

Another moment: The fifth grade teacher at the BIA school was keeping me after school because she wanted to learn the Tewa language. My great-grandmother noticed that I was coming home long after other children had passed her house. When I explained, she very emphatically said, "No, we don't do that! We do not give our language to other people who will lay it on the table, cut it into pieces, and study it. When we, as a group of people, are ready to die, our language must go with us."

Organicism, or a lack of focus on durability or permanency, is a major characteristic of Pueblo thought which is reflected in the view of language and also how houses are built and treated. Houses and all other structures are viewed as expressions of the life force, as are humans, plants, and other animals. They contain the life force, or *po-wa-ha*, as certainly as does the human, and therefore must be fed, blessed, healed — and allowed to die. Houses are, then, given the ultimate respect of having life and death cycles.

Additionally, houses have the power of interaction. Peter Nabokov, a non-Indian, studying Acoma Pueblo in the 1980s, had a fleeting sense of Pueblo house structures:

> Then I noticed a room up on a third story.... In that little chamber I could not stand up straight.... For the first time I got a palpable sense of Pueblo living space. A niche was hollowed out of the wall. A horizontal pole for bedding and clothes hung from the slender vigas across the low ceiling. The walls bent at the corners.... The walls rippled around as in a cocoon softened and renewed by the annual caress of women's hands.... I felt how safe and warm it would be to sleep in such a place....[2]

The recognized gentle character of Pueblo architecture is not surprising with the knowledge that women and children, mostly, built the houses. They also maintained — plastered annually — the structures. The focus in that world on the feminine, or softer, qualities of life is clearly expressed in the entire Pueblo physical environment by the kind of materials chosen, the manner in which the materials were used, and even in the contextual ordering of the physical space. The entire Pueblo cosmos is ordered around the *nan-sipu*, the place of connection with the other three levels of existence within the earth bowl out of which the people emerge and into which they return. The breath flows in and out of the *nan-sipu* and through every part of this fourth level of existence so that everything and everybody breathes the breath. Consistently, houses, or even the community form, also breathes the breath and does not stand alone. They are always regarded within the context of the larger natural environment — the surrounding fields, mesas, hills, and mountains. They constantly

Mesa and Pueblo of Acoma, sheet 1 of 3, HABS. Julsing J. Lamsam, del. 1965–73 (NM-6).

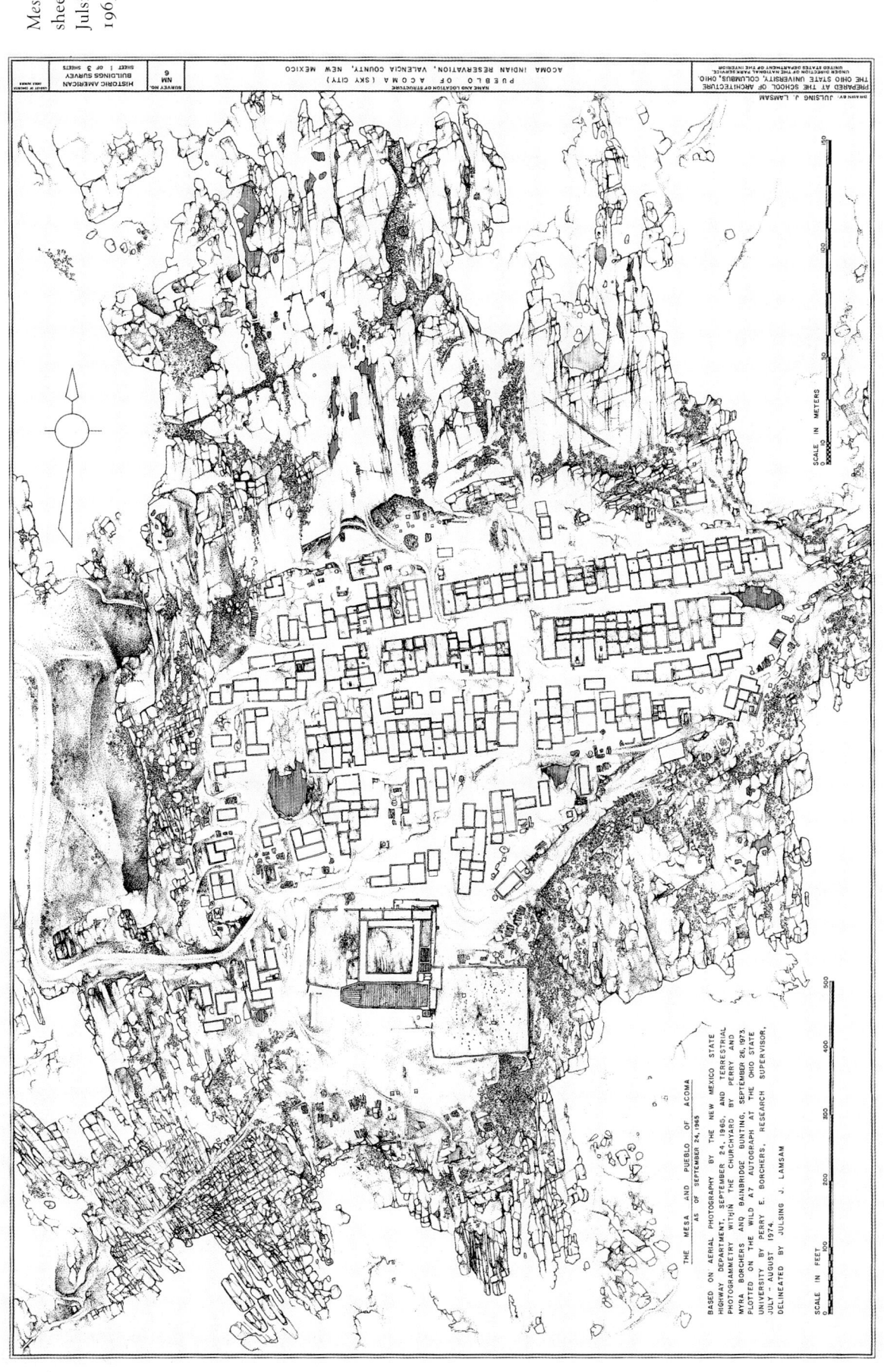

(opposite) *Acoma Pueblo,* copy photograph of photogrammetric plate, photograph 1-87. Perry E. Borchers, photographer. 1965 (NM-6).

American Buildings Survey, which was conceived in 1933 during the New Deal era when the federal government provided funds for unemployment relief. Aside from the federal government providing work for the great number of unemployed architects and draftsmen, HABS aimed at "the creation of a permanent graphic record of the existing architectural remains of the early dwellers in the country."[5]

There were 83 sheets and 85 photographs made of Acoma Pueblo. In addition to the pueblo structures, the adjacent Mission of San Estevan del Rey was documented by 31 sheets of drawings and 34 photographs. The pueblo of Laguna was not as thoroughly documented, with only 4 sheets and 3 photographs; the mission of San José de Laguna had 21 sheets and 21 photographs. Other pueblos or ruins recorded between 1934 and 1940 include the Nambé kiva, the Bandelier ceremonial cave and large kiva, the Pecos Mission, the San Geronimo Mission at Taos Pueblo, and two Chaco Canyon sites of Kin Klizhin and Pueblo Bonito. None of them, however, received the focused attention that Acoma did.

The group at Acoma recorded as "diligently and precisely as possible its parts and surfaces but without a key to explain how the whole town functioned as an integrated organism."[6] An architect recalled that "we set stakes and strung lines as close to parallel and perpendicular as the [rough and irregular] building plan permitted."[7] It would have been as easy for them to measure the rock cliffs and protrusions from which the pueblo structures grew. In fact, they often joked about having to remeasure everything after each rainstorm.

They also discovered that "whenever two walls join, one is always butted against the other but never bond-

Acoma Pueblo, interior of House 3, Block 1, photograph 1-14, HABS. M. James Slack, photographer. 1934 (NM-6).

group in Acoma Pueblo was especially strange given the Pueblo view that structures derive their primary meaning from their connectedness to the larger natural context. As Nabokov states, "In a sense, the outsiders were like the blind men describing an elephant . . ."[3] Aside from not knowing or sensing the larger context of the structures, an architect recalled that the "the walls were out of line and plumb and square, and floors and roofs were out of level,"[4] which was unusual to the drafters and architects assigned to thoroughly measure and document all of the pueblo's ecclesiastical and domestic structures. The project was part of the 1934 Historic

and continuously reverberate the natural forms within the well-defined world boundaries. They are not an end unto themselves but exist within the ordering of the cosmos. They do not call attention to themselves as separate entities or receive individualized focus, except for the role that they play in the larger whole.

The house-to-house survey done by the 1934 HABS

RECORDING A VANISHING LEGACY

ed."⁹ Structural durability and permanence were, obviously, not the major concern for the women and the children who erected the walls being measured and documented by the professional architects and the draftsmen.

The 1970s HABS recordings again included 2 sheets each of Acoma and Laguna. Other pueblos photographed and recorded during the session between 1972 and 1977 include Zuni, Santa Clara, Tesuque, Taos, San Ildefonso, San Juan, Zía, Santa Ana, Jémez, Nambé, and Picuris.

The careful and tedious measuring techniques of the house-to-house survey of the 1930s project were replaced in the 1970s by "photogrammetry from air and ground," as described by Perry E. Borchers:

Considerable improvement in accuracy and diversity of data could result from the new aerial stereophotogrammetry of the pueblos which would produce stereoscopic optical models, scaled, leveled and oriented to the three-coordinate systems within photogrammetric plotting instruments. . . . [Additionally, photogrammetric recording could] measure complex and fluid forms of architecture with unstable and dangerous structures, minimum intrusion on privacy, and minimum disruption of activities.¹⁰

Aerial photogrammetry, which is a kind of remote sensing, had taken the 1970s recording far beyond the 1930s process in accuracy and precision of measurement and recording. The goal of obtaining a permanent record to facilitate possible restoration of the structures to what they were was undoubtedly achieved with minimum direct human contact with the structures and with minimum intrusion or disruption of community activities. Everything was identified and recorded in the greatest detail. The resultant drawings are exquisite, as were those from the 1930s. They are wonderful for what they are — incredibly detailed and beautiful line representations of what was.

But what does it mean in the Pueblo world, where detail is traditionally minimalized and all lines must point to the larger whole; where the structures are connected to each other and to the earth and related to the far mountains and valley; where connectedness is both physical and spiritual; where the spiritual is the real focus; where recognition of the breath flowing through house and community forms is synonymous with the flow happening through the mountains, rain, plants, humans? All are related — interconnected. Those qualities are, of course, unmeasurable. Spirit cannot be measured. As we may know the proportions of one human body and have those to compare with every other human body, the spirit of each or of the whole cannot be known by measuring. It can, however, begin to be hinted at by the complete drawing or the photograph that can capture the peculiar look or gaze, gesture, stance or posture — and so with the structures.

I think that the value of the recordings for the Pueblo communities lies not so much in the accuracy of recording the slightest details of the structures and lines of the community forms but in the whole gesture — the attitudes of the buildings and town forms so that the greater whole is glimpsed. The goal of recording, then, could come together with the Pueblo worldview when recording is seen as not being about the material stuff of the structures but about gaining a sense of the greater whole that recognizes life and death cycles and the interconnectedness of all life-forms.

GEORGE CLAYTON PEARL

Since the late 1950s, George Clayton Pearl has shaped New Mexico through his contributions to both architectural design and historic preservation. Like Bainbridge Bunting, he has had a profound interest in domestic architecture, the subject of this chapter. Here he examines the changing technology and traditions that have influenced Native American, Spanish, and American settlement.

Pearl first considers the concept of architectural measurement and its relevance to New Mexico buildings. Although the state has the oldest continuous tradition of building for human habitation in the nation, he notes that it is ironic that the materials, forms, and techniques of this tradition do not lend themselves to the precise measuring techniques of HABS as do buildings produced after the arrival of Anglo-Americans. He concludes with recommendations for future HABS documentation and the warning that few of the Territorial Period houses that existed in the state in the 1950s survive today.

George Clayton Pearl, a fellow of the American Institute of Architects, began his career as an architect in 1950 and has been a principal with the Albuquerque firm of Stevens, Mallory, Pearl & Campbell since 1959. He has volunteered service in many community and professional organizations from the Archbishop of Santa Fe's Task Force for the Preservation of New Mexico Churches and the Albuquerque Landmarks and Urban Conservation Commission to the National Trust for Historic Preservation and the National American Institute of Architects' Committee on Historic Resources. Among his honors are more than thirty awards in design and historic preservation from governmental and private organizations, including the Silver Medal from the Western Mountain Region of the American Institute of Architects and the 1999 Person of the Year Award by the Albuquerque Conservation Association. In 2000 the University of New Mexico honored Pearl by naming the new architectural school after him. Currently, he serves on the Board of Directors of the Cornerstones Foundation.

CHAPTER 8
RESIDENTIAL RECORDING

GEORGE CLAYTON PEARL

That the architectural heritage of New Mexico was prominent in the establishment and earliest work of the Historic American Buildings Survey was as rare as it was appropriate. It was rare in that New Mexico's cultural heritage fits so awkwardly into national patterns that it is often overlooked or set aside. It was appropriate in that ours is not only the oldest continuous tradition of building for human habitation in this country but is also a tradition unlike any other.

Our having the oldest continuous building tradition for human habitation is an elaborate claim requiring justification. Many architectural historians might say that the first seven or eight centuries, from Basketmaker II times up to Pueblo II (roughly from about the time of Christ to the tenth century A.D.), produced no *architecture*. It is very pleasing to me that the founders of HABS made no fine distinctions between *building* and *architecture*, since I acknowledge no such distinctions. There would be little basis for conversation between me and anyone who did not admit the tipi of the Plains tribes or the pueblo of Acoma into the realm of great architecture.

Similarly, many archaeologists might question the idea of continuity, since I am using patterns from many cultural variations and ignoring many gaps in southwestern prehistory. This deliberate oversimplification is justifiable to me, however, in that it is possible to arrange selected archaeological sites in a sequence that demonstrates, almost cinematically, or as in the apparent motion seen through the peephole of a 1900 nickelodeon, an evolution of a thousand years' duration. Beginning with clusters of partly subterranean pithouses, the evolutionary pattern moves upward to stone masonry storage structures at ground level. These surface structures developed into the living places until, by Pueblo II times (about 900 A.D.), the Anasazi were living entirely above ground and the pithouse survived only as a communal social and ceremonial place. By the tenth century the masonry houseblocks reached the elaboration seen in several great sites in Chaco Canyon and elsewhere in New Mexico and Arizona.

In spite of the distinguished age of this building tradition, very little has survived which lends itself to the measuring techniques of HABS from before the invasion of ideas and tools from the United States in the mid-nineteenth century. The precise recording of profiles of eroded or leaning walls, for example, which are either accidental or possibly predictable by new fractal geometric techniques, is probably irrelevant. In understanding a sand dune or a cloud, it is fundamentally significant to realize that they are in motion. It is less important to record their specific shape at a specific time. Also, because of the lack of articulate detail and ornament, the most significant data from any site is largely a matter of village form and artifacts of material culture. These elements contribute to an understanding of the culture's evolution and are best analyzed by

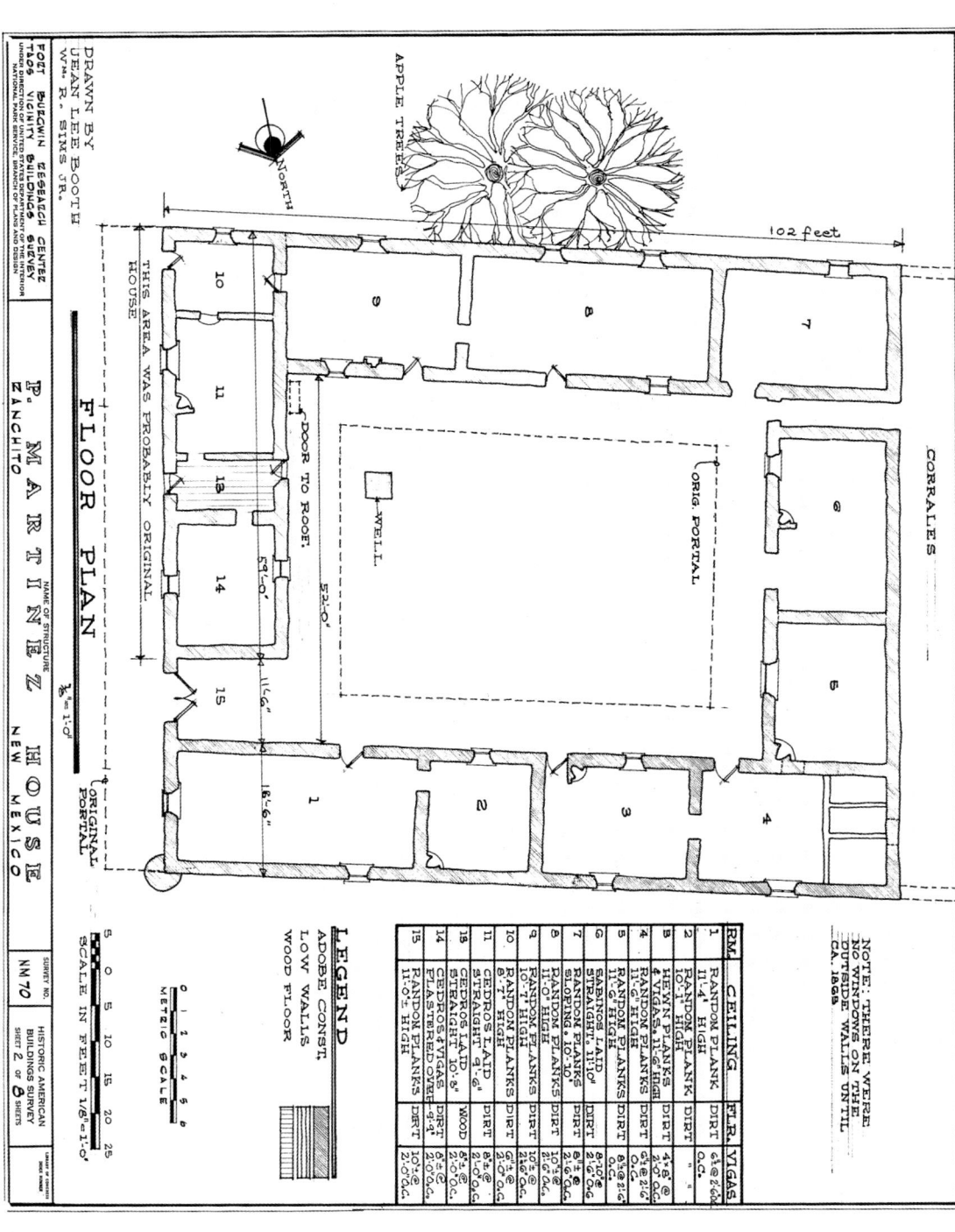

Martinez Hacienda, Ranchito, floor plan, sheet 2 of 8, HABS. Jean Lee Booth and William R. Sims, Jr., dels. 1963 (NM-70).

RECORDING A VANISHING LEGACY

slight. It was limited primarily to the introduction of molded adobe building blocks and the interior fireplace flue that exhausted smoke more effectively. Previously, mud was not formed into bricks. Walls were built up slowly in layers which were left to dry between courses. The influence of the indigenous building technology upon the traditions which the Spanish brought with them was probably more significant than the converse, since the Spanish had little choice but to strive for their building aspirations within the limits of indigenous building skills.

The formed adobe block made it possible to build walls of greater strength and to build them more quickly. The *fogón* (fireplace), or more specifically the *chiflón* (flue), probably had a much greater effect than the adobe block upon the interior environment of human habitations in the Southwest. Previously, fires were built on the floor, and the smoke escaped only through an opening in the roof. It is reasonable to assume that in the pre-Spanish Southwest only the choice between winter cold and smoke-filled rooms existed.

The Spanish also brought metal tools, totally new to the Southwest, which made it possible to manipulate wood more precisely, producing longer spans for roof beams and therefore larger rooms. Metal gouges and chisels also made it possible to embellish wooden members with ornament, although I know of no residential application of this capability.

The Spanish introduced a larger residential scale and a plan form which, despite the dearth of articulate detail, is to some extent a proper subject for conventional measurement and recording. Rooms of consistent width and variable length, largely self-sufficient and unspecialized as to function, are arranged in series that form rows, ells, "C" shapes, or complete rectangles

archaeological techniques. Only with the constructions of Pueblo II and the evidence of preconceived and rigidly followed village plans do the methods of architectural measurement become relevant.

The effect of the Spanish invasion upon the technology and the form of building for human habitation was

Plaza del Cerro, Chimayó, plan, sheet 1 of 2, HABS. Jack W. Schafer and Michelle F. Lewis, dels. 1975 (NM-128).

Plaza del Chimayó, Chimayó, aerial photograph. John Gaw Meem Archive of Southwestern Architecture, Bainbridge Bunting Collection, University of New Mexico.

and *dispensas* and very rare family chapels in Spanish houses are exceptions.

This pattern of unspecialized rooms, either *ensuite* or entered only from the outside, prevailed with little change or development until the mid-nineteenth century when influences from the United States brought about a plan form unprecedented in New Mexico. Rooms dedicated to such special purposes as cooking, eating, and sleeping, accessed by hallways or more communal space, became popular or at least extant in New Mexico. Houses built for the military at Fort Union and Fort Marcy and by affluent merchants from the United States were primary influences.

The most typical early example which I have seen of this new plan form consists of a central long space that gives access to discrete rooms on both sides. In this sala plan, the central space might be so narrow that it serves only as a passageway, or it might be wide enough to accommodate various other social and communal functions.

In those houses built of adobe or of stone in adobe mortar, the element of change is enigmatic. Pre-Spanish urban morphology is best considered in terms of centuries. Hispanic houses and settlements, the proper subject of more precise measurements, require the recognition of the importance of more rapid change. Adobe buildings require such continuous and extensive maintenance that it is reasonable to consider them as being continuously under construction. Similarly, adobe construction was a craft so available and so well understood by the cultures using it that adding additional rooms or demolishing existing ones or allowing them to erode away was an easy decision.

I remember Dr. W. W. Hill's description, in an anthropology seminar during the 1950s, of a series of photographs taken annually for many years from the same spot in the pueblo of Santa Clara. Although I did not see the photographs, Dr. Hill's verbal description of the constant changes that they showed causes me to use the cinematic analogy again. The changes resulting from new construction, demolition, erosion, and repair are so great that the buildings seem to move as if they were living organisms. A short series of photographs of Santa Clara Pueblo in Peter Nabokov and Robert Easton's book *Native American Architecture* demonstrates this same point.[1]

Two conclusions derived from this element of change are inescapable. First, apart from relatively stabilized archaeological sites, very little remains in New Mexico of pre-Anglo-American invasion building that has not been drastically changed. Second, any measured drawing or photograph of a traditional adobe (or stone in adobe mortar) building is of limited value unless one also knows the time at which the drawing was made or the photograph taken.

Between 1960 and 1980 Dr. Bainbridge Bunting was responsible for the documentation of many New Mexico buildings by students at the University of New Mexico. These drawings, many of domestic architecture, are of considerable value today. But there are several reasons why it is unfair to compare their quality to that of the work done during the 1930s by experienced professionals, splendidly supervised, who devoted their full time to the effort. The work for which Dr. Bunting was responsible was produced by students whose architectural and technical training varied greatly. It was done a bit at a time, as dictated by academic schedules. This discontinuity of effort was a severe limitation. It is essential to remember that Dr. Bunting's responsibility and primary interest was in training people to make

around interior courtyards. Certainly these plan configurations existed in pre-Spanish Pueblo architecture, but they probably existed only in communal settlements. The internal courtyard of Pueblo villages offering a degree of security from enemy raids was perpetuated by the Spanish and is best suggested today by what remains of the Plaza del Cerro in Chimayó and San Juan del Vado on the Pecos. The Spanish used the same form for exurban habitations for extended families and their retainers, continuing a very long tradition extending back in time through Mexico, Spain, and the Near East.

Like the rooms in Pueblo villages, those Spanish rooms were largely self-sufficient and unspecialized. In any such room a family unit cooked, ate, slept, entertained visitors, and did whatever work had to be done indoors. Storage rooms and kivas in Pueblo houseblocks

Ranchito de Arboles

Ranchito de Arboles is an architectural replication of an "historically designated" Santa Fe casita from the early 1900s, previously existing within the compound. Ranchito de Arboles replicates the streetscape profile of the original casita and is rebuilt in the traditional, northern New Mexico style with pitched tin roofs, Territorial style small windows and low ceiling portals.

- A complete replication of an early 1900s traditional northern New Mexico casita.
- 1400 + square feet – 2 bedrooms/1 bath
- Vaulted Ceiling living room with territorial style fireplace and wood plank floors
- Pitched tin roofs, Territorial style small windows and low ceiling portals.
- Extended covered portal, courtyards and orchard-like gardens
- Chimayó kitchen with built-in *horno* and modern high end Wolf appliances
- Double adobe wall construction with mud stucco finish
- Radiant heating, remote controlled electrical and heating systems, air conditioning, security system

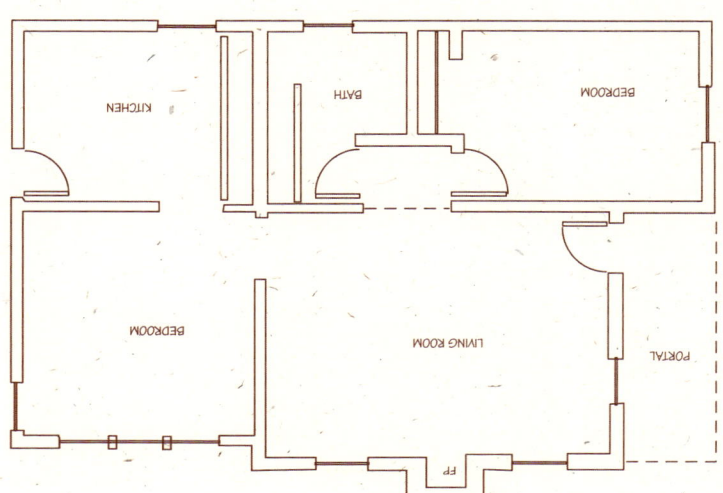

603 Acequia Madre

Casita Nativa, Casita Alhambra

Casita Nativa tastefully blends features from select Native American Indian architecture and materials. The interior wall finishes are mud plaster, accented with stenciled Indian designs around corner kiva fireplaces.

Casita Alhambra adopts a Mediterranean theme with architectural features and materials found in the villages of old Spain. The interior uses tinted plasters, Moorish tiles and colorful ceramics found in old world residences in Granada and Sevilla.

The majestic Spanish Pueblo portals of both casitas will maintain continuity with the compound. Each casita can be custom built to fit the needs of the buyer.

- Approximately + 1700 square feet – 2 bedroom / 2 bath
- All adobe construction, kiva fireplaces and/or Venetian finished fireplaces.
- Accented imported lighting fixtures, hand-carved cabinets and hand-painted tiles.
- Kitchen features custom hand-carved cabinets, granite countertops, Wolf appliances, hand-painted tiles
- Radiant floor heat, air conditioning and remote controlled electrical and heating optional
- Private courtyards with fountains and elegant flowering gardens.

Nativa: 347 Delgado Street   Alhambra: 605 Acequia Madre

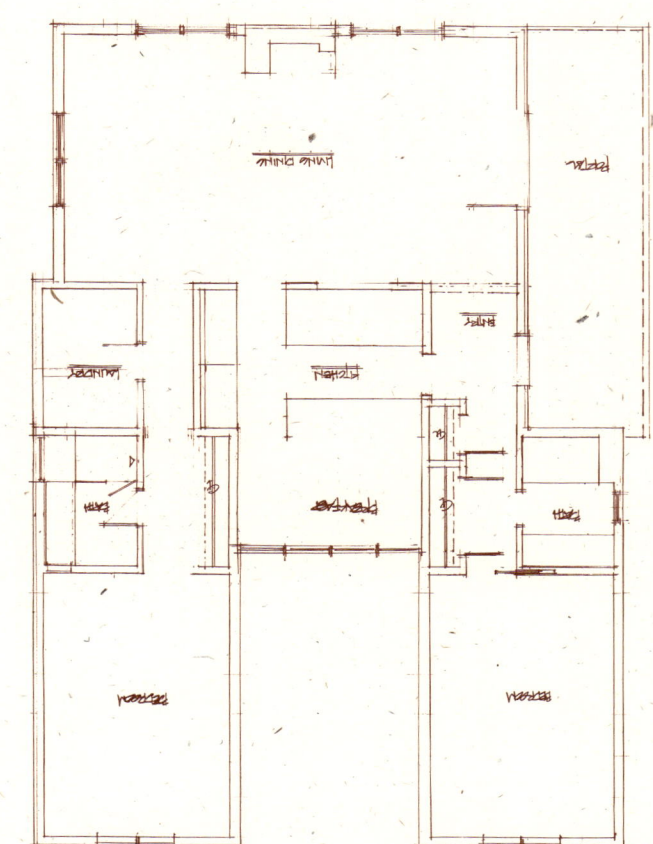

Ortiz de Velarde
COMPOUND

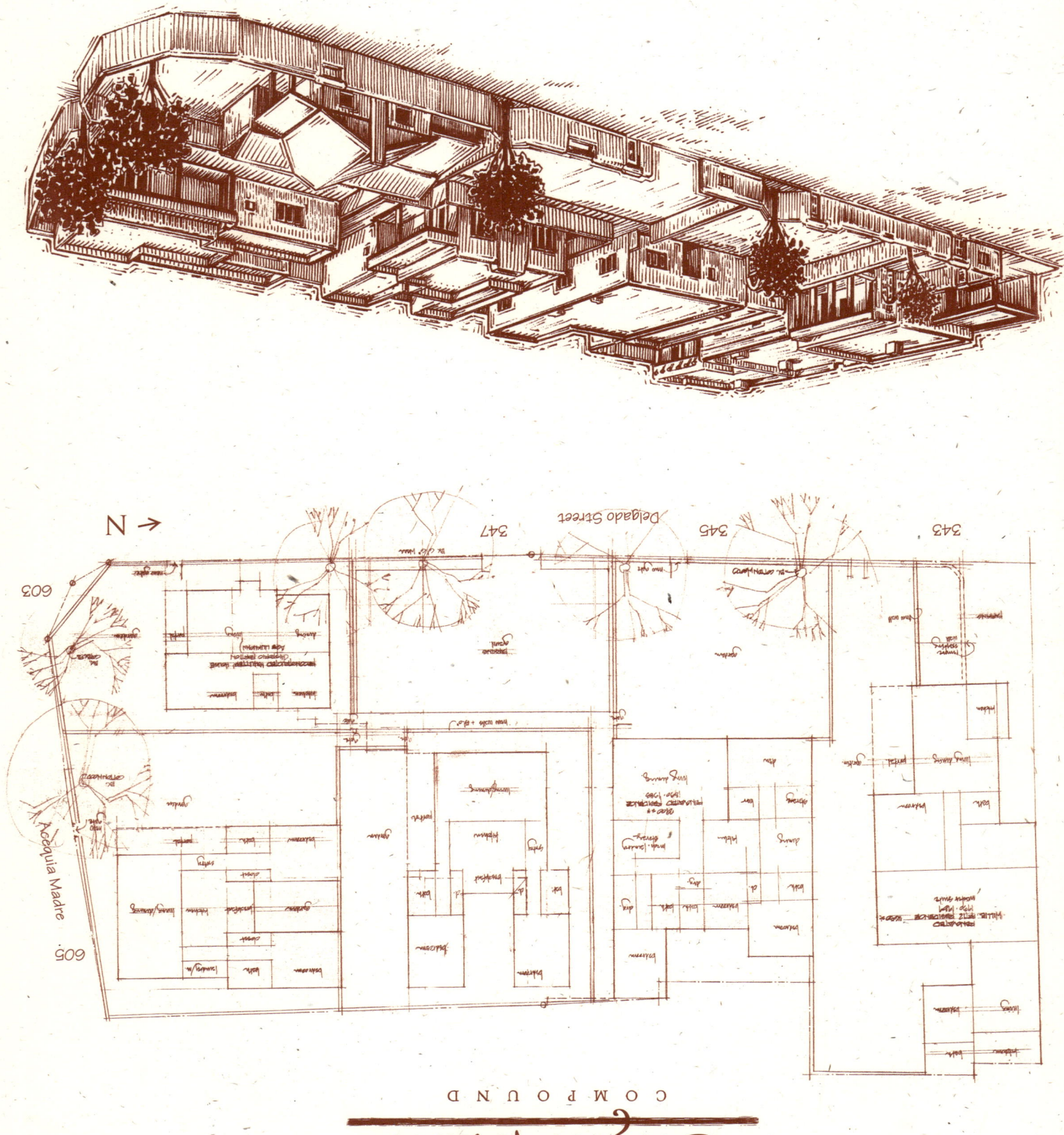

Contact: Reynaldo Ortiz

Telephone 303.393.0713 ■ Fax 303.322.3250 ■ Mobile 303.669.9383

339 1/2 Delgado St. Santa Fe, New Mexico 87501

Hacienda de los Tejedores

This charming hacienda dates back to 1920 and has been completely restored in the Spanish Colonial architectural theme. The main house and quaint detached guesthouse are connected and surrounded by four distinct courtyard gardens, each designed as an extended exterior room. Landscaped courtyards offer solitude, with flowering trees and plants, a fountain, and restored hand-painted wall murals.

- Completely restored 1920s Spanish Pueblo Revival adobe
- 2571 square feet – Main house with master suite including 2 bedrooms and 2 baths and 4 kiva fireplaces, carport
- Detached guesthouse – 1 bedroom and 1 bath, kiva fireplace
- Kitchen features custom hand-carved cabinets, granite countertops, Wolf appliances, hand-painted tiles
- 4 private courtyards, mature trees, stone work and trellis
- Forced air heat, optional air conditioning system
- System-controlled watering and exterior lighting, wired for intercom and gate access, security system
- Restored *sombra* or sitting area covered with *latillas*, hand-carved corbels, beams and lintels
- Utility Room leads to secure walk-in steel vault

Casa de Colores

Beautifully restored 1890s historically designated Southwestern style home with double adobe walls, viga ceilings, original kiva fireplaces with bancos. Vibrant color accents of Moorish and Spanish influence abound, and the façade features a restored painted floral mural surrounding the door under the historic portal. Master suite includes a cozy *sala* or sitting area with kiva fireplace.

- 2581 square feet – Main house has 2 bedrooms and 2 baths and 2 kiva fireplaces
- Attached guest quarters – 1 bedroom and 1 bath mini-cantina and separate laundry room
- 3 distinct courtyards, mature trees, fountain, elegant stone work
- Kitchen features custom hand-carved cabinets, granite countertops, Wolf appliances, hand-painted tiles
- Restored antique light fixtures, recessed ceiling lights and Spanish sconces
- New forced air heating system with separate controls for guest quarters, optional air conditioning
- Top-of-the-line bath fixtures, tubs and showers with decorative Moroccan tiles
- System controlled watering and exterior lighting
- Wired for intercom, gate access and security system

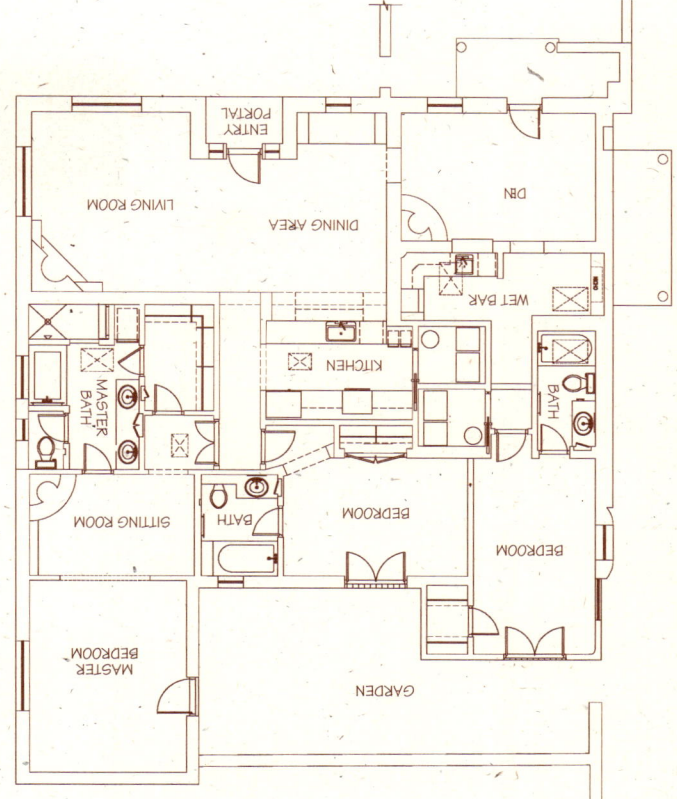

345 Delgado Street

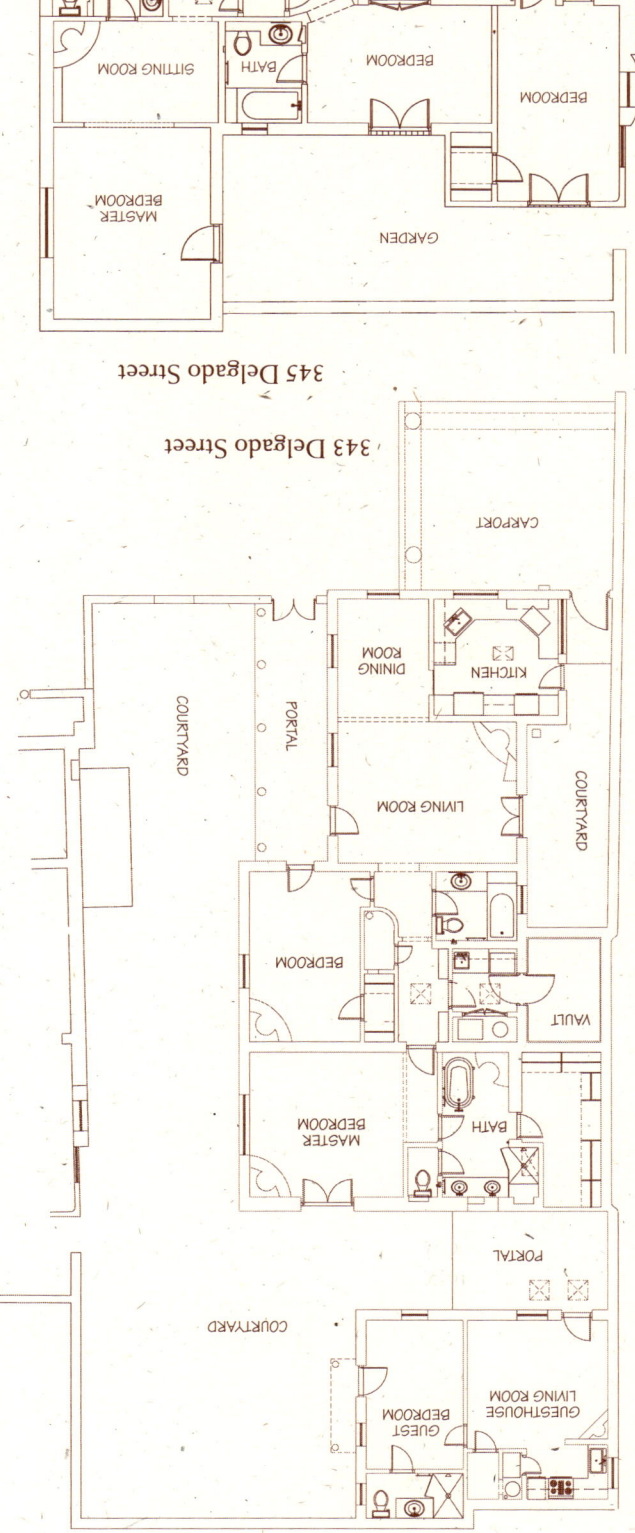

343 Delgado Street

Ortiz de Velarde
COMPOUND

measured drawings of buildings, as much as in preserving records of the buildings themselves. Although many student drawings may have errors in measurement, they nevertheless convey the sense of buildings that, in many cases, have been demolished. For that reason, they are now irreplaceable.

There is probably general agreement that the most appealing stage of New Mexico residential architecture occurred during the early Territorial Period as a result of influences from the United States. The two most essential of these influences were the introduction of the Greek Revival style, which manifested itself primarily in the treatment of doors and windows, and the increasing freedom from fear of attack, which made it possible to use the window glass which the Santa Fe Trail was beginning to supply. It is an exaggeration to say that the dark, cold, and inarticulate fortifications in which people lived suddenly opened out into light, comfortable, and humane dwellings. The stylistic changes occurred slowly, and it was near the end of the century before the need for protection from various enemies largely disappeared.

It is not surprising that the earliest and best examples of the Greek Revival influence in New Mexico resulted from applying the new doors, windows, brick copings, wood floors, etc. to existing buildings. Possibly the richest single aspect of this development is the treatment of the new openings cut through the thick walls of adobe or *terrón* or stone set in adobe mortar. Usually cased in painted wood, often in vertical boards, and sometimes divided into recessed panels, these deep window jambs form, for me, the primary symbol of the Territorial Period and of New Mexico architecture. Fortunately, several of the best examples of this type of house were documented thoroughly during the early HABS work. Most unfortunately, however, of the dozens of such houses which I knew as late as the 1950s, almost none exist today in a reasonably unchanged condition.

For many years, Bainbridge Bunting asked me, and probably others, for lists of buildings which I felt should be recorded, and I made my selections based on my opinion of the historic value of the site. In our discussions of sites that should have full HABS documentation, one of the things which both Dr. Bunting and I most regretted was the lack of attention given to New Mexico ranch complexes, especially the great cattle- and sheep-raising establishments of the mid to late nineteenth century. As far as I know, only the main house at the Watrous Ranch (now the Doolittle Ranch) has been adequately measured and photographed by HABS. One visit which Dr. Bunting and I made to the Bell Ranch and the Sanchez Ranch near Conchas Lake and the Mitchell Ranch near Mosquero, convinced us of the differences that exist among these sites and their counterparts in other parts of the West.

After forty years of unsystematic exploration in rural New Mexico, I still do not know the state well enough to make a definitive list of these ranch headquarters. Even so, I am aware of a score of uniquely New Mexican ranch headquarters that are little known, undocumented, and are a vital part of our architectural heritage. A thorough study of this category should have a high priority in the effort to record the historic architecture of New Mexico.

I am also aware of the importance of the many identifiable local styles extant throughout New Mexico and the lack of sufficient research to preserve the knowledge of their existence. These local styles were primarily the result of the isolation of communities, and in

Unidentified building [Our Lady of Angels School], Albuquerque, door in eroded adobe wall, photograph 1-2, HABS *1940 (NM-32).*

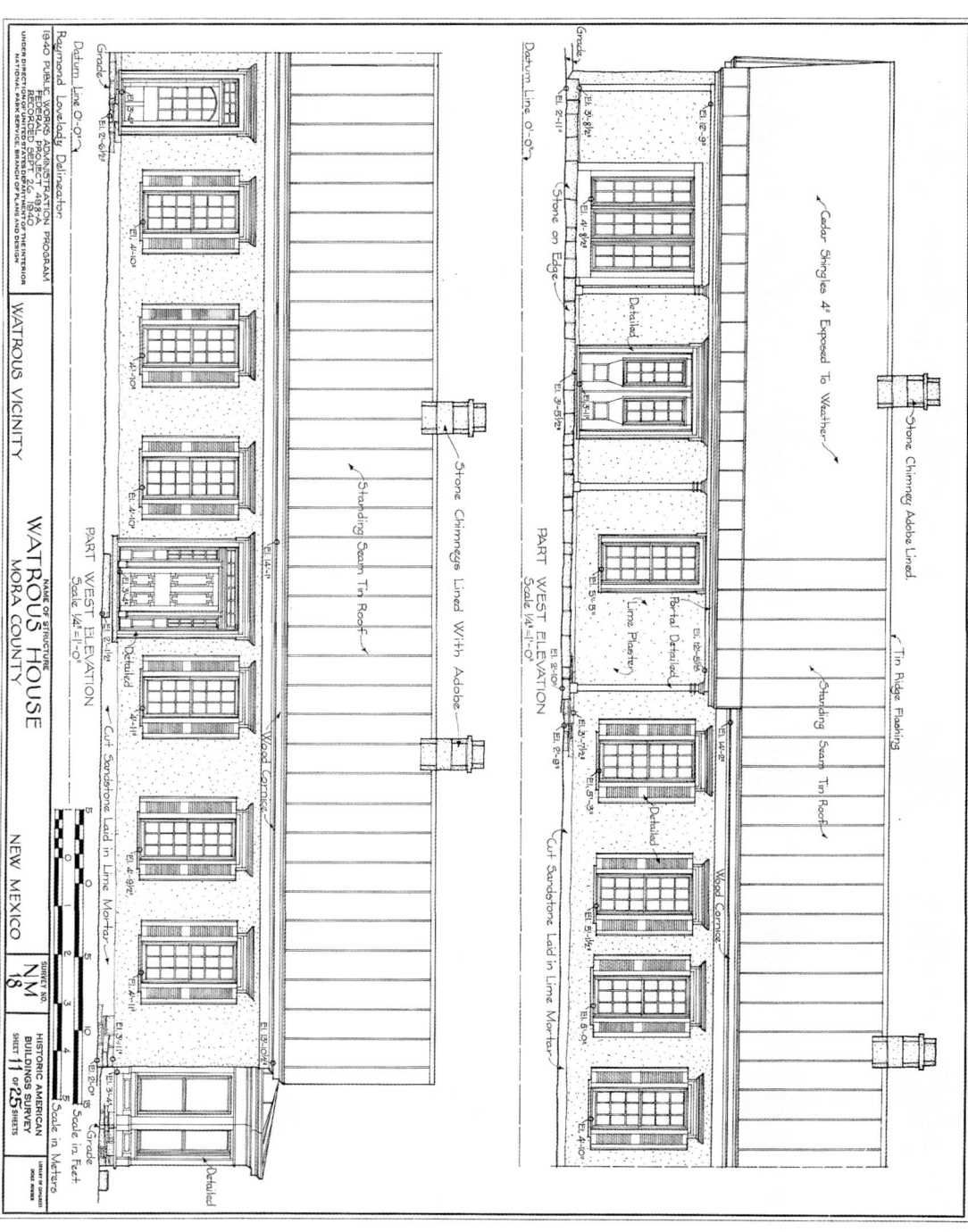

Watrous House, Watrous vicinity, west elevation, sheet 11 of 25, HABS. Raymond T. Lovelady, del. 1940 (NM-18).

from Chacón to Shakespeare, and from Puerta de Luna to Gallup.[2]

An interestingly debatable question is the importance of New Mexico houses built in the several styles which contact with the United States made available in the mid-1800s. The arrival of the railroad in the 1880s brought not only increased awareness but also equipment, tools, and materials that made these styles achievable here. What is the significance of these isolated examples of Second Empire, Queen Anne, Italianate, Stick Style, Shingle Style, Craftsman Style, Prairie Style, World's Fair Classic, and Bungalow, which exist in abundance in most other parts of the country? I once thought that it was only their rarity here which gave them apparent, but not actual, significance. Why do more than record the existence of a Second Empire house in Silver City or a Queen Anne house in Las Vegas when more pure examples of these styles exist elsewhere?

Possibly, it is precisely these impurities of style that warrant extraordinarily thorough documentation and accurate measurement of detail. It is the way in which various styles were used in the same house in the same phase of construction, the way in which the desired details were improvised and local materials and skills used, which make the houses peculiarly New Mexican. They become more important in the extent to which they vary from national norms. After the advent of the railroad, New Mexicans were able to choose from a great variety of plans, styles, and materials. It is not surprising that plans and styles were mixed in the same house more often than a single style was carried out consistently.

Should funds again become available for continuing the HABS documentation of residential structures in many cases, of the influence of a specific builder or craftsman. The Tierra Amarilla—Los Ojos—Los Brazos area is probably the most conspicuous example of the sense of a specific and unique place derived from the houses as much as from the landscape and the inhabitants, but many such areas exist in New Mexico,

New Mexico, three categories of houses come immediately to my mind. First, there is a great need to continue with the recording of prominent houses that have survived reasonably intact. In Socorro alone, at least a dozen significant houses with minimal change still exist from the 1880s and 1890s. They warrant full documentation. The unrecorded survivals in Raton, Las Vegas, and Silver City are even more numerous, to mention only the most conspicuous cities and neglect the great number of smaller towns, which contain fewer but equally significant examples.

A second category has received little attention: the houses which were not prominent but represented the living style of the majority of the inhabitants in the era. As in the early archaeological investigations of Mexico and the Holy Land, the sensational and the imminently exhibitable aspects of the cultures were studied, and the artifacts of the majority of the people were neglected. A distorted view of the prehistory of those cultures was the result. The vernacular houses in Northern New Mexico studied by Beverly Spears in her 1986 book *American Adobes: Rural Houses of Northern New Mexico* are exemplary of the type of house which I feel has been so much overlooked.[3]

A third category is perhaps the most significant: houses that have grown by accretion, continuing elements of so many styles and eras that they are often described as having lost their architectural integrity. The temporally one-dimensional characteristic of conventional measurement might be supplemented by archaeological techniques if the essence of New Mexico residential architecture is to be recorded.

CHRIS WILSON

In this chapter, Chris Wilson makes use of HABS drawings to document the religious architecture of New Mexico from the traditional Pueblo plaza and Spanish Colonial mission compound to the Gothic Revival Protestant churches of the turn of the century. v teams in New Mexico have recorded over thirty religious structures, primarily churches and chapels but also kivas, Pueblo missions, and Penitente moradas.

Wilson makes the interesting point that scholars have only just begun to identify and record the variety of ways in which religious significance manifests itself in the environment. In the Pueblo world, for example, sacredness connects the plaza, kivas, houseblocks, and surrounding natural landscape. A circle of stones may be a Pueblo shrine. In the Spanish Colonial landscape, religion is expressed not only through churches but also domestic shrines, outdoor temporary altars, and even religious place-names. Although HABS has periodically issued guidelines for recording, from the first bulletin of 1933 to John A. Burns's field instructions of 1989, they have not addressed such manifestations, which are often ephemeral.

A student of Bainbridge Bunting's at the University of New Mexico in the late 1970s, Chris Wilson is now one of the state's leading architectural historians. In 1993, the Society of Architectural Historians honored his La Tierra Amarilla: Its History, Architecture, and Cultural Landscape, coauthored with David Kammer, with its Antoinette Downing Award for the year's best publication resulting from an architectural survey. His recent book, The Myth of Santa Fe: Tourism, Ethnic Identity, and the Creation of a Modern Regional Tradition, received the Villagra Award from the Historical Society of New Mexico and the Cummings Award from the Vernacular Architecture Forum. In 1999 he was appointed the J. B. Jackson Professor of Cultural Landscape Studies at the University of New Mexico

CHAPTER 9
RELIGIOUS ARCHITECTURE AND SITES

CHRIS WILSON

From its beginning in 1934, the Historic American Buildings Survey specialized in pre-industrial, folk buildings. Such localized building traditions frequently have only two or three building types: a residential form, a religious structure, and often a barn or other agricultural building type. In New Mexico, HABS National Advisory Board member John Gaw Meem included a healthy selection of Spanish missions among the first buildings documented. He also included a few prehistoric *kivas* but only one historic kiva, probably because of the defensive secrecy surrounding many Pueblo religious practices. While HABS has focused on architectural monuments, we have begun to realize that religion has been so central to Pueblo and Spanish communities that religious significance has also been projected in less tangible ways throughout the environment, ways that have only recently begun to be recognized, documented, and preserved.

Religion permeates a traditional Pueblo environment in ways unimaginable to contemporary European-Americans. The most sacred site, the *sipapu* — the point of emergence from the spirit underworld to the present world — is a small, circular hole, a few inches across and deep. Positioned at the center of the traditional Pueblo world, the sipapu is typically framed by concentric rings of buildings, sacred hills, and mountains. It may be located in a ceremonial chamber, known as a kiva, which is often located in a plaza, or in the village plaza itself, marked only by an inconspicuous ring of stones.

The Pueblo plaza is not primarily a commercial or social space, as it is in the European tradition, but it is a religious precinct where the annual cycle of ritual dances are performed. Pueblo houseblocks are religious structures in the sense that they are positioned to protect the sipapu, to frame the dance, and to provide a platform from which to view the dance. Beyond each pueblo, four sacred hills and four sacred mountains further encircle the sipapu. These and other ritual sites, such as springs, are frequently defined by rocks arranged in geometric forms on the ground. A keyhole-shaped rock shrine might be positioned on a hill southeast of a village, for instance, to channel the energy of the rising sun toward the sipapu.

The most architecturally distinctive Pueblo religious structure is the kiva. Kivas are found at archaeological sites dating from A.D. 900. The classic kiva was circular and subterranean; it was entered through a smoke hole in the roof and equipped with a separate ventilator shaft bringing air to a fire pit in the floor. A low deflector wall normally shielded the fire from direct air flow. At the center of the floor was a small circular hole, sometimes found, centuries later, still filled with clean sand or other ritual materials.

Not all of these features occur in contemporary kivas: some kivas are above ground; others, square; and still others lack a recognizable sipapu. Indeed, a few pueb-

83

RECORDING A VANISHING LEGACY

generally have one or two large, circular, aboveground kivas. Taos, with its six subterranean kivas, is the notable departure from this pattern.

HABS documented an aboveground kiva at Nambé, north of Santa Fe, in 1934. It measures approximately 30 feet in diameter and has projecting piers which carry the log roof beams. The staircase, engaged to the side of the kiva, narrows as it rises. The depth of the treads and the height of the risers also diminish as they approach the roof of the kiva, as if to slow the progress and focus the attention of anyone approaching the roof, where a tall ladder leads down the smoke hole to the sacred chamber.

Although the term "mission" is sometimes used as a synonym for church, the Spanish Colonial mission consisted of both a church and an attached residential courtyard, often with a walled forecourt known as an *atrio*. This mission form developed in sixteenth-century Mexico and was transplanted to New Mexico the following century by Franciscan missionaries. The courtyard, known as a *convento*, resembles other large residences of the era. Rows of rooms, one room deep, form four or sometimes three sides of the courtyard (in which case the church completes the enclosure). Typically, each room opens onto the covered porch that rings the courtyard. Here the Franciscan missionary friars lived, preached Catholicism, and imparted Spanish culture and technology to the Pueblos, for the convento typically contained not only living quarters but also a school, workshops, and a kitchen garden within the courtyard.

In his classic study *The Religious Architecture of New Mexico*, George Kubler traced New Mexican, Spanish Colonial church forms to sixteenth-century Mexico

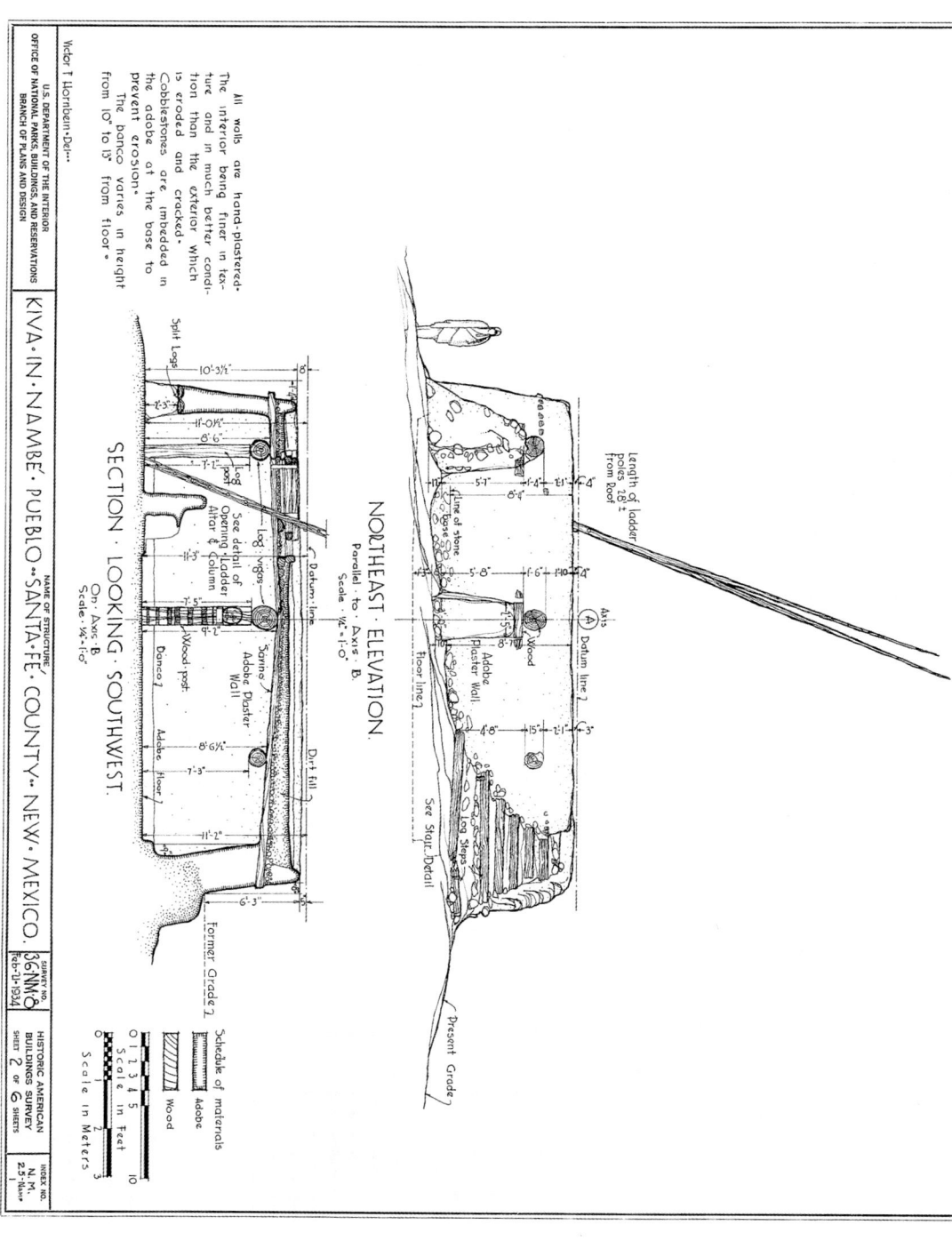

Kiva, Nambé Pueblo, sheet 2 of 6, HABS. Victor Hornbein, del. 1934(NM-8).

los lack kivas altogether. The western Pueblo villages — those of the Laguna, Acoma, Zuni, and Hopi — typically have several rectangular kivas that are often integrated into a multistory houseblock. The eastern Pueblos along the Rio Grande and its immediate tributaries

and beyond to the French fortified churches of the late Middle Ages. In New Mexico, walls are of massive adobe or unfinished stone construction, which favors simple single nave or cruciform plans without the structural elaboration of side aisles common to Romanesque and Gothic churches. The locally available roofing timbers determine the width of church naves, which generally are between 25 and 35 feet wide. A tower to either or both sides of the entrance or an *espadaña* (a stepping parapet wall with an opening for a bell) are the typical facade treatments.

Windows are few and small: usually one over the main door lighting the choir loft at the rear of the church and two or perhaps three on one side of the nave. The Franciscan friars working with the Pueblo builders stepped their flat roofs up two or so feet just before the sanctuary of single nave churches or at the transept of cruciform churches. Here they inserted a final window. The ingenious adaptation of the transept dome into humble adobe and log beams approximates the elaborate lighting schemes of Baroque Counter-Reformation churches: in the otherwise dimly lit interiors of New Mexican churches, light from the clerestory window floods the altar. A railing, steps to a raised altar, and the narrowing of a polygonal apse (preceded, in cruciform churches, by the opening out of the space at the transepts) further articulate and help focus attention on the sanctuary.

Spanish villages did not require missions since the population was already Catholic. As a result parish churches stand alone without attached residential courtyards. Frequently, however, a small, one-story baptistry is attached to one side of the nave near the entrance, while a one-room sacristy connects to the

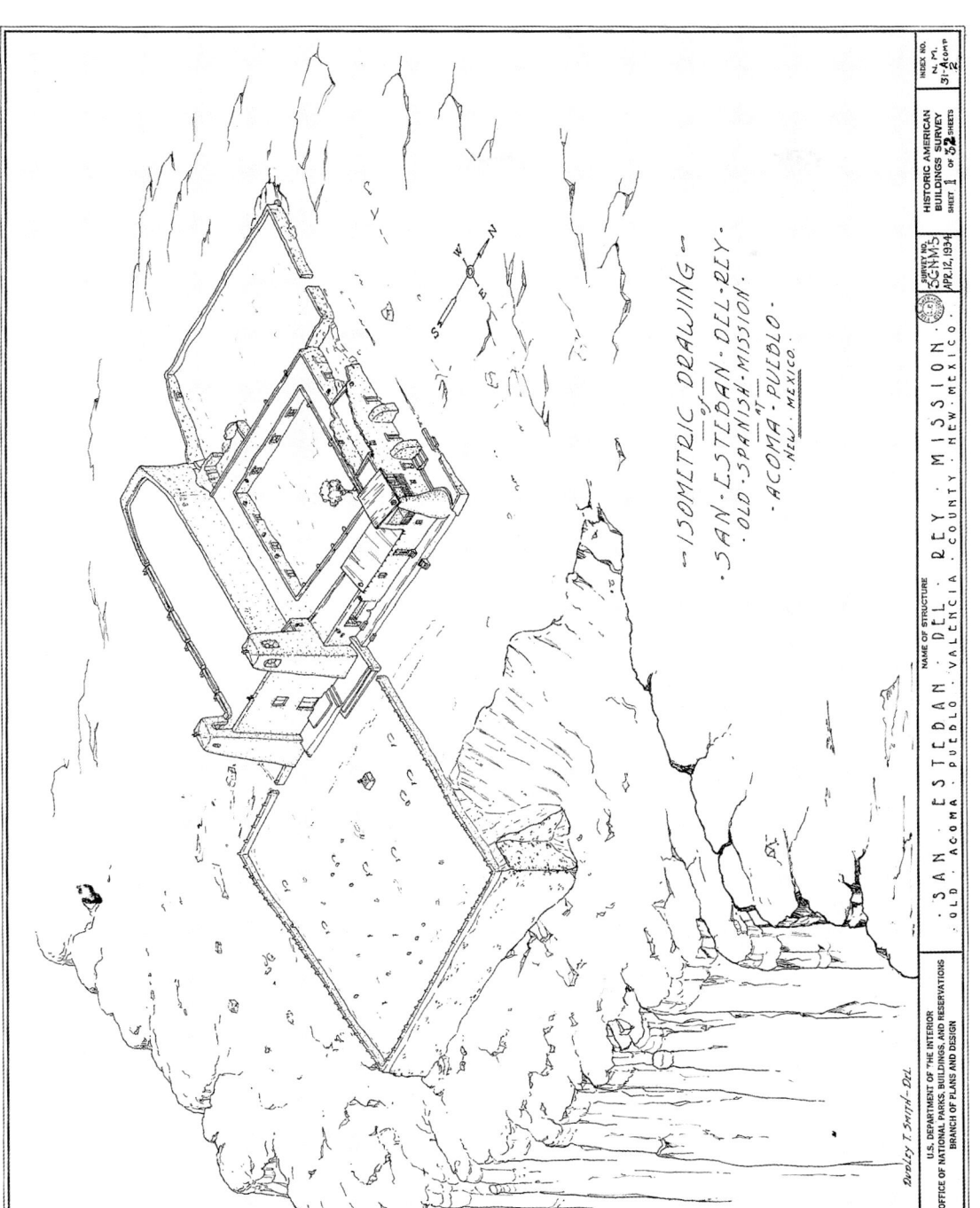

San Esteban del Rey Mission (Catholic), Acoma Pueblo, sheet 1 of 32, HABS. Dudley T. Smith, del. 1934 (NM-5).

opposite side near the apse. Cruciform plans predominate in the larger Spanish and Mexican communities such as Albuquerque, Santa Fe, Santa Cruz, San Miguel de Vado, Socorro, and El Paso del Norte (now Ciudad Juárez). In smaller villages, especially those settled in

RELIGIOUS ARCHITECTURE AND SITES

PREDOMINANT CHARACTERISTICS OF NEW MEXICAN CATHOLIC CHURCHES

	SIMILARITIES		DIFFERENCES	
	1750–1815	*1880–1930*	*1750–1815*	*1880–1930*
	masonry construction (adobe, stone)	masonry construction (adobe, stone)	flat roof	pitched roof
	cruciform or single nave plan	cruciform or single nave plan	facade tower(s)	roof belfry or tower(s)
	distinctive apse termination (polygonal or round)	distinctive apse termination (hipped roof compared to gabled front, some polygonal apses)	windows on one side of nave	windows on both sides of nave
			transept windows infrequent	transept windows common
	choir window	choir window in large minority	clerestory window	no clerestory window
			no additional facade windows	no additional facade windows
	sanctuary accented (raised, railing, double corbelling, narrower)	sanctuary accented (raised, railing, double corbelling, narrower)	choir loft	choir loft infrequent
			flat ceiling	curved ceiling
	East orientation (south and west less common, north infrequent)	East orientation (south and west less common, north infrequent)	vigas exposed	roof trusses covered
	attached sanctuary	attached sanctuary	attached baptistery	no baptistery
	walled atrio/camposanto	walled or fenced camposanto		

the nineteenth century, the single nave plan is most common.

Following the annexation of New Mexico to the United States and the arrival of French-born Bishop Jean Baptiste Lamy in 1851, new materials and a different set of ideas about church design reached the region. Milled lumber, window glass, and metal roofing combined with the Gothic and Romanesque Revival styles to transform religious architecture in the territory. Pitched roofs were added, and arched windows were cut into existing churches and became standard components of the dozens of new churches constructed by Lamy and the clergy he recruited primarily from France. The typical village church built in the late nineteenth and early twentieth century continued the Hispanic traditions with adobe or stone construction, a cruciform or single nave plan, orientation to the east or southeast, and an enclosed *camposanto* forecourt. The new pitched roofs, however, shrouded the clerestory windows, which were compensated for by the addition of larger glass windows on both sides of the nave at the end of transepts. Approximately half of the characteristics of churches before 1815 continue in the typical village church built between about 1880 and 1930 (table). The church form changed more rapidly in a few decades than it had in the previous two centuries but nevertheless demonstrated a significant cultural continuity in the face of dramatic economic, political, and religious change.

The chronic shortage of Catholic clergy in eighteenth- and early nineteenth-century New Mexico, exacerbated by the dramatic expansion of both Hispanic population and settled areas during the following century, contributed to the growth of a lay religious fraternity known as the Penitentes. Although the

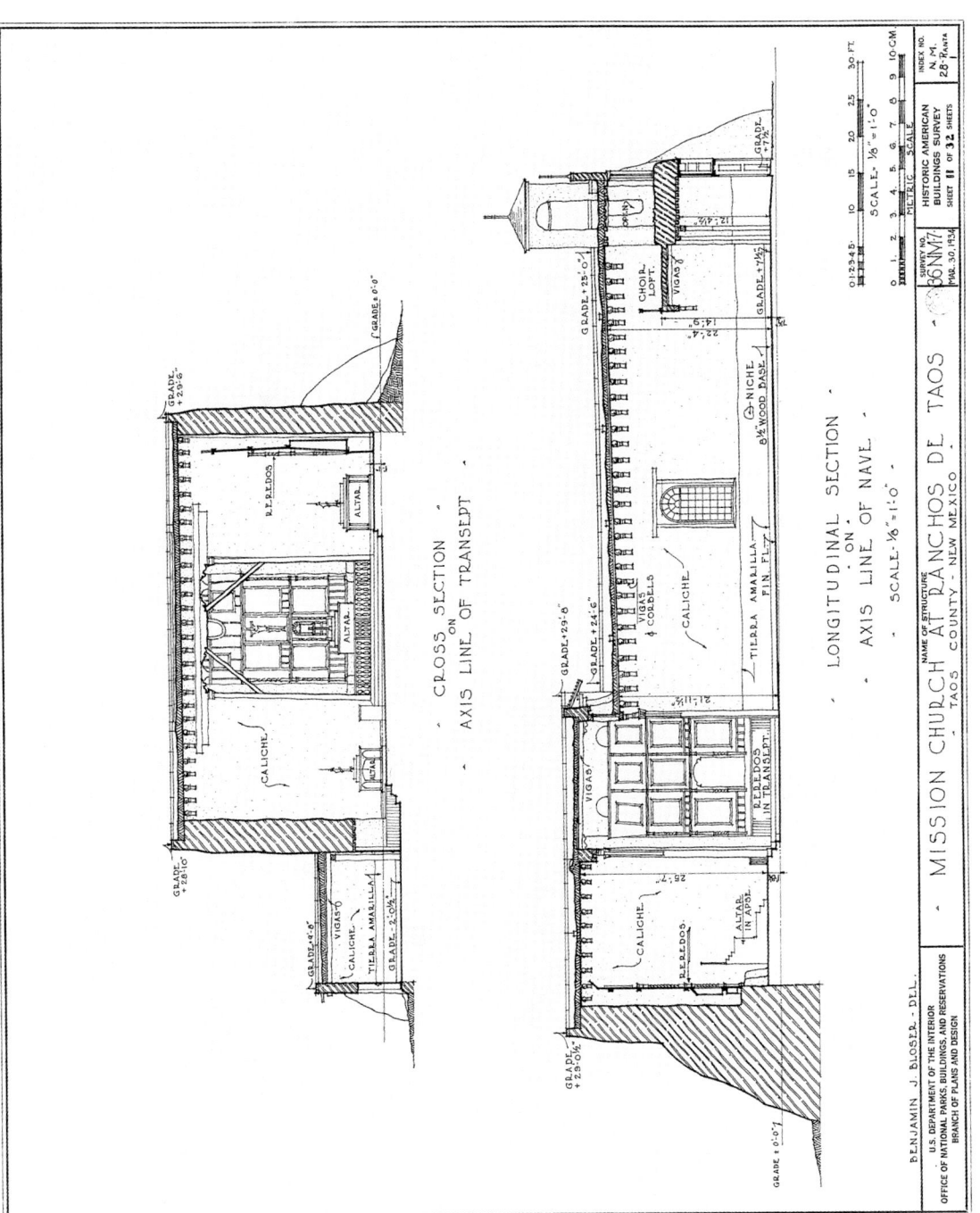

San Francisco Church (Catholic), Ranchos de Taos, sheet 11 of 32, HABS, Benjamin J. Bloser, del. 1934 (NM-7).

Penitentes are best known for their acts of penance during Holy Week, they also performed religious functions in the absence of clergy, such as burials, and served as an informal mutual aid society. Their meeting lodges, known as *moradas*, are typically two- or three-room structures built of adobe or stone with flat or pitched

RELIGIOUS ARCHITECTURE AND SITES

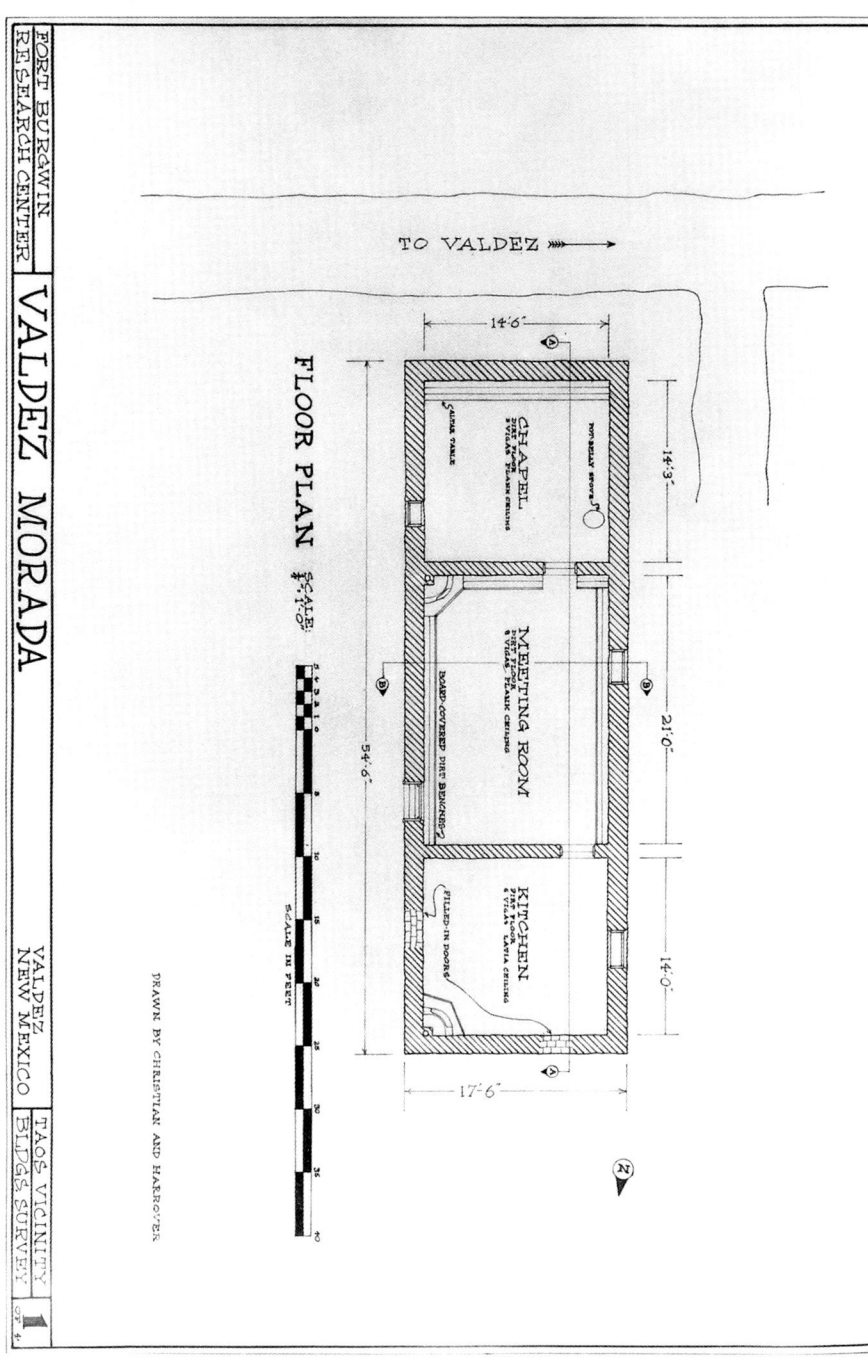

Morada, Valdez, sheet 1 of 4. Christian and Harrover, dels. (Architecture 261–62). ca. 1961. Bainbridge Bunting student drawings, John Gaw Meem Archive of Southwestern Architecture, University of New Mexico.

Moradas are usually located beside a cemetery and in a remote location to provide privacy for religious observances.

Private chapels, home devotional altars and statuary wall niches, religious processions, processional altars, shrines, and religious place-names joined with missions, churches, and moradas to project religion into the entire Spanish Colonial landscape. Private chapels ranged from ones as large as a parish church, such as El Santuario de Chimayó, to ones as small as the single room of a house set aside for devotion. Temporary altars were erected under exterior porches or under freestanding shade houses as stopping points for annual Corpus Cristi processions. Processional paths for Holy Week observances, known as *Via Crucis*, or the Way of the Cross, also developed in conjunction with moradas. These paths typically led from the morada to a local hill topped by three white crosses, a Mount Calvary, or *Calvario*, where the Passion of Christ was reenacted on Good Friday. The bronze, life-size stations of the cross under construction in the early 1990s on the mesa above San Luis, Colorado, continue this Hispanic religious observance.

Too few Protestants lived in towns during the nineteenth century and in rural areas into this century to justify the construction of separate, denominational churches. Often a single community or union church or only one church of the strongest denomination, generally Presbyterian, Methodist, Baptist, or Episcopalian, was erected. A few early adobe churches were built, although wood frame structures with clapboard or, increasingly in this century, stuccoed exteriors became more common.

Typically, Protestant churches are rectangular, gable-metal roofs. Often only a small cupola over an entrance in the long side of the building, and the building's few, relatively small windows distinguish a morada on the exterior from a residence. A large room, sometimes with a polygonal end, serves as a chapel known as an *oratorio*. Attached to this is a meeting room with a corner fireplace or cast-iron stove and built-in masonry *bancos*. Frequently, a third room is added for records or storage. These rooms are most often arranged in a single file, although L- and T-shaped plans also emerged.

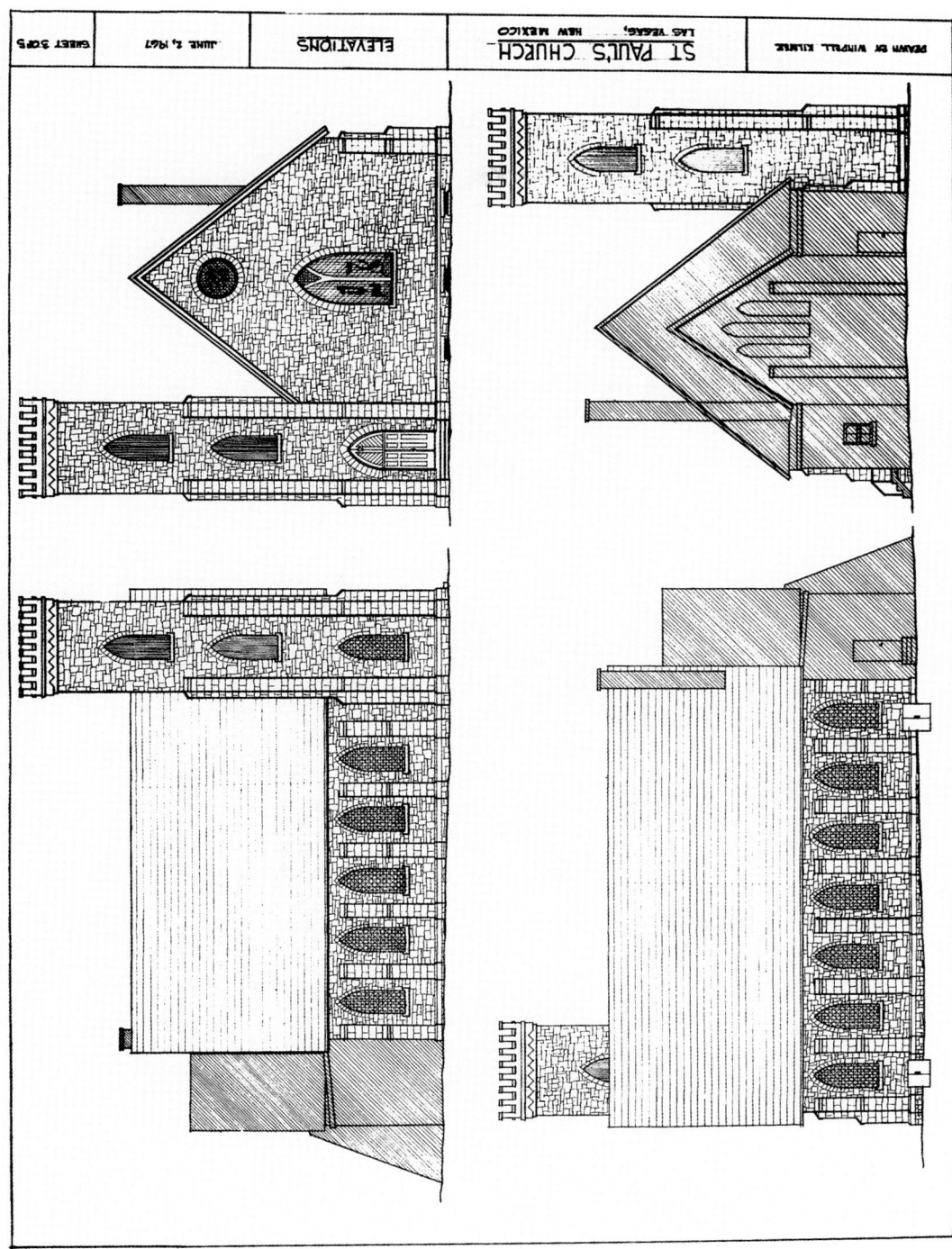

St. Paul's Church (Episcopalian), Las Vegas, sheet 3 of 5. Wimpell Kilmer, del. (Architecture 261–62). 1967. Bainbridge Bunting student drawings, John Gaw Meem Archive of Southwestern Architecture, University of New Mexico.

roofed structures with the entrances centered on the gable end and windows in both of the long sides. The proportions of this form, in particular the gable end with eaves returns and sometimes a bit of Greek Revival or other classical detailing, give the church the form of a classical temple with its implied emphasis of rationality over ritual. Only the Presbyterian Mission erected in West Las Vegas in 1872 fully realizes the form of a Greek temple. The more numerous, simple Protestant churches, such as the community church in James Canyon east of Cloudcroft, convey the purity and simplicity of the nineteenth-century American Protestant white temple in the wilderness. Frequently there is no altar or pulpit, as many denominations deemphasized ritual in favor of preaching by the priesthood of all believers. The very simplicity of the building and lack of liturgical trappings also made these churches suitable as schools or for community meetings.

Episcopalians and Catholics led the reaction against this Protestant simplicity in the nineteenth century. They reemphasized church ritual and revived the Gothic and Romanesque Revival styles, thereby evoking the great medieval cathedrals. In the 1870s, Catholic Bishop Lamy erected the Romanesque St. Francis Cathedral and the Gothic Revival Loretto Chapel in Santa Fe, while the substantial Gothic Revival church, Our Lady of Sorrows, was built of stone in West Las Vegas between 1862 and 1869. St. Paul's Episcopal Church, built in east Las Vegas in 1886–88, typifies Protestant attempts to evoke English Gothic parish churches — a movement fostered in the mid-nineteenth century by the architect Richard Upjohn and the Camden Society. St. Paul's pointed, ogee arches and dark, rough-faced, random ashlar sandstone, its stepped buttresses, tower crenellations, and steeply pitched roof, and inside, its dark woodwork and scissors trusses all contribute to its Gothic atmosphere.

While the Spanish Crown had granted the Church first choice of the most prominent location on the plaza, the speculative grid of Anglo-American railroad towns made no special provisions for churches. How-

RELIGIOUS ARCHITECTURE AND SITES

Corpus Cristi altar in front of Sena Plaza Santa Fe, about 1920. Museum of New Mexico Photo Archives, neg. no. 8137.

required a staircase that was frequently designed into a modest processional entrance with flights of stairs pausing at landings, sometimes splitting to move to the sides and then reforming at a tower entrance or entry vestibule. The use of the basement for Sunday school classes, dinners, and recreational activities, reflected the growing importance of social functions in many Protestant churches.

The Gothic Revival remained the preeminent church style well into the twentieth century, although usually executed with a lighter palette of buff sandstone or tan brick and fewer rustic surfaces. The restoration of the great Spanish missions in the 1920s and the growing interest in the history and traditions of New Mexico fostered the Spanish Pueblo and Spanish Colonial styles, which soon became popular for churches. The leading preservationist of the 1920s was John Gaw Meem, an Episcopalian, who, as already noted, guided the New Mexico HABS program in the 1930s. His intimate knowledge of the Spanish missions, gained through preservation and documentation, led Meem to specialize in revival style churches, such as Santa Fe's Cristo Rey Catholic Church of 1939. In its adobe construction, Cristo Rey represents the continuation of the Spanish tradition, while Meem's eclectic mixing of features from a variety of historic churches reflects a self-conscious return to local religious traditions.

The monuments of Pueblo and Spanish architecture that Meem selected for documentation in 1933 and 1934 had already become major prototypes of the Santa Fe style, also known as the Pueblo Revival. But in the second half of the 1930s, Meem and fellow architect Gordon Street turned to the provincial Greek Revival of mid-nineteenth century, Territorial New Mexico for ever, churches sometimes were clustered on a "church row" or "Zion Hill," and town developers occasionally offered free building lots to the congregations. Many Protestant churches also gained prominence from a street corner location and an entry tower at the corner of the basic, gabled church form. The nave was often raised atop a partially excavated basement. This

inspiration in developing an appropriate regional classicism for New Deal government buildings. When Meem selected a second set of buildings for HABS documentation in 1939, his role in the development of this Territorial Revival style led him to emphasize Territorial style buildings that revealed the impact of the newly arrived Anglo-Americans. But the parallel combination of medieval revivalism and adobe construction initiated by Archbishop Lamy and the French clergy did not enter the twentieth-century revival vocabulary, nor did Meem choose any of these "Adobe Gothic" hybrids for HABS documentation (excepting only the relatively minor accretions to essentially Spanish Colonial monuments such as the church at Ranchos de Taos).

Only in the 1960s and 1970s did Bainbridge Bunting begin to direct his students at the University of New Mexico to document the churches and moradas of the late nineteenth century. Even then, the greatest monument of the Adobe Gothic, San Felipe de Neri Church in Albuquerque, was only documented by HABS in the early 1990s. As for the less tangible manifestations of religion in New Mexico — the stone shrines of the Pueblos or the Via Crucis of the Penitentes — HABS has not attempted to document these, which is probably for the best. After all, how would one document the Tewa life force, *po-waha*, or the presence of the Holy Ghost?

CHARLES D. BIEBEL

Although Charles D. Biebel does not limit civic buildings to government-owned structures but defines them broadly as structures used for communitywide purposes, this brings the number documented by HABS in New Mexico between 1934 and 1940 to a mere seven. He evaluates the techniques and methods of HABS in that era and points out some of the survey's shortcomings. Biebel's comparison of three structures central to different systems of governance in the state since the seventeenth century demonstrates in what ways political structures are also indicative of social and cultural change.

In the 1930s John Gaw Meem personally selected priority sites for HABS documentation. Biebel insightfully criticizes the choice of sites and recording process, pointing out that the scope of HABS documentation has not been comprehensive and that entire regions of the state have been neglected. Neither is the range of functions representative; civic buildings, for example, make up less than 5 percent of the total.

In part this is a matter of definition: within traditional New Mexican cultures buildings were not strictly differentiated by function and often combined spiritual and civic purposes. Often the documentation is not complete, consisting of a few photographs and no measured drawings. Biebel, like Rina Swentzell, comments that the siting of a building is a crucial dimension that has been ignored by HABS.

As a longtime student of American culture and institutions, Charles D. Biebel, emeritus associate professor of American Studies at the University of New Mexico, has a keen interest in understanding the impact of physical monuments on the social landscape and their symbolic importance in history. He is the author of Making the Most of It: Public Works in Albuquerque during the Great Depression, 1929–42, published by the Albuquerque Museum (1989). Currently, he is living in Maine, where he works as a consultant affiliated with the University of Maine-Orono.

CHAPTER 10

CIVIC BUILDINGS

CHARLES D. BIEBEL

Arguably, a chapter concentrating on the civic buildings included in the early Historic American Buildings Survey in New Mexico could be very brief. For civic buildings, that is, public government-owned structures used in the political affairs of citizens, commanded a rather low priority for HABS officials in late 1933 and early 1934. When NPS architect Charles E. Peterson, the "father" of HABS, first discussed the need for a nationwide architectural survey in November 1933, he specifically focused on New Mexico's Pueblo villages and the ruins at Chaco Canyon as examples of the nation's neglected and rapidly "mutating" heritage that deserved immediate documentation.[1] And given HABS National Advisory Board member John Gaw Meem's preoccupation in the late 1920s with the preservation of New Mexico's picturesque and rapidly disappearing religious architecture, it should perhaps not be surprising that civic buildings were not emphasized when the lists of New Mexico structures to be surveyed were drawn up early in 1934 by Meem and HABS Southwest District Officer A. Leicester Hyde.[2]

Progress in New Mexico came slowly, however. Indeed, all HABS work in the state ceased in 1934 because the number of unemployed architects and drafters on welfare rolls in New Mexico was insufficient to justify allocation of federal relief funds to implement local surveys. When funding did finally resume in New Mexico, the pressure to document pueblos, mission churches, and deteriorating adobe residential structures was even more intense. Of the twelve "Priorities for Immediate Measurement in New Mexico" listed on a September 1939 memo to HABS headquarters in Washington, for example, three were Pueblo structures, two were churches or chapels, and seven were domestic complexes: no civic structures were identified.[3]

The full extent of this obvious lack of interest in civic buildings in New Mexico becomes apparent when one realizes that of some 115 or so buildings or sites surveyed by HABS architectural workers in the 1930s and 1940s, only about a half a dozen can be designated as primarily civic in function. And that six or seven can only be reached if one considerably stretches the conventional definition of "civic" used by HABS authorities. For by the strict meaning of civic, only four structures singled out in the first decade of HABS work would qualify: the Palace of the Governors in Santa Fe, the meeting house in Old Laguna Pueblo, the old Colfax County courthouse in Cimarron, and the old stone jail in Cimarron. To double the subjects for this discussion, therefore, we suggest broadening the contemporary meaning of civic to include either nongovernment or government-owned structures utilized primarily for communitywide purposes. By so doing, we can include the *torreón* in Manzano, the government trading store

93

El Palacio Real (Palace of the Governors), Santa Fe, front view from the southwest, photograph 2-2, HABS. M. James Slack, photographer. 1934 (NM-1934).

cal justification for such an emphasis and particularly so if one's mission were primarily to document as much as possible of the Pueblo and older Hispanic architectural record. The inclusion, however, of only three buildings in Doña Ana County, two in Otero County, and five in Socorro County suggests a rather skewed and incomplete documentation of the state's material culture.

The paucity of civic buildings in general in the earliest years of HABS activity occurred not only because New Mexico officials believed in the necessity of selecting the most spectacular pueblos, Spanish Colonial churches, and Spanish Pueblo residences as subjects for documentation and, therefore, for federal funding. There were also significant historical, social, and cultural reasons for what today we consider an important omission. Prior to the nineteenth century, New Mexican cultures seldom distinguished between civic, that is, secular activities, and the religious or sacred. Concepts of public and private were considerably more integrated in Native American and Spanish Colonial societies than in that of the early twentieth-century United States. The "private" kivas, mission churches, and family chapels which are treated in a separate religious architecture chapter in this volume were not only "sacred" buildings. At a time when distinctions between the political and spiritual realms were far less rigidly defined, they also often served important community functions that today we might relegate to the civic realm, that is, public ceremony, education, deliberation, or judicial decision making. It simply would not have occurred to earlier cultures that there was a need to create separate, discrete spaces or specialized architectural forms for these activities.

Therefore, a considerable number of the pre-twenti-

eth-century buildings used for civic activities were, and often still are, religious structures. From the elaborate Spanish Colonial mission churches in pueblos such as Laguna and Acoma to the small, humble family chapels in northern New Mexican villages, religious buildings also were—and in many cases still are—the site of community gatherings and decision making. Even the plaza spaces in front of the mission churches and in the centers of the pueblos functioned as important gathering places for civic purposes.

Nevertheless, certain buildings and spaces were clearly used for non-religious activities and, as such, deserve special documentation. It is therefore unfortunate that HABS activity in this area was and remains so limited. For instance, the Palace of the Governors in Santa Fe is documented only by two photographs taken in 1934 (photograph 2-2). There are no photographs of this important structure in any other collection of HABS photographs, and, to the best of my knowledge, the Palace of the Governors has never been measured and drawn as a HABS project. Similarly, the *torreón*, or defensive tower, in Manzano, New Mexico, is represented only by two small photographs, and the meeting house in Old Laguna is documented only by an exterior photograph.

There is also no evidence of HABS documentation of the grade school at Loretto Academy. There are no drawings available for the three civic buildings in Colfax County, and no accessible documentation exists other than a single photograph of each building taken in the 1930s. Fortunately, many years ago Professor Bainbridge Bunting had copies of early HABS photographs duplicated by the National Archives, and a full collection of these can be found among his collected papers in the John Gaw Meem archives at the University of New Mexico.

An additional selection bias evident in the early years of HABS history might be mentioned at this point. In looking at the original inventories, one is struck by the fact that the preponderance of structures chosen for measured drawings or photo documentation, including all the civic buildings, are located in the northern half of the state and primarily in the Rio Arriba region of New Mexico. There is, of course, considerable histori-

grade school at Loretto Academy in Cimarron, and the grade school at Loretto Academy in Santa Fe.

This dearth of examples of civic structures is problematic in another way as well. We tend to assume that the familiar multiple sheets of detailed scaled drawings of all 115 early HABS entries on New Mexico are available to scholars today. In seeking reproductions of the drawn treatments of each of the examples of early civic buildings, however, I discovered that sheets of drawings exist only for the Palace of the Governors, the meeting house in Old Laguna, the torreón in Manzano, and the

eth-century structures documented by HABS workers and discussed elsewhere in this volume as examples of residential architecture also served as sites for public meetings, community celebrations, and other activities of civil government in an age when social contexts were less specialized and differentiated. The inclusion of Pueblo Bonito and Kin Klizhin in Chaco Canyon and the entire pueblos of Zuni, Santa Ana, Acoma, and Nambé and the central portions of Santa Clara, Taos, and Tesuque pueblos perhaps attests to this unity of forms and functions inherent in the Pueblo worldview.

While few unaltered examples of Hispanic residential building remained from the Spanish Colonial and Mexican periods, HABS architects did document numerous examples of house complexes, such as the Los Luceros house in Rio Arriba County, the Chavez house in Belén, the Don José Albino Baca house near Las Vegas, and a half-dozen domestic structures in Taos County, all of which often provided civic, social, economic, and political focus for their communities or regions. Frontier Territorial Period residences constructed by Anglo-Americans after 1821 likewise often served as sites for similar multiple civic activities, particularly prior to the construction of transcontinental railroads in New Mexico in the late 1870s and early 1880s. Perhaps the best-known examples on the HABS inventories are the Horace G. Long house in Ranchos de Taos and the Watrous house in Mora County.[4]

Though severely limited in number, then, the seven civic buildings initially selected for HABS documentation nonetheless provide a number of interesting points for comparison and analysis. The Palace of the Governors, the Old Laguna meeting house, and the old Colfax County courthouse and jail, for example, all were central at one time to political governance in

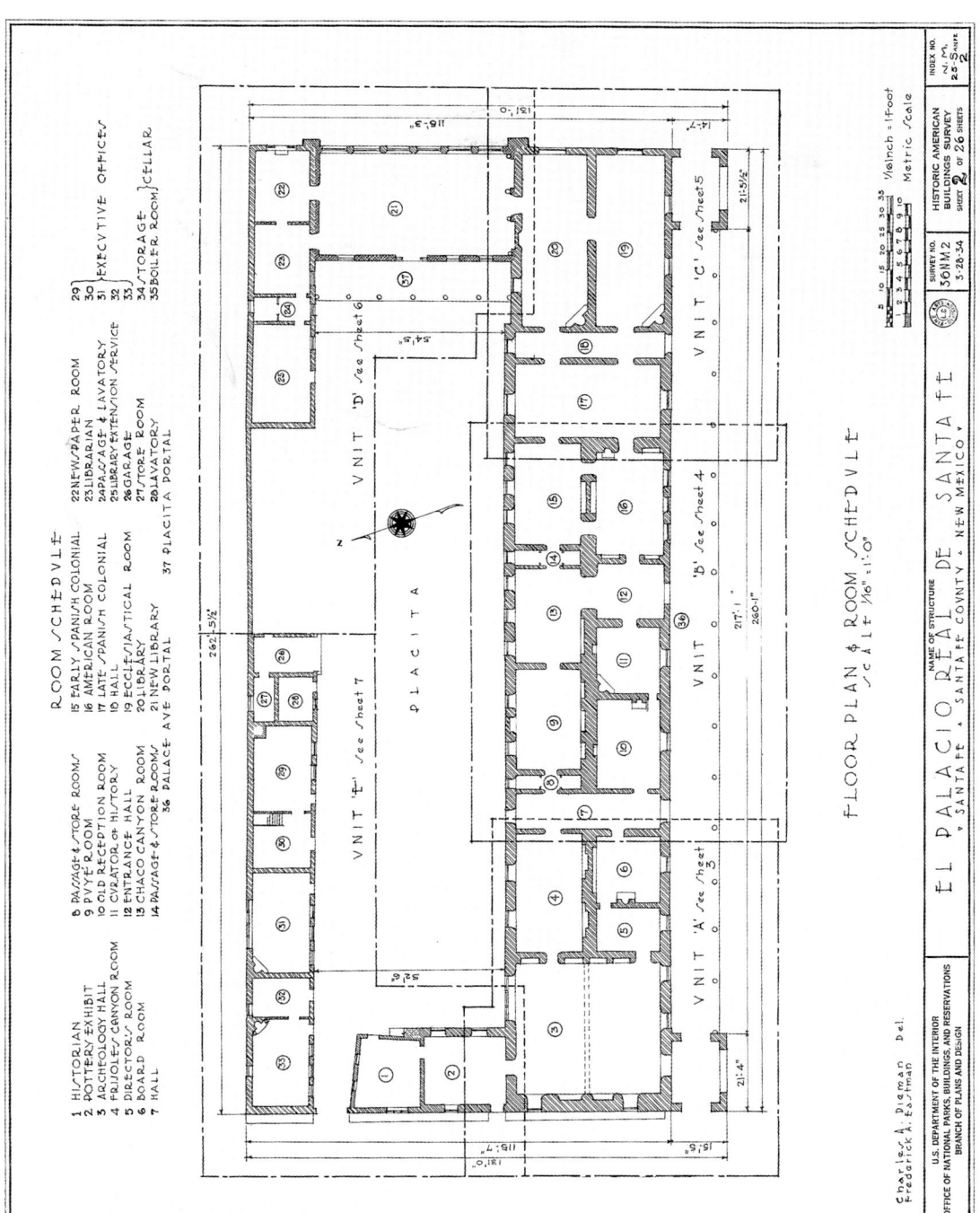

El Palacio Real de Santa Fe, Santa Fe County, New Mexico. Floor plan and room schedule. Charles A. Digman, del.; Frederick A. Eastman. HABS, sheet 2 of 26 sheets (NM-2).

three different New Mexican social and cultural contexts.

In size and as a center for the exercise of temporal power, the Palace of the Governors reigned as the premier civic building in New Mexico for almost three centuries. From its initial construction, which may

Old Laguna Meeting House, longitudinal section, Old Laguna Pueblo, sheet 2 of 4, HABS. Byron M. Kaufman, del. 1934 (NM-4).

CIVIC BUILDINGS

RECORDING A VANISHING LEGACY

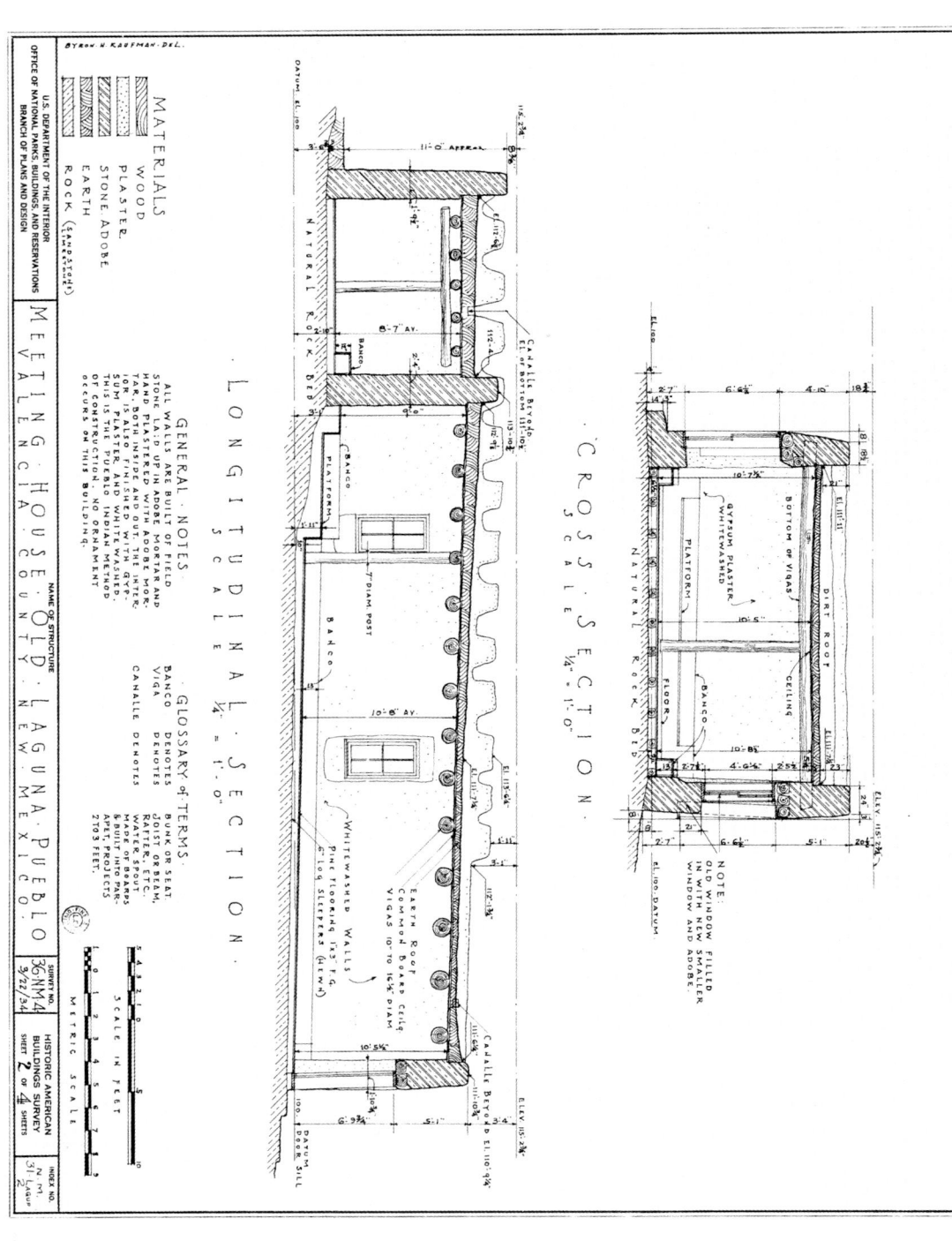

Old Laguna Meeting House, longitudinal section, Old Laguna Pueblo, sheet 2 of 4, HABS. Byron M. Kaufman, del. 1934 (NM-4).

rule, the palace continued to accommodate the governors' executive offices and until 1885 served as the seat of the Territorial legislatures. Even after completion of the new capitol building in 1885, the palace continued as the governor's residence for another twenty-four years. Then, after considerable restoration, its remaining twenty-nine one-story, adobe walled rooms, traditionally clustered around an interior courtyard and fronted by a substantial new Spanish Colonial portal, were utilized for other public functions as museum and library space. A HABS field survey team of imported, unemployed Colorado architects and drafters measured the palace in January and February of 1934. With the loss of federal money the next year because of new Works Projects Administration regulations, the survey measurements were not transformed into finished drawings until March of 1939.

Those 26 sheets of drawings, of course, in essence capture a temporal skeletal snapshot of the palace as it existed in the early depression era, a monument to the emerging tastes of the promoters of the Spanish Pueblo Revival and the renovators of 1909–13.[5] There is little hint of the structure's initial construction in accordance with the royal decrees of the Spanish Crown's 1573 City Planning Ordinances of the Laws of the Indies. Nor is there an evolving record of the continual building and rebuilding of the palace over the centuries in response to changing civic needs and altered social realities. These additional snapshots would include the major residential adaptation of the building by victorious Pueblo Indian occupants between 1680 and 1692, the erection of massive eighteenth-century presidio towers, and the installation of milled lumber Victorian porch details and Classical Revival ornamentation by

have begun as early as the winter of 1609–10, El Palacio Real housed various changing executive, judicial, legislative, military, and other civic offices, which themselves reflected the changing roles and civic needs of various successive governments. Under United States

U.S. government builders in the latter half of the nineteenth century.

HABS drawings also often do not reveal another important element significant in the comparison of these three civic structures. The palace did not stand randomly in its setting. As the first major building constructed at the new administrative seat of Spanish authority, its siting had been consciously determined by royal regulation and almost a century of prior colonization experience in the New World. Along with the church and convent of San Francisco, the palace was the central focus of a plaza that itself formed the contextual core of habitation and the center of communal economic and social activity.

In contrast to the relative antiquity and organic, evolutionary development of the Palace of the Governors in Santa Fe, the old Laguna meeting house paradoxically had been in use for just sixty years when it was measured in March of 1934. Mandated by the U.S. government (like the Spanish in 1610 a fairly recent external conqueror), the meeting house was constructed in 1874 to accommodate meetings of the newly legislated Laguna tribal council. As the Palace of the Governors, the meeting house was constructed of indigenous materials and included many traditional vernacular building elements. Like most Laguna structures of the time, its walls were built of local fieldstone and adobe, which were topped by an earthen roof supported by pine vigas. The latter, however, did not project beyond the exterior walls. In contrast to the multiroomed and much, altered seat of Territorial government in Santa Fe, the Laguna meeting house in 1934 consisted of a single simple 28- by 34-foot rectangular space, the interior walls of which were plastered with gypsum and whitewashed.

Old Laguna Meeting House, view from northeast, Old Laguna Pueblo, photograph 2-2, HABS. M. James Slack, photographer. 1934 (NM-4).

Unlike other Laguna structures, however, the west end of the meeting house included a raised 7-foot-deep platform that served to elevate council members both physically and symbolically above their peers, who could sit on wooden benches built into the bases of the remaining three walls. The latter walls were each punctuated by two small windows, and the east wall opposite the council's platform included a small door. By 1931 the floors of the meeting house were covered with milled white pine flooring, and a 12- by 13-foot storeroom, also constructed of fieldstone and adobe, was attached

CIVIC BUILDINGS

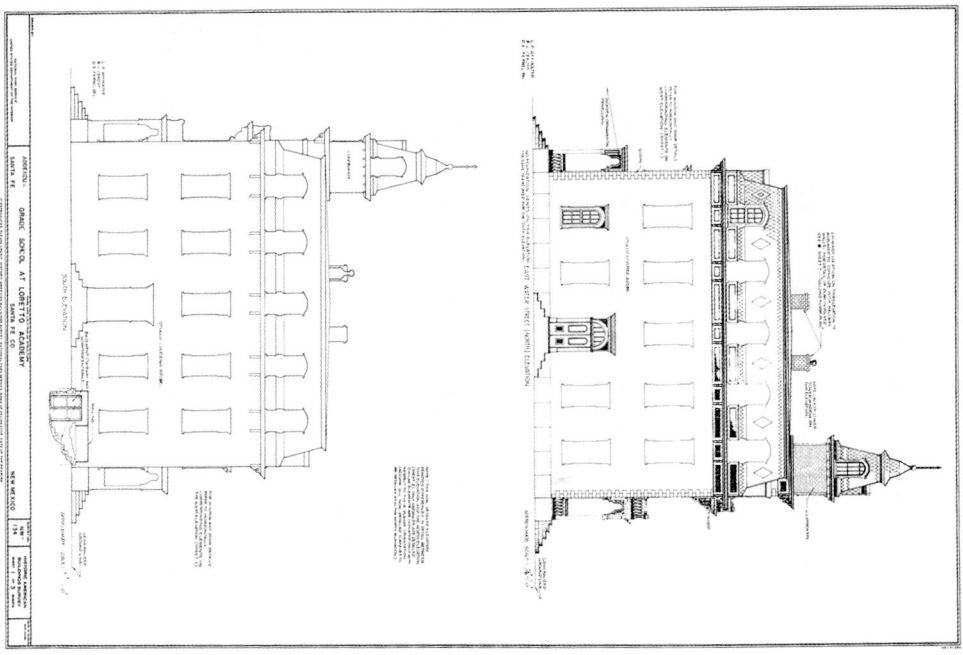

Grade School at Loretto Academy, Santa Fe, sheet 1 of 6, HABS. L. P. Affholter, B. J. Cekosh, and D. E. Ferro, dels. (Architecture 261–62). 1966–67 (NM-134).

to the west end of the building. With the exception of one corner fireplace, the interior of the meeting house was devoid of extraneous decoration or, for that matter, any elements indigenous to Laguna tradition.

As with its interior design, the external siting failed to reflect any connection with or centrality to the ritual spaces of older structures. Similar to the nearby San José de Laguna Mission Church (also surveyed and drawn by HABS workers), the meeting house stood as a late nineteenth-century monument to new forms of cultural imposition.

Finally, in its form and construction materials, the old Colfax County courthouse in Cimarron also echoed the simplicity and unobtrusiveness of the Laguna meeting house. Slightly older than the latter, the history and use of the courthouse interestingly enough reflect not so much radical change in political values but the response of a growing community to the rapid economic fluctuation and social shifts common to portions of late nineteenth-century Territorial New Mexico. Strategically astride the route of the Santa Fe Trail, in the 1860s and 1870s the northeast quadrant of New Mexico was emerging as one of the territory's richest mining and livestock raising areas. Reflecting the increased tempo of economic activity and an attendant increase in population and political power, Colfax County was created north of Mora County in 1896 with Elizabethtown (E-Town) as the county seat. The following year the prospering trading center of Cimarron was designated as the new county seat. Significantly, the county's first actual courthouse was an adapted single-story vernacular adobe dwelling. Though similar to the Palace of the Governors in the use of indigenous construction materials and vernacular forms, the courthouse remained consistent with an older tradition of nondifferentiated building forms. Its random siting, moreover, was more consistent with the Laguna meeting house. As an adaptive structure, it possessed little symbolic significance or distinctive scale to set it apart from its vernacular neighbors.

Within the next decade, the tracks of the Atchison, Topeka and Santa Fe Railway transected the northeast counties of New Mexico, bringing a further influx of prosperity, Anglo-American immigrants, and heightened eastern architectural expectations. By 1882, Cimarron's importance was surpassed by Springer, a town located only 20 miles to the southeast but adjacent to the main tracks of the AT&SF. With its more strategic economic location and a larger population base, Springer soon succeeded in being designated the new county seat of Colfax County. Accordingly, an "appropriately" designed new courthouse was built as the focal point in the center of a "proper" new courthouse square. Unlike its more prosaic neighboring commercial structures, the new courthouse was a two-story edifice constructed in the Second Empire style that had been particularly popular for civic buildings in midwestern counties a decade earlier. Its "modern" distinctiveness in the New Mexico Territory stood in proud contrast to the older, adapted Cimarron County courthouse or even to the ancient Palace of the Governors. It was, in short, an acceptably grand stylistic form for the new county seat's most important governmental building, at least until 1897, when the county seat was moved once again, this time to the booming town of Raton.

While the origin and use of the Palace of the Governors, the Laguna meeting house, and the Colfax

Torreón, Manzano, west elevation, photograph 1-4, HABS. Jesse Nusbaum, photographer. 1916 (NM-11).

County courthouse spanned several hundred years, similarities in form and construction of the three civic structures are suggestive. Their common characteristics reveal the strength of tradition and continuity of pre-twentieth-century New Mexican cultural attitudes about civic architecture. The resiliency of vernacular forms and indigenous materials during this period reflects an undifferentiated and nonspecialized stability that stands in sharp contrast to the innovation and technological change of the last quarter of the nineteenth century.

The torreón in Manzano, the jail and government trading post in Cimarron, and the grade school at Loretto Academy in Santa Fe also reflect this dialectic. The torreón and Cimarron structures are vernacular buildings, again employing local materials and traditional construction practice and design. The Loretto Academy, on the other hand, introduces the newer stylistic forms and materials that began to increase dramatically as the Anglo-American population rapidly grew in the last quarter of the nineteenth century.

Similar tensions between public/private and civic/community meanings attend the functions of these structures, from the communal defense functions of the torreón to the civic-economic role of the trading post and the quasi-"public" school role played by the Loretto Academy in the years before the Territorial legislature defined more precisely what "public" meant in the 1891 public school laws.

Shortly after the HABS crew finished measuring the torreón in Manzano, it should be noted, an official New Mexico State road construction crew moved in and destroyed the structure in the process of widening an adjacent county road. The loss of the historic torreón, which had previously been featured on a popular hand-tinted postcard for tourists, was symptomatic of the higher priority of road building as a form of public welfare programs in the depression era. It was also reflective of the increasingly pervasive impact of the automobile in New Mexico by the late 1930s and symbolic of the enormous potential of the automobile to transform an older set of physical and cultural landscapes.

In sum, the wholesale omission of civic buildings from the earliest lists of fragile New Mexico architectural gems that needed HABS documentation tells us a great deal about the then dominant values of architects

CIVIC BUILDINGS

and preservationists. The omission also underscores the historically fluid nature of public life in pre-twentieth-century New Mexico and the attendant lack of buildings specifically designed and dedicated for civic activities in New Mexican communities.

Happily, in subsequent years a wider range of appropriate structures neither residential nor religious were added to the HABS inventories. Still not entirely civic in function, these examples continued to underscore the disjunction between eastern cultural categories and the wide diversity of New Mexican social experiences. There were important commercial buildings, for example, such as the Alvarado Hotel in Albuquerque, the old Aztec mill, the opera house and Baca's store in Socorro, a blacksmith shop in Cimarron, and a warehouse and stables in San Miguel. All were privately owned commercial establishments of remarkably varied technological and economic complexity which provided spaces for significant quasi-civic activities and services within their communities. Other similar structures such as government schools, community irrigation projects, Navajo trading posts, and numerous railroad structures and airfields across the state should rightfully find their place on the inventories. Together with their earlier, more conventional counterparts, they strikingly reveal the state's unique civic architectural adaptations and cultural patterns. Their inclusion would serve greatly to fulfill the original HABS challenge to document the rich material evidence of the civic values of a people and a region.

CONCLUSION

SALLY HYER

In his 1969 speech to the Colonial Dames of Colorado, Alan B. Fisher remembered that in 1934 La Capilla de Talpa "... stood with an almost innate desire within its very perishable self for destruction and with an inclination to return to the adobe floor of land upon which it stood." The chapel has not survived, and, according to HABS chief Robert Kapsch, neither have approximately one-third to one-half of the buildings documented by HABS and HAER nationwide.

Charles E. Peterson in 1933 realized that the nation's architectural heritage was inexorably disappearing; his colleagues and successors in New Mexico, from John Gaw Meem and Bainbridge Bunting to Perry E. Borchers, have shared this conviction. To resist the destruction they created records on paper, some of which have outlasted the structures documented. These architects' passion, energy, and devotion to creating accurate records of the past have set standards for architectural recording today and laid the groundwork for the nation's historic preservation movement.

To Santa Clara Pueblo architect Rina Swentzell, buildings have a natural life span and should be allowed to be born, live to maturity, and die. They are part of the spirit of the whole, which cannot be measured or drawn. She sees concern with accuracy, detail, and permanence as being at odds with the Pueblo sense of respect for the interconnectedness of all life. The authors of the essays collected here recognize that buildings disappear, but their opinions about the value of storing information in the form of drawings on paper reflect profound cultural differences that have barely been addressed in HABS' decades in New Mexico, beliefs that shaped the very architecture being documented. Yet the survey cannot be faulted for failing to achieve a goal it never planned to meet.

While the discrepancy between the cultural traditions and values of the original builders of New Mexican pueblos and the raw HABS recruits may be striking, some HABS architects intuitively appreciated the concept of buildings as organic beings, as Fisher's remarks clearly show. Bainbridge Bunting's first Native American architecture students led the way for others to enter the field. Architects, archaeologists, and historians may gain greater insights into Pueblo concepts from them, just as Pueblo scholars may come to appreciate the idea of creating a permanent record of the past from their non-Indian colleagues. The work of the three generations of HABS architects described in this book we hope will be the starting point for a more profound understanding between builders and recorders of New Mexico's vanishing legacy of historic architecture.

PART FOUR
HABS INVENTORY FOR NEW MEXICO

HOW TO USE THE INVENTORY

The entries in this inventory are based on the HABS/HAER Inventory Index of the Library of Congress documenting all material received through August 8, 1993. Records that were being processed at that time are not included in this list.

In the inventory, records are arranged alphabetically by town, city, or nearest vicinity. Counties are also listed. Individual entries are arranged alphabetically within a geographic location by the historic name of the structure. Secondary names are given following the main entry. Following the name of the building is the HABS number, e.g., NM-18. These numbers should be used when inquiring about a structure or when ordering reproductions from the Library of Congress.

The entries begin with a listing of records in the New Mexico HABS collection at the Library of Congress. This is followed by a summary of the administrative organization of the project under which the documentation was made. The general format for each entry is as follows:

- **Town, city, pueblo, or nearest vicinity county**
- Historic **name** and alternate names
- **HABS number** for the structure (e.g., NM-18), control number, and Library of Congress shelf code number (e.g., NM, 22-BLAND.V.2-).
- Number and date of HABS **sheets** (measured drawings of plans, sections, elevations, and details), **photographs**, **data pages**, and **photocopies** compiled for each entry.
- Names of **team members**: architects, delineators, plotters, photographers, students, and/or historians involved in documentation.
- **Administrative organization** of the project, including information on funding and personnel when available.

ABBREVIATIONS, TERMS, AND SYMBOLS USED IN THE INVENTORY

Data pages		Information on the structure
(NM-18)		HABS number assigned to site
Photos		Photographs in the files of HABS
Sheets		Sheets of measured drawings recorded for each entry
Illustrated		An entry that is illustrated in the text
NM, 22-BLAND.V,2-		Library of Congress shelf code number
n.d.		The date has not been determined
Photocopy		Photographic copies or reproductions include facsimiles of old photographs and other historical material pertaining to each recorded structure. When known, the date is given.
Photogrammetric images		When noted the inventory, "photos" may consist of copy photos of photogrammetric plates and "data pages" of a list of photogrammetric images. Glass photogrammetric plates are not reproducible without special permission. The Photogrammetric Images Project at the Library of Congress in 1985–86 incorporated photogrammetric images into the HABS/HAER collections. Inventories of the images were compiled and filed as data pages for each structure recorded. A reference print and film copy negative were made from one plate of each stereopair and from the most informative plates in sequential sets. The reference prints and copy negatives were then incorporated into the formal HABS/HAER photograph collections.

HABS INVENTORY FOR NEW MEXICO

SALLY HYER

ABÓ
TORRANCE COUNTY
Misión San Gregorio de Abó (NM-146)
Control Nr. NM0151; LC Shelf Code NM, 29-ABOP, 1-.

14 sheets (1985, including isometric drawing, plans, elevations, sections).

The Salinas National Monument documentation project was undertaken by the Washington, DC, office of HABS and sponsored by the Southwest Regional Office of NPS. The 1985 summer documentation was conducted by the HABS/HAER Division, Robert J. Kapsch, Chief, and was organized and directed by Kenneth L. Anderson, Principal Architect, HABS, in conjunction with Barry Sulam, Chief, Division of Conservation, Southwest Cultural Resources Center, and Thomas B. Carroll, Superintendent, Salinas National Monument.

The 1985 summer documentation of Misión San Gregorio de Abó was produced by Project Supervisor Leonard M. Kliwinski (University of Chicago). The site was measured and drawn by Kenneth L. Anderson and architecture technicians John P. Jennings (Texas Tech University) and Rudd M. Long (University of Texas at Arlington).

ACOMA PUEBLO
VALENCIA COUNTY
(became Cibola County in 1982)
Acoma, Pueblo of (Sky City) (NM-6)
Control Nr. NM0095; LC Shelf Code NM, 31-ACOMP, 1-.

1934 PROJECT:
83 sheets (1934, including plans, elevations, sections, details); 75 ext. photos (1934), 1 photo of aerial view showing pueblo and church with identifying block numbers (n.d.), 1 ext. photo with label: "photograph of an aerial photograph bought at the Kimo curio shop in Albuquerque in 1928," 9 int. photos (1934); 4 data pages (1936).

This project was undertaken by HABS, NPS, Branch of Plans and Design, USDOI. It was approved by Acoma Pueblo Governor Bautisto Pino and prepared under the direction of John Gaw Meem, HABS National Advisory Board member and A. Leicester Hyde, District Officer for District 36 (Utah, Colorado, New Mexico).

The leaders were: C. Truman St. Clair, General Squad Leader; Bradley P. Kidder, Field Squad Leader; and E. S. Mosher, Drafting Squad Leader. B. A. Reuter was in charge of Indian relations. Sketching was by F. O. Kellman, Stanley H. Kent, Arthur G. Longfellow, and A. E. Jack. Measuring was by B. H. Kaufman, A. B. Willison, B. A. Reuter, O. G. Stromquist, Bradley P. Kidder, Edwin B. Clarke, Urie McCleary, William Kraemer, M. James Slack, A. E. Jack. Transit: C. Truman St. Clair and J. T. M. Kidder.

Drafting squad members were Alan B. Fisher, Dudley T. Smith, W. Howard Speer, O. G. Stromquist, C. Truman St. Clair, F. O. Kellman, M. James Slack, and Edwin B. Clark. Inking and lettering were by E. S. Mosher, Arthur Hoyer, Stanley H. Kent, Victor F. Hornbein, H. P. Atchison, A. E. Jack, and Arthur G. Longfellow.

The 1934 photos were taken by M. James Slack. The 1936 data pages were prepared by A. Leicester Hyde.

1973 PROJECT:
3 sheets (1973, including plan, section, elevation); 1 ext. photo (1965, copy photo of photogrammetric plate); 2 data pages (1985–86).

This project was undertaken by the NPS, USDOI. It was approved by the Acoma Pueblo Governor and Tribal Council. The drawings were prepared at the School of Architecture, OSU, under the direction of Perry E. Borchers, Research Supervisor.

Aerial photography was by the New Mexico State Highway Department in 1965. Terrestrial photogrammetry within the churchyard was by Perry and Myra Borchers and Bainbridge Bunting in 1973. Drawings were plotted on the Wild A7 Autograph at OSU by Perry E. Borchers and delineated by Julsing J. Lamsam (OSU) in 1974.

The exterior photo was taken by Perry E. Borchers in 1965. The data pages are an inventory of photogrammetric images prepared by the Photogrammetric Images Project (1985–86). They consist of four 9.5 × 9.5-inch glass plate diapositives, survey control contact prints, and survey control information and reduced image prints for some plates.

ACOMA PUEBLO
VALENCIA COUNTY
(became Cibola County in 1982)
San Esteban de Rey Mission (NM-5)
Control Nr. NM0067; LC Shelf Code NM, 31-ACOMP, 2-.
32 sheets (1934, including plans, elevations, sections, details, restoration, color sheet); 19 ext-photos (1934), 15 int. photos (1934); 5 data pages (1934).

This project was undertaken by HABS, NPS, Branch of Plans and Design, USDOI. It was approved by Acoma Pueblo Governor Bautisto Pino and prepared under the direction of John Gaw Meem, HABS National Advisory Board member and A. Leicester Hyde, District Officer for District 36 (Utah, Colorado, New Mexico).

The Squad Leaders were Bradley P. Kidder and M. James Slack; the field party was Dudley T. Smith and C. Truman St. Clair; others involved were B. A. Reuter, Arthur E. Jack, B. M. Kaufman, Arthur G. Longfellow, E. S. Mosher, W. Howard Speer. The photos were taken by M. James Slack. The data pages were prepared by A. Leicester Hyde.

ALAMOGORDO VICINITY
OTERO COUNTY
La Luz, Town of (NM-141)
Control Nr. NM0133; LC Shelf Code NM.8-LAUZ.1-.
3 ext. photos (1976, copy photos of photogrammetric plates); 3 data pages (1985–86).

This project was undertaken by the New Mexico State Historic Preservation Division and the Office of Archaeology and Historic Preservation, NPS, USDOI. It was prepared under the direction of Perry E. Borchers of the School of Architecture, OSU.

The photos are copies of photogrammetric plates by Perry E. Borchers. The data pages are an inventory of photogrammetric images prepared by the Photogrammetric Images Project (1985–86). They consist of four 5 × 7-inch glass plate diapositives (two stereopairs) and six 9.5 × 9.5-inch glass plate aerial diapositives.

ALBUQUERQUE
BERNALILLO COUNTY
Alvarado Hotel (NM-123)
Control Nr. NM0081; LC Shelf Code NM.1-ALBU.5-.
22 ext. photos (1969), 11 int. photos (1969).

This structure was photographed by Fred Mang, Jr., of NPS in 1969.

ALBUQUERQUE
BERNALILLO COUNTY
Charles Ilfeld Company Warehouse (NM-105)
Control Nr. NM0093; LC Shelf Code NM.1-ALBU.3-.
14 ext. photos (1977), 11 int. photos (1977); 5 data pages (1979).

This project was undertaken by the U.S. Department of Housing and Urban Development in compliance with Executive Order 11593 and a Memorandum of Agreement with the Advisory Council on Historic Preservation as a mitigative effort in demolition. John A. Burns, AIA, was the project coordinator. Photos were taken by Jerry Goffe. Research was conducted by Michael McCachren and data pages prepared by Mary Beth Betts.

ALBUQUERQUE
BERNALILLO COUNTY
Building (NM-32)
Control Nr. NM0002; LC Shelf Code NM.1-ALBU.1-.
3 ext. photos (1940).

These photos were taken by Delos H. Smith. Smith, a consulting architect with HABS in the Washington, DC, office, emphasized the importance of photographic documentation of sites. He worked briefly in New Mexico in 1940 and produced photos of five buildings in Albuquerque, Peralta, and the Valencia vicinity that are now part of the HABS inventory. In 1940, HABS documentation was funded by the Works Progress Administration and by Public Works appropriations.

ALBUQUERQUE
BERNALILLO COUNTY
House (NM-33)
Control Nr. NM0003; LC Shelf Code NM.1-ALBU.2-.
1 ext. photo (1940).
See Albuquerque, Building (NM-32).

ALBUQUERQUE
BERNALILLO COUNTY
1-25 Hazeldine Plaza (Building) (NM-22)
Control Nr. NM0117; LC Shelf Code NM.1-ALBU.4-.
1 ext. photo (1980).

The photographer Walter Smalling, Jr., took 11 photos of structures at Albuquerque, Taos, Chimayó, Las Trampas, and Los Alamos for HABS in 1980.

ALBUQUERQUE
BERNALILLO COUNTY
Kimo Theater (NM-20)
Control Nr. NM0115; LC Shelf Code NM.1-ALBU.6-.
1 ext. photo (1980).
See Albuquerque, 1-25 Hazeldine Plaza (Building)(NM-22).

ALBUQUERQUE
BERNALILLO COUNTY
Rosenwald Brothers Building (NM-26)
Control Nr. NM0121; LC Shelf Code NM.1-ALBU.7-.
1 ext. photo (1980).
See Albuquerque, 1-25 Hazeldine Plaza (Building) (NM-22).

ALBUQUERQUE
BERNALILLO COUNTY
St. Anthony's Orphanage (NM-149)
Control Nr. NM0154; LC Shelf Code 1989(HABS):15.
7 photos (unprocessed, n.d.); 22 data pages (unprocessed, n.d.).
(The materials on St. Anthony's Orphanage have not been processed and are not available to the public.)

ALBUQUERQUE
BERNALILLO COUNTY
St. Anthony's Orphanage, Classroom and Dormitory (NM-149-A)
Control Nr. NM0155; LC Shelf Code 1989 (HABS):15.
11 photos (1989); 22 data pages (1989).

ALBUQUERQUE
BERNALILLO COUNTY
St. Anthony's Orphanage, Auditorium (NM-149-B)
Control Nr. NM0156; LC Shelf Code 1989 (HABS):15.
7 photos (1989).

ALBUQUERQUE
BERNALILLO COUNTY
St. Anthony's Orphanage, Chapel (NM-149-C)
Control Nr. NM0157; LC Shelf Code 1989 (HABS):15.
11 photos (1989).

ALBUQUERQUE
BERNALILLO COUNTY
San Felipe de Neri Church, Old Town Plaza,nw, (NM-176)
LC Shelf Code NM,1-ALBU,11.
7 measured drawings.

ALBUQUERQUE
BERNALILLO COUNTY
U. S. Veterans' Administration Medical Center (NM-133)
Control Nr. NM0118; LC Shelf Code NM.1-ALBU.8-.
19 ext. photos (1983); 1 int. photo (1983); 1 data page (1985); 2 photocopies of photos (1932), 4 photocopies of photos (1 each from 1933, 1939, 1940, 1956), 1 photocopy of site plan (ca. 1982), 1 photocopy of drawing (ca. 1982).
This project was undertaken by the Washington, DC, office of HABS. The int. and ext. photos were taken by Terry L. Brian and Herman O. Tafoya, Jr. The data page was prepared by historian Alison K. Hoagland of the Washington office of HABS.

ALBUQUERQUE
BERNALILLO COUNTY
Wool Warehouse (NM-21)
Control Nr. NM0116; LC Shelf Code NM.1-ALBU.9-.
1 photo (1980).
The photographer Walter Smalling, Jr., took 11 photos of structures at Albuquerque, Taos, Chimayó, Las Trampas, and Los Alamos for HABS in 1980.

ALCALDE
RIO ARRIBA COUNTY
Alcalde Village (NM-83)
Control Nr. NM0106; LC Shelf Code NM.20-ALCA.1-.
2 ext. photos (1936).
These photos were taken by Frederick D. Nichols of the Washington office of HABS. In August 1936 and July–September 1937, Nichols took 42 photos of structures in the counties of Santa Fe, Taos, Rio Arriba, San Miguel, Colfax, Doña Ana, and Otero. Each structure was documented with four or fewer photos. Nichols, an architecture graduate from Yale University, was a leading employee at the Washington office of HABS from 1933 until he joined the navy during World War II. He compiled the HABS 1941 catalog. In 1936 HABS documentation was funded by the Works Progress Administration.

ALCALDE
RIO ARRIBA COUNTY
Church (NM-84)
Control Nr. NM0009; LC Shelf Code NM.20-ALCA.2-.
1 ext. photo (1936).
See Alcalde, *Alcalde Village* (NM-83).

ALCALDE
RIO ARRIBA COUNTY
Los Luceros Chapel (NM-54)
Control Nr. NM0105; LC Shelf Code NM.20-LOLUC.2-.
5 sheets (ca. 1960–65, including plans, elevations, sections, details).
This project was prepared under the direction of Bainbridge Bunting, Associate Professor of Art History, University of New Mexico Art History Department. The measured drawings are by architecture student Leon J. Holecheck and were submitted as a term project for Architecture 261–262. Due to insufficient information at the time of editing, they may not conform to HABS standards. The reproduction rights were acquired by HABS under the direction of James C. Massey, Chief, in 1971.

ALCALDE
RIO ARRIBA COUNTY
Los Luceros House (NM-53)
Control Nr. NM0085; LC Shelf Code NM.20-LOLUC.1-.
9 sheets (ca. 1960–65, including plans, elevations, sections, details).
This project was prepared under the direction of Bainbridge Bunting, Associate Professor of Art History, University of New Mexico Art History Department. The measured drawings are by architecture students Leon J. Holecheck, Manuel Hernandez, and Phillip A. Hendren and were submitted as a term project for Architecture 261–262. Due to insufficient information at the time of editing, they may not conform to HABS standards. The reproduction rights were acquired by HABS under the direction of James C. Massey, Chief, in 1971.

ALCALDE
RIO ARRIBA COUNTY
Merrill House (Door) (NM-34)
Control Nr. NM0042; LC Shelf Code NM.200-ALCA.3-.
2 ext. photos (n.d.).
These photos are undated and unattributed. They do not appear in the 1941 HABS catalog but are in the 1959 catalog. However, it is unlikely that they date from between 1941 and 1959, a period during which HABS was inactive in New Mexico. It is probable that the photos were taken by one of the three

HABS administrators from the Washington, DC, office who photographed in New Mexico in the late 1930s: Frederick D. Nichols (1936, 1937), John P. O'Neill (1937), or Delos Hamilton Smith (1940); or by photographer Donald W. Dickensheets (1940). Of these, only Nichols is recorded as having photographed in Rio Arriba County. Between 1936 and 1941 HABS documentation was funded by the Works Progress Administration.

ARROYO HONDO
TAOS COUNTY
Upper Penitente Morada Chapel (Penitente Morada) (NM-60)

Control Nr. NM0025; LC Shelf Code NM, 20-ARROY, 1-.
6 sheets (1963, including plan, elevations, sections, details); 1 ext. photo (1961), 4 int. photos (1961); 4 data pages (1962).

This project was prepared by the Fort Burgwin Research Center, Fred Wendorf, Director, in cooperation with the Museum of New Mexico. Charles S. Pope, Supervising Architect, Historic Structures, Western Office of Design and Construction, NPS, assisted in preparing the drawings for the HABS collection at the Library of Congress.

The structure was measured and drawn in 1960–61 under the direction of Bainbridge Bunting, Associate Professor of Architectural History, University of New Mexico, by Jean Lee Booth and William R. Sims, Jr., students at the University of New Mexico. Presentation modifications of 1964 were by NPS student architect Mark Steele, University of Kentucky. The project was financed from funds of the "Mission 66" Program, NPS, Branch of Plans and Design, USDOI.

The photos were taken by John E. Boucher of the HABS Washington office. The data pages were prepared by Bainbridge Bunting and approved by Charles S. Pope.

BELÉN
VALENCIA COUNTY
Chavez House (NM-35)

Control Nr. NM0114; LC Shelf Code NM, 31-BEL, 1-.
2 ext. photos (n.d.).

These photos are undated and unattributed. They do not appear in the 1941 HABS catalog but are in the 1959 catalog. However, it is unlikely that they date from between 1941 and 1959, a period during which HABS was inactive in New Mexico. It is probable that the photos were taken by one of the three HABS administrators from the Washington, DC, office who photographed in New Mexico in the late 1930s: Frederick D. Nichols (1936, 1937), John P. O'Neill (1937), or Delos Hamilton Smith (1940); or by photographer Donald W. Dickensheets (1940). Of these, O'Neill and Smith are recorded as having photographed in Valencia County. Between 1936 and 1941, HABS documentation was funded by the Works Progress Administration.

BLAND VICINITY
SANDOVAL COUNTY
Ceremonial Cave (Bandelier National Monument) (NM-17)

Control Nr. NM0007; LC Shelf Code NM,22-BLAND.V.2-.
2 sheets (1939, including plans, sections, restoration); 8 ext. photos (1940); 1 data page (1940).

This was undertaken as a Public Works Administration Project, Federal Project 498-A, and prepared under the direction of NPS, Branch of Plans and Design, USDOI. The delineator was R. P. McClung. The data pages were taken by Donald W. Dickensheets. The data pages were prepared by Trent Thomas, Architect in Charge, HABS, Southwest Unit, and approved by John Gaw Meem, District Officer.

BLAND VICINITY
SANDOVAL COUNTY
Kiva, Large (Bandelier National Monument) (NM-16)

Control Nr. NM0008; LC Shelf Code NM,22-BLAND.V.1-.
2 sheets (1939, including plan, sections, details); 4 ext. photos (1940); 1 data page (1940).

See Bland Vicinity, *Ceremonial Cave (Bandelier National Monument* (NM-17).

CAÑONCITA [CAÑONCITO]
SANTA FE COUNTY
Church (NM-36)

Control Nr. NM0046; LC Shelf Code NM,25-CANCI,1-.
1 ext. photo (n.d.).

This photo is undated and unattributed. It does not appear in the 1941 HABS catalog but is in the 1959 catalog. However, it is unlikely that it dates from between 1941 and 1959, a period during which HABS was inactive in New Mexico. It is probable that the photo was taken by one of the three HABS administrators from the Washington, DC, office who photographed in New Mexico in the late 1930s: Frederick D. Nichols (1936, 1937), John P. O'Neill (1937), or Delos Hamilton Smith (1940); or by photographer Donald W. Dickensheets (1940). Of these, Nichols and Dickensheets are recorded as having photographed in Santa Fe County. Between 1936 and 1941 HABS documentation was funded by the Works Progress Administration.

EL CERRITO
SAN MIGUEL COUNTY
El Cerrito, Village of (Spanish-American Villages of the Pecos River) (NM-127)

Control Nr. NM0089; LC Shelf Code NM,24-ELCERT,1-.
5 sheets 1975, including photomosaic, plans, sections, elevations); 1 ext. photo (1975, copy photo of photogrammetric plate); 3 data pages (1985–86).

This project was undertaken by the HABS, under the direction of John C. Poppeleirs, Chief, in cooperation with the New Mexico State Planning Office. It was sponsored by the New Mexico State Historic Preservation Division and the Office of Archaeology and Historic Preservation, NPS, USDOI. The project was completed during the summer of 1975 at the HABS field office, Pecos, New Mexico, by Project Supervisor Perry E. Borchers, the School of Architecture, OSU.

Survey control was by the Pecos Valley Team in 1975. The text was by Perry E. Borchers. The drawings were plotted at OSU by Muzzafir El-Ghazali and drawn by Project Foreman Jack W. Schafer (University of Cincinnati) and student assistant architects Joseph J. Bilello (Washington State University) and Michele F. Lewis (Rhode Island School of Design) in 1975.

The photo is a copy of a photogrammetric plate by Perry E. Borchers. The data pages are an inventory of photogrammetric images prepared by the Photogrammetric Images Project (1985–86). They consist of eleven 9.5 x 9.5-inch glass plate aerial diapositives, with survey control contact prints and survey control information for each plate.

CHACO CANYON
SAN JUAN COUNTY
Bonito, Pueblo (Chaco Canyon National Monument) (NM-30)
Control Nr. NM0107; LC Shelf Code NM.23-_____.1- (no shelf code assigned).
9 sheets (1940, including plans, elevations, sections, details).

This project was prepared by the Southwestern National Monuments, Civilian Conservation Corps (CCC), Indian Mobile Unit, under the direction of the NPS, Branch of Plans and Design, USDOI. The delineator was Herbert K. Boone.

CHACO CANYON
SAN JUAN COUNTY
Pueblo del Arroyo (NM-163 [WASO])
Control Nr. NM0171; LC Shelf Code DLC/PP-1992:NM-5.

This documentation project was undertaken by the Southwest Washington office of HABS and sponsored by the HABS/HAER Regional Office of NPS. It was conducted by the HABS/HAER Division, Kenneth L. Anderson, Chief; Morgan A. Rieder, Supervisor (School of Architecture and Planning, University of New Mexico); and Jim G. Duran, Architecture Technician (School of Architecture and Planning, University of New Mexico). Aerial photogrammetry was by Jim Walker (Brigham Young University).

CHACO CANYON VICINITY
SAN JUAN COUNTY
Kin Klizhin (Chaco Canyon National Monument) (NM-31)
Control Nr. NM0108; LC Shelf Code NM.23-_____.2- (no shelf code assigned).
5 sheets (1939, including elevations, sections, details).

This project was prepared by the Southwestern National Monuments, Civilian Conservation Corps (CCC), Indian Mobile Unit, under the direction of the NPS, Branch of Plans and Design, USDOI. The delineator was Herbert K. Boone.

CHACO, CROWNPOINT VICINITY
MCKINLEY COUNTY
Chaco Outliers (HABS NOS. NM-179-A, NM-179-B, NM-180–181)
Control Nr. NM0192-0195
8 drawings (n.d.), 74 photos (n.d.).

This project was undertaken by the Rocky Mountain Regional Office, National Park Service, under the direction of National Historical Architect Thomas G. Keohan. Documentation was completed during the summer of 1994 by the Historic Resources Imaging Laboratory, College of Architecture, Texas A&M University, David G. Woodcock, Director. Documentation was completed by Project Director William C. Barbee and architectural technicians Coye Wardell and Robert Gauper. Archaeological consultation was provided by the Bureau of Land Management archaeologist Peggy Gaudy. Funding was provided by the Bureau of Land Management, Farmington District.

CHAMITA
RIO ARRIBA COUNTY
House Next to Church (NM-37)
Control Nr. NM0010; LC Shelf Code NM.20-CHAM.1-.
1 ext. photo (n.d.).

This photo is undated and unattributed. It does not appear in the 1941 HABS catalog but is in the 1959 catalog. However, it is unlikely that it dates from between 1941 and 1959, a period during which HABS was inactive in New Mexico.

It is probable that the photo was taken by one of the three HABS administrators from the Washington, DC, office who photographed in New Mexico in the late 1930s: Frederick D. Nichols (1936, 1937), John P. O'Neill (1937), or Delos Hamilton Smith (1940). Of these, only Nichols is recorded as having photographed in Rio Arriba County. Between 1936 and 1941 HABS documentation was funded by the Works Progress Administration.

CHIMAYÓ
RIO ARRIBA COUNTY
Plaza del Cerro (Plaza de San Buenaventura) (NM-128)
Control Nr. NM0035; LC Shelf Code NM.20-CHIM.1-.
2 sheets (1975, plan, elevation); 3 data pages (1975; 1985–86).

This project was undertaken by HABS, under the direction of John C. Poppeliers, Chief, in cooperation with the New Mexico State Planning Office. It was sponsored by the New Mexico State Historic Preservation Division and the Office of Archaeology and Historic Preservation, NPS, USDOI. The project was completed during the summer of 1975 at the HABS field office, Pecos, New Mexico, by Project Supervisor Perry E. Borchers, the School of Architecture, OSU.

Aerial photography was by Koogle & Pouls Engineering, Inc., Albuquerque. Images were plotted on the Wild A7 Autograph at OSU and drawn by Project Foreman Jack W. Schafer (University of Cincinnati) and student assistant architect Michele F. Lewis (Rhode Island School of Design). The plotting was supervised by Perry E. Borchers.

The data pages were written by project historian Nelson Arroyo-Ortiz (Cornell University). Susan McCowan, a HABS architectural historian in the Washington, DC, office, edited the report in 1983 for preparation of transmittal to the Library of Congress.

The photo is a copy of a photogrammetric plate by Perry E. Borchers. The data pages are an inventory of photogrammetric images prepared by the Photogrammetric Images Project (1985–86). They consist of eleven 9.5 x 9.5-inch glass plate aerial diapositives, with survey control contact prints and survey control information for each plate.

CHIMAYÓ
SANTA FE COUNTY
El Santuario del Señor Esquípula (NM-9)
Control Nr. NM0047; LC Shelf Code NM.25-CHIM.1-.

PROJECT 1:
32 sheets (1934, including plans, elevations, sections, details, color sheets; 8 ext. photos (1934), 9 int. photos (1934); 2 data pages (1934).

This project was prepared under the direction of John Gaw Meem, HABS National Advisory Board member, and A.

Leicester Hyde, District Officer for District 36 (Utah, Colorado, New Mexico). It was undertaken by HABS, Office of National Parks, Buildings, and Reservations [NPS], Branch of Plans and Design.

The delineators were Edwin B. Clarke, A. B. Willison, William H. Kraemer, Urie McCleary, Neal W. Cash, Victor F. Hornbein, Arthur Hoyer, and Stanley H. Kent. The photos were taken by M. James Slack. The data pages were prepared by A. Leicester Hyde.

PROJECT 2:
2 ext. photos (1980), 2 int. photos (1980).

The photographer Walter Smalling, Jr., took 11 photos of structures at Albuquerque, Taos, Chimayó, Las Trampas, and Los Alamos for HABS in 1980.

CIENEGA
OTERO COUNTY
House, Double (NM-82)
Control Nr. NM0041; LC Shelf Code NM.18-CIENEG.1-.
2 ext. photos (1937).

The photos were taken by Frederick D. Nichols of the Washington office of HABS. In August 1936 and July–September 1937, Nichols took about 45 photos of structures in the counties of Santa Fe, Taos, Rio Arriba, San Miguel, Colfax, Doña Ana, and Otero. Each structure was documented with four or fewer photos. Nichols, an architecture graduate from Yale University, was a leading employee at the Washington office of HABS from 1933 until he joined the navy during World War II. He compiled the HABS 1941 catalog. In 1937 HABS documentation was funded by the Works Progress Administration.

Doña Ana, and Otero. Each structure was documented with four or fewer photos. Nichols, an architecture graduate from Yale University, was a leading employee at the Washington office of HABS from 1933 until he joined the navy during World War II. He compiled the HABS 1941 catalog. In 1936 HABS documentation was funded by the Works Progress Administration.

CIMARRON
COLFAX COUNTY
Blacksmith Shop (NM-38)
Control Nr. NM0012; LC Shelf Code NM.4-CIM.2-. 1 ext. photo (n.d.).

This photo is undated and unattributed. Although it does not appear in the 1941 HABS catalog, it is in the 1959 catalog. However, it is unlikely that it dates from between 1941 and 1959, a period during which HABS was largely deactivated. It is probable that the photo was taken by one of the three HABS administrators from the Washington, DC, office who photographed in New Mexico in the late 1930s: Frederick D. Nichols (1936, 1937), John P. O'Neill (1937), or Delos Hamilton Smith (1940). Of these, only Nichols is recorded as having photographed in Colfax County. Between 1936 and 1941 HABS documentation was funded by the Works Progress Administration.

CIMARRON
COLFAX COUNTY
Cimarron Church (NM-114)
Control Nr. NM0027; LC Shelf Code NM.4-CIM.3-.
3 ext. photos (1936).
See Cimarron, *Aztec Mill, Old* (NM-119).

CIMARRON
COLFAX COUNTY
County Courthouse, Old (NM-118)
Control Nr. NM0013; LC Shelf Code NM.4-CIM.4-.
2 ext. photos (1936).
See Cimarron, *Aztec Mill, Old* (NM-119).

CIMARRON
COLFAX COUNTY
Aztec Mill, Old (NM-119)
Control Nr. NM0014; LC Shelf Code NM.4-CIM.1-.
2 ext. photos (1936).

These photos were taken by Frederick D. Nichols of the Washington office of HABS. In August 1936 and July–September 1937, Nichols took about 45 photos of structures in the counties of Santa Fe, Taos, Rio Arriba, San Miguel, Colfax,

Colfax, Doña Ana, and Otero. Each structure was documented with four or fewer photos. Nichols, an architecture graduate from Yale University, was a leading employee at the Washington office of HABS from 1933 until he joined the navy during World War II. He compiled the HABS 1941 catalog. In 1937 HABS documentation was funded by the Works Progress Administration.

CIMARRON
COLFAX COUNTY
Government Trading Store (NM-116)
Control Nr. NM0029; LC Shelf Code NM.4-CIM.6-.
2 ext. photos (1936).
See Cimarron, *Aztec Mill, Old* (NM-119).

CIMARRON
COLFAX COUNTY
Jail, Old Stone (NM-117)
Control Nr. NM0030; LC Shelf Code NM.4-CIM.5-.
3 ext. photos (1936).
See Cimarron, *Aztec Mill, Old* (NM-119).

CIMARRON
COLFAX COUNTY
St. James Hotel (Diego, Don, Hotel) (NM-115)
Control Nr. NM0028; LC Shelf Code NM.4-CIM.7-.
1 ext. photo (1936), 3 int. photos (1936).

The ext. photo was taken by Frederick D. Nichols of the Washington office of HABS. See Cimarron, *Aztec Mill, Old* (NM-119).

The int. photos are unattributed. Although the 1940 HABS catalog lists four photos of the hotel dating from 1936 and 1940, it does not specify the photographer. It is probable that they were taken by one of the three HABS administrators from the Washington, DC, office who photographed in New Mexico in the late 1930s: Frederick D. Nichols (1936, 1937), John P. O'Neill (1937), or Delos Hamilton Smith (1940). Of these, only Nichols is recorded as having photographed in Colfax County. Between 1936 and 1941 HABS documentation was funded by the Works Progress Administration.

DULCE VICINITY
RIO ARRIBA COUNTY
Pueblitos of Dinetah (HABS NOS. NM-153-162, NM-167-171)
Control Nr. NM0161-0169; NM0179-183.

Project undertaken by the Rocky Mountain Regional Office, National Park Service, under the direction of historical architect Thomas G. Keohan. Documentation was completed during the summer of 1993 by the Historic Resources Imaging Laboratory, College of Architecture, Texas A&M University, David G. Woodcock, Director. Documentation was completed by Project Director William C. Barbee and architectural technicians Verner W. Laird III, Kirtimalini S. Dharmadhikar, and Hadiba Zareen. Archaeological consultation was provided by the Bureau of Land Management archaeologist Peggy Gaudy. Funding was provided by the Bureau of Land Management, Farmington District. Field office space was provided by San Juan College through Judith Wooderson, AutoCAD Training Center manager.

GALISTEO
SANTA FE COUNTY
House (NM-39)
Control Nr. NM0048; LC Shelf Code NM.25-GAL.1-.
1 ext. photo (n.d.).

This photo is undated and unattributed. It does not appear in the 1941 HABS catalog but is in the 1959 catalog. However, it is unlikely that it dates from between 1941 and 1959, a period during which HABS was inactive in New Mexico.

It is probable that the photo was taken by one of the three HABS administrators from the Washington, DC, office who photographed in New Mexico in the late 1930s: Frederick D. Nichols (1936, 1937), John P. O'Neill (1937), or by photographer Donald W. Hamilton Smith (1940); or by photographer Donald W. Dickensheets (1940). Of these, Nichols and Dickensheets are recorded as having photographed in Santa Fe County. Between 1936 and 1941 HABS documentation was funded by the Works Progress Administration.

GALISTEO
SANTA FE COUNTY
Lucero House (NM-129)
Control Nr. NM0034; LC Shelf Code NM.25-GAL.2-.
6 sheets (1966, including plans, elevations, details).

This project was prepared under the direction of Bainbridge Bunting, Associate Professor of Art History, University of New Mexico Art History Department. The measured drawings are by architecture students Donald Mackel, Pat McClernon, and Arthur Torres, and were submitted as a term project for Architecture 261–262. Due to insufficient information at the time of editing, they may not conform to HABS standards. The reproduction rights were acquired by HABS under the direction of James C. Massey, Chief, in 1971.

GILA
GRANT COUNTY
L. C. Ranch Headquarters (NM-144)
Control Nr. NM0136; LC Shelf Code NM.9-GILA.1A-.
1 ext. photo (1976, copy photo of photogrammetric plate); 2 data pages (1985–86).

This project was sponsored by the New Mexico State Historic Preservation Division and the Office of Archaeology and Historic Preservation, NPS, USDOI. It was prepared under the direction of Perry E. Borchers, School of Architecture, OSU.

The photo is a copy of a photogrammetric plate by Perry E. Borchers. The data pages are an inventory of photogrammetric images prepared by the Photogrammetric Images Project (1985–86). They consist of two 5 x 7-inch glass plate negatives (one stereopair) and one reference print made from plates in the Library of Congress collection.

GRAN QUIVIRA
SOCORRO COUNTY
Missions of San Buenaventura and San Isidro (Church of San Isidro) (NM-147)
Control Nr. NM0152; LC Shelf Code NM.27-GRAQI, 1-.
11 sheets (1986, including plans, elevations, sections).

The Salinas National Monument documentation project was undertaken by the Washington office of HABS and sponsored by the Southwest Regional Office of the NPS. The 1986 summer documentation was undertaken by the HABS/HAER Division, Robert J. Kapsch, Chief. It was organized and directed by Kenneth L. Anderson, AIA, Chief, HABS, in conjunction with Barry Sulam, Chief, Division of Conservation, Southwest Cultural Resources Center, and Thomas B. Carroll, Superintendent, Salinas National Monument.

The 1986 documentation of San Buenaventura and San Isidro was produced by Project Supervisor Morgan Rieder (School of Architecture and Planning, University of New Mexico) and architectural technicians Jean L. Pike (School of Architecture, Yale University) and Daniel A. Hernandez (School of Architecture and Urban Planning, University of California at Los Angeles).

HILLSBORO
SIERRA COUNTY
Hillsboro, Town of (NM-142)
Control Nr. NM0134; LC Shelf Code NM, 26-HILLSB, 1-.
5 ext. photos (1976, copy photos of photogrammetric plates); 3 data pages (1985–86).

This project was sponsored by the New Mexico State Historic Preservation Division and the Office of Archaeology and Historic Preservation, NPS, USDOI. It was prepared under the direction of Perry E. Borchers, the School of Architecture, OSU.

The photos are copies of photogrammetric plates by Perry E. Borchers. The data pages are an inventory of photogrammetric images prepared by the Photogrammetric Images Project (1985–86). They consist of four 5 x 7-inch glass plate negatives (two stereopairs), with survey control contact prints and survey control information for each plate; ten 9.5 x 9.5-inch glass plate diapositives (two stereopairs and six aerial photos), one survey control contact print, and survey control information for each stereopair.

ISLETA PUEBLO
BERNALILLO COUNTY
House, Adobe (Recessed Portal) (NM-122)
Control Nr. NM0005; LC Shelf Code NM.1-ISLEP.2-.
1 ext. photo (1937).

This photo was one of five taken by John P. O'Neill in 1937 at Isleta and Laguna pueblos. HABS documentation was funded by the Works Progress Administration in 1937.

Since 1933, O'Neill had been employed by the NPS as a manager at the Washington HABS office. Before joining HABS, he studied architecture at Notre Dame University and participated in an archaeological dig in Central America sponsored by the Carnegie Institution, Washington, DC.

ISLETA PUEBLO
BERNALILLO COUNTY

House, Adobe and Sod (NM-79)
Control Nr. NM0001; LC Shelf Code NM.1-ISLEP.1-.
1 ext. photo (1937).
See Isleta Pueblo, House, Adobe (Recessed Portal) (NM-122).

ISLETA PUEBLO
BERNALILLO COUNTY

House, Adobe (Walled Forecourt) (NM-121)
Control Nr. NM0006; LC Shelf Code NM.1-ISLEP.3-.
1 ext. photo (1937).
See Isleta Pueblo, House, Adobe (Recessed Portal)(NM-122).

ISLETA PUEBLO
BERNALILLO COUNTY

Houses, Row of, and Sod Wall (NM-120)
Control Nr. NM0004; LC Shelf Code NM.1-ISLEP.4-.
1 ext. photo (1937).
See Isleta Pueblo, House, Adobe (Recessed Portal) (NM-122).

JÉMEZ PUEBLO
SANDOVAL COUNTY

Jémez, Pueblo of (NM-145)
Control Nr. NM0137; LC Shelf Code NM.22-JEMEP.1-.
5 ext. photos (1976, copy photos of photogrammetric plates); 4 data pages (1985–86).

This project was sponsored by the New Mexico State Historic Preservation Division and the Office of Archaeology and Historic Preservation, NPS, USDOI. It was prepared under the direction of Perry E. Borchers, the School of Architecture, OSU.

The photos are copies of photogrammetric plates by Perry E. Borchers. The data pages are an inventory of photogrammetric images prepared by the Photogrammetric Images Project (1985–86). They consist of fourteen 9.5 x 9.5-inch glass plate diapositives, with survey control contact prints and survey control information for each plate.

LAGUNA PUEBLO
VALENCIA COUNTY (became Cibola County in 1982)

Houses (Near Mission) (NM-97)
Control Nr. NM0070; LC Shelf Code NM, 31-LAGUP, 3-.
1 ext. photo (1937).

This photo was one of five taken by John P. O'Neill in 1937 at Isleta and Laguna pueblos. HABS documentation was funded by the Works Progress Administration in 1937.

Since 1933, O'Neill had been employed by the NPS as a manager at the Washington HABS office. Before joining HABS, he studied architecture at Notre Dame University and participated in an archaeological dig in Central America sponsored by the Carnegie Institution, Washington, DC.

LAGUNA PUEBLO
VALENCIA COUNTY (became Cibola County in 1982)

Laguna, Pueblo of (NM-27)
Control Nr. NM0130; LC Shelf Code NM, 31-LAGUP, 4-.
1 ext. photo (1974, copy photo of photogrammetric plate); 5 data pages (1985–86).

This project was undertaken by the New Mexico State Historic Preservation Division and NPS, USDOI. It was approved by the Laguna Pueblo governor and tribal council. The recording was prepared under the direction of Perry E. Borchers, the School of Architecture, OSU.

Aerial photography was by the New Mexico Department in 1974. The ext. photo is a copy of a photogrammetric plate by Perry E. Borchers. The data pages are an inventory of photogrammetric images prepared by the Photogrammetric Images Project (1985–86). They consist of twenty-five 9.5 x 9.5-inch glass plate aerial diapositives, with survey control contact prints and survey control information for each plate.

LAGUNA PUEBLO
VALENCIA COUNTY (became Cibola County in 1982)

Meeting House (NM-4)
Control Nr. NM0068; LC Shelf Code NM, 31-LAGUP, 2-.
4 sheets (1934, including plan, elevations, sections); 2 ext. photos (1934); 2 data pages (1936).

This project was undertaken by HABS, NPS, Branch of Plans and Design, USDOI. It was approved by the governor of Laguna Pueblo and prepared under the direction of John Gaw Meem, HABS National Advisory Board member and A. Leicester Hyde, HABS District Officer for District 36 (Utah, Colorado, New Mexico).

The squad leader was C. Truman St. Clair. The field party was made up of Arthur E. Jack, Byron M. Kaufman, E. S. Mosher, and W. Howard Speer. The photos were taken by M. James Slack; the data pages were prepared by A. Leicester Hyde.

LAGUNA PUEBLO
VALENCIA COUNTY (became Cibola County in 1982)

San José de Laguna Mission Church and Convento (NM-3)
Control Nr. NM0069; LC Shelf Code NM, 31-LAGUP, 1-.
22 sheets (1934, including plans, elevations, sections, details, color sheet); 9 ext. photos (1934); 12 int. photos (1934); 3 data pages (1934).

This project was undertaken by HABS, NPS, Branch of Plans and Design, USDOI. It was approved by the governor of Laguna Pueblo and prepared under the direction of John Gaw Meem, HABS National Advisory Board member and A. Leicester Hyde, HABS District Officer for District 36 (Utah, Colorado, New Mexico).

The squad leader was C. Truman St. Clair. The field party was made up of Byron M. Kaufman, E. S. Mosher, and W. Howard Speer. The photos were taken by James M. Slack [M. James Slack?]; the data pages were prepared by A. Leicester Hyde.

LAS CRUCES
DONA ANA COUNTY

Ascarate, Frank, House (NM-80)
Control Nr. NM0011; LC Shelf Code NM.7-LACRU.1-.
2 ext. photos (1937), 3 ext. photos (n.d.).

Of the five photos, two were taken by Frederick D. Nichols of the Washington office of HABS in 1937, and three are undated and unattributed. It is probable that the unattributed photos were taken by one of the three HABS administrators from the Washington, DC, office who photographed in New Mexico in the late 1930s: Frederick D. Nichols (1936, 1937), John P. O'Neill (1937), or Delos Hamilton Smith (1940). Of these, only Nichols is recorded as having photographed in Doña Ana County. In 1937 HABS documentation was funded by the Works Progress Administration.

LAS CRUCES
DOÑA ANA COUNTY
House Nr. 127 (House opposite Amador Hotel) (NM-81)
Control Nr. NM0074; LC Shelf Code NM.7-LACRU.2-.
1 ext. photo (1937).
See Las Cruces, *Ascarate, Frank, House* (NM-80).

LAS VEGAS
SAN MIGUEL COUNTY
Castaneda Hotel (NM-29)
Control Nr. NM0132; LC Shelf Code NM.24-LAVEG.2-.
5 ext. photos (1976, copy photos of photogrammetric plates); 3 data pages (1985–86).

This project was undertaken by the New Mexico State Historic Preservation Division and the Office of Archaeology and Historic Preservation, NPS, USDOI. It was prepared under the direction of Perry E. Borchers, the School of Architecture, OSU.

The photos are copies of photogrammetric plates by Perry E. Borchers. The data pages are an inventory of photogrammetric images prepared by the Photogrammetric Images Project (1985–86). They consist of four 5 x 7-inch glass plate negatives (two stereopairs), with survey control contact prints and survey control information for each plate; and eight 9.5 x 9.5-inch glass plate diapositives, with survey control contact prints and survey control information for each plate.

LAS VEGAS
SAN MIGUEL COUNTY
Las Vegas City Hall (Las Vegas City Police and Fire Department) (NM-99)
Control Nr. NM0122; LC Shelf Code NM.24-LAVWG.1-.
3 ext. photos (1981), 1 int. photo (1981); 7 data pages (1982).

This project was completed under the direction of the New Mexico State Historic Preservation Bureau. The photos were taken by Betsy Swanson. The data pages were prepared by Kathleen Brooker, Deputy State Historic Preservation Officer, Historic Preservation Bureau, Santa Fe.

LAS VEGAS VICINITY
SAN MIGUEL COUNTY
Baca, Don José Albino, House (NM-12)
Control Nr. NM0043; LC Shelf Code NM.24-LAVEG.V.1-.
19 sheets (1940, including plans, elevations, sections, details); 14 ext. photos (1940), 1 int. photo (1940); 4 data pages (1940).

This was undertaken as a Public Works Administration Project, Federal Project 498-A, and prepared under the direction of NPS, Branch of Plans and Design, USDOI.

The delineators were R. P. McClung, Raymond T. Lovelady, Cecil James, and Trent Thomas. The photos were taken by Donald W. Dickensheets. The data pages were prepared by Trent Thomas, Architect in Charge, HABS, Southwest Unit, and approved by John Gaw Meem, District Officer.

LAS VEGAS VICINITY
SAN MIGUEL COUNTY
Montezuma Hotel (NM-28)
Control Nr. NM0131; LC Shelf Code NM.24-LAVEG.V.2-.
10 ext. photos (1976, copy photos of photogrammetric plates); 4 data pages (1985–86).

This project was undertaken by the New Mexico State Historic Preservation Division and the Office of Archaeology and Historic Preservation, NPS, USDOI. It was prepared under the direction of Perry E. Borchers, the School of Architecture, OSU.

The photos are copies of photogrammetric plates by Perry E. Borchers. The data pages are an inventory of photogrammetric images prepared by the Photogrammetric Images Project (1985–86). They consist of ten 5 x 7-inch glass plate negatives (two stereopairs and two stereoprints), with one survey control contact print for each plate and survey control information for each pair/triplet; and 16 9.5 x 9.5-inch glass plate diapositives (five stereopairs and six aerial views), with one survey control contact print and survey control information for each plate.

LLANO QUEMADO
TAOS COUNTY
Fernandez, Sofio, House (NM-67)
Control Nr. NM0024; LC Shelf Code NM.28-LLANO, 1-.
4 sheets (1963, including plans, elevation).

This project was prepared by the Fort Burgwin Research Center, Fred Wendorf, Director, in cooperation with the Museum of New Mexico. Charles S. Pope, Supervising Architect, Historic Structures, Western Office of Design and Construction, NPS, assisted in preparing the drawings for the HABS collection at the Library of Congress.

The structure was measured and drawn in 1963 under the direction of Bainbridge Bunting, Associate Professor of Architectural History, University of New Mexico, by Jean Lee Booth and William R. Sims, Jr., students at the University of New Mexico. Presentation modifications of 1964 were by NPS student architect Mark Steele, University of Kentucky. The project was financed from funds of the "Mission 66" Program of the NPS, Branch of Plans and Design, USDOI.

LORDSBURG
HIDALGO COUNTY
Shakespeare, Town of (NM-23)
Control Nr. NM0126; LC Shelf Code NM.12-LORDBU.V.1-.
1 ext. photo (1976, copy photo of photogrammetric plate); 2 data pages (1985–86).

This project was sponsored by the New Mexico State Historic Preservation Division and the Office of Archaeology and Historic Preservation, NPS, USDOI. It was prepared under the direction of Perry E. Borchers, the School of Architecture, OSU.

The photos are copies of photogrammetric plates by Perry E. Borchers. The data pages are an inventory of photogrammetric images prepared by the Photogrammetric Images Project (1985–86). They consist of two 5 x 7-inch glass plate negatives (one stereopair), with one survey control contact print for each plate and survey control information for the pair. Plates 1004L and 1004R are missing. Survey control information and survey control contact prints are included in the collection of stereopairs.

HABS INVENTORY FOR NEW MEXICO

113

LOS ALAMOS

LOS ALAMOS COUNTY
Fuller Lodge (NM-25)
Control Nr. NM0120; LC Shelf Code NM-32-LOSAL.1-.
1 ext. photo (1980).

The photographer Walter Smalling, Jr., took 11 photos of structures at Albuquerque, Taos, Chimayó, Las Trampas, and Los Alamos for HABS in 1980.

LOS ALAMOS VICINITY

LOS ALAMOS COUNTY
Romero Cabin (NM-148)
Control Nr. NM0153; LC Shelf Code NM.32-LOSAL.V.1-.
3 sheets (1984–85, including plans, elevations).

This site was documented as part of a U.S. Department of Energy Restoration Project. The field data was collected in 1984–1985 by Louis Anderson and A. Crosby. The drawings were by Louis Anderson, NPS, USDOI.

MANZANO

TORRANCE COUNTY
Torreón, the (NM-11)
Control Nr. NM0066; LC Shelf Code NM, 29-MANZ, 1-.
3 sheets (1939, including plans, sections, elevations); 2 ext. photos (1940); 4 data pages (1940); 2 photocopies of historic photographs (1885, 1916).

This was undertaken as a Public Works Administration Project, Federal Project 498-A, and prepared under the direction of NPS, Branch of Plans and Design, USDOI.

The delineator was Raymond T. Lovelady. The photos were taken by Donald W. Dickensheets. Reproductions are included of a photograph by Charles T. Lummis of the Southwest Museum, Los Angeles (1885), and one by Jesse Nusbaum of the Museum of New Mexico, Santa Fe (1916). The data pages were prepared by Trent Thomas, Architect in Charge, HABS, Southwest Unit, and approved by John Gaw Meem, District Officer.

NAMBÉ PUEBLO

SANTA FE COUNTY
Kiva (NM-8)
Control Nr. NM0049; LC Shelf Code NM.25-NAMP.1-.
6 sheets (1934, including plans, elevations, sections, details); 4 ext. photos (1934); 1 data page (1934).

This project was undertaken by HABS, Office of National Parks, Buildings, and Reservations [NPS], Branch of Plans and Design, USDOI. It was approved of by the governor of Laguna Pueblo and prepared under the direction of John Gaw Meem, HABS National Advisory Board member and A. Leicester Hyde, District Officer for District 36 (Utah, Colorado, New Mexico).

The delineators were Edwin B. Clarke, Victor F. Hornbein, Stanley H. Kent, and Urie McCleary. The photos were taken by M. James Slack; the data pages were prepared by A. Leicester Hyde.

NAMBÉ PUEBLO

SANTA FE COUNTY
Nambé, Pueblo of (NM-107)
Control Nr. NM0101; LC Shelf Code NM.25-NAMP.2-.
2 sheets (1977, including plan, restoration drawings); 1 ext. photo (1974, copy photo of photogrammetric plate); 2 data pages (1985–86).

This project was undertaken by the New Mexico State Historic Preservation Division and the Office of Archaeology and Historic Preservation, NPS, USDOI. It was approved by the Nambé Pueblo governor and tribal council. It was prepared under the direction of Perry E. Borchers, the School of Architecture, OSU.

Aerial photography was by the New Mexico State Highway Department in 1974. Terrestrial photography with a Galileo-Santoni phototheodolite was by Perry E. Borchers and family in 1977. Images were oriented and plotted on the Wild A7 Autograph at OSU in 1977 and drawn by Varathorn Bookaman in 1978.

The photos are copies of photogrammetric plates by Perry E. Borchers. The data pages are an inventory of photogrammetric images prepared by the Photogrammetric Images Project (1985–86). They consist of four 9.5 x 9.5-inch glass plate aerial diapositives produced by Borchers in 1974, with survey control information and survey control contact prints.

PECOS

SAN MIGUEL COUNTY
Pecos Church (Ruins) (*Pecos National Monument*) (NM-85)
Control Nr. NM0044; LC Shelf Code NM.24-PECO.1-.

PROJECT 1:
4 ext. photos (1936), 3 ext. photos (n.d.).

The four ext. photos were taken by Frederick D. Nichols. In August 1936 and July–September 1937, Nichols took about 45 photos of structures in the counties of Santa Fe, Taos, Rio Arriba, San Miguel, Colfax, Doña Ana, and Otero. Each structure was documented with four or fewer photos. Nichols, an architecture graduate from Yale University, was a leading employee at the Washington office of HABS from 1933 until he joined the navy during World War II. He compiled the HABS 1941 catalog.

PROJECT 2:
14 sheets (1979, including plans, elevations, sections, details).

The delineators were Dan Frank Irick and Richard Charles Schalk. This site was measured and drawn for the Division of History Studies, Washington, DC, by Walter A. Gathman, AIA Architect, Albuquerque, NM, under the direction of NPS, USDOI.

PEÑASCO

TAOS COUNTY
Romero House (NM-73)
Control Nr. NM0094; LC Shelf Code NM, 28-PENA, 1-.
6 sheets (1963, including plan, elevations, sections, details).

This project was prepared by the Fort Burgwin Research Center, Fred Wendorf, Director, in cooperation with the Museum of New Mexico. Charles S. Pope, Supervising Architect, Historic Structures, Western Office of Design and Construction, NPS, assisted in preparing the drawings for the HABS collection at the Library of Congress.

The structure was measured and drawn in 1960–61 under the direction of Bainbridge Bunting, Associate Professor of Architectural History, University of New Mexico, by Jean Lee Booth and William R. Sims, Jr, students at the University of New Mexico. Presentation modifications of 1964 were by NPS student architect Mark Steele, University of Kentucky. The project was financed from funds of the "Mission 66" Program of NPS, Branch of Plans and Design, USDOI.

PERALTA
VALENCIA COUNTY
Alvarete House (Door and Zaguán) (NM-41)
Control Nr. NM0072; LC Shelf Code NM, 31-PERAL, 2-.
1 ext. photo (1940).

This photo was taken by Delos H. Smith. Smith, a consulting architect with HABS in the Washington, DC, office, emphasized the importance of photographic documentation of sites. He worked briefly in New Mexico in 1940 and produced photos of five buildings in Albuquerque, Peralta, and the Valencia vicinity that are now part of the HABS inventory. In 1940 HABS documentation was funded by the Works Progress Administration and by Public Works appropriations.

PERALTA
VALENCIA COUNTY
Our Lady of Guadalupe Church at Peralta (NM-40)
Control Nr. NM0033; LC Shelf Code NM, 31-PERAL, 1-.

PROJECT 1:
1 ext. photo (1940).

This photo was taken by Delos H. Smith. Smith, a consulting architect with HABS in the Washington, DC, office, emphasized the importance of photographic documentation. He worked briefly in New Mexico in 1940 and produced photos of five buildings in Albuquerque, Peralta, and the Valencia vicinity that are now part of the HABS inventory.

PROJECT 2:
11 sheets (1967, including plans, elevations, sections, details).

This project was prepared under the direction of Bainbridge Bunting, Associate Professor of Art History, University of New Mexico. The measured drawings are by architecture students Frank Neal Gaskin, Jr., and Greg B. Putnam and were submitted as a term project for Architecture 261–62. Due to insufficient information at the time of editing, they may not conform to HABS standards. The reproduction rights were acquired by HABS under the direction of James C. Massey, Chief, in 1971.

PICURÍS
TAOS COUNTY
Picurís, Pueblo of (San Lorenzo Pueblo) (NM-100)
Control Nr. NM0127; LC Shelf Code NM, 28-PICUP, 1-.
1 ext. photo (1974, copy photo of photogrammetric plate); 2 data pages (1985–86).

This project was undertaken by the New Mexico State Historic Preservation Division and HABS, NPS, USDOI. It was approved by the Picurís Pueblo Governor and Tribal Council. The documentation was prepared under the direction of Perry E. Borchers, the School of Architecture, OSU.

The photo is a copy of a photogrammetric plate by Perry E. Borchers. The data pages are an inventory of photogrammetric images prepared by the Photogrammetric Images Project (1985–86). They consist of seven 9.5 x 9.5-inch glass plate aerial diapositives, with survey control information and survey control contact prints for each plate.

PLACITA DE TAOS
TAOS COUNTY
La Capilla de Nuestra Señora de Dolores (Chapel at Placita de Taos) (NM-93)
Control Nr. NM0065; LC Shelf Code NM, 28-TAO.V, 1-.
2 ext. photos (1936).

The photos were taken by Frederick D. Nichols of the Washington office of HABS. In August 1936 and July–September 1937, Nichols took about 45 photos of structures in the counties of Santa Fe, Taos, Rio Arriba, San Miguel, Colfax, Doña Ana, and Otero. Each structure was documented with four or fewer photos. Nichols, an architecture graduate from Yale University, was a leading employee at the Washington office of HABS from 1933 until he joined the navy during World War II. He compiled the HABS 1941 catalog. In 1936 HABS documentation was funded by the Works Progress Administration.

POJOAQUE VICINITY
SANTA FE COUNTY
Bouquet Ranch (NM-88)
Control Nr. NM0050; LC Shelf Code NM.25-POJU.V, 1-.
3 ext. photos (n.d.).

These photos are undated and unattributed. The 1941 HABS catalog lists three photos of the Bouquet Ranch dated 1940 but does not specify the photographer.

It is probable that the photo was taken by one of the three HABS administrators from the Washington, DC, office who photographed in New Mexico in the late 1930s: Frederick D. Nichols (1936, 1937), John P. O'Neill (1937), or Delos Hamilton Smith (1940); or by photographer Donald W. Dickensheets (1940). Of these, only Nichols is recorded as having photographed in Santa Fe County. Between 1936 and 1940 HABS documentation was funded by the Works Progress Administration.

PUERTO DE LUNA
GUADALUPE COUNTY
House (NM-138)
Control Nr. NM0080; LC Shelf Code NM.10-PUEDEL, 1-.
6 sheets (1964, including plan, elevations, details).

This project was prepared under the direction of Bainbridge Bunting, Associate Professor of Art History, University of New Mexico Art History Department. The measured drawings are by architecture student Donald A. Krueger and were submitted as a term project for Architecture 261–262. Due to insufficient information at the time of editing, they may not conform to HABS standards. They were purchased by HABS under the direction of James C. Massey, Chief, in 1971.

RANCHITO
TAOS COUNTY
Martínez, José María, House (NM-71)
Control Nr. NM0021; LC Shelf Code NM, 28-RANCHI, 3-.
8 sheets (1963, including plan, elevations, sections, details).

This project was prepared by the Fort Burgwin Research Center, Fred Wendorf, Director, in cooperation with the Museum of New Mexico. Charles S. Pope, Supervising Architect, Historic Structures, Western Office of Design and Construction, NPS, assisted in preparing the drawings for the HABS collection at the Library of Congress.

The structure was measured and drawn in 1960–61 under the direction of Bainbridge Bunting, Associate Professor of Architectural History, University of New Mexico, by Jean Lee Booth and William R. Sims, Jr., students at the University of

HABS INVENTORY FOR NEW MEXICO

New Mexico. Presentation modifications of 1964 were by NPS student architect Mark Steele, University of Kentucky. The project was financed from funds of the "Mission 66" Program of NPS, Branch of Plans and Design, USDOI.

RANCHITO
TAOS COUNTY
Martinez, Leandro, House (NM-64)
Control Nr. NM0023; LC Shelf Code NM, 28-RANCHI, 1-.
7 sheets (1963, including plan, elevations, details).
See Ranchito, *Martinez, José María, House* (NM-71).

RANCHITO
TAOS COUNTY
Martinez, Pascual, House (NM-70)
Control Nr. NM0060; LC Shelf Code NM, 28-RANCHI, 2-.
8 sheets (1963, plans, elevations).
See Ranchito, *Martinez, José María, House* (NM-71).

RANCHOS DE TAOS
TAOS COUNTY
Caretaker's House (NM-94)
Control Nr. NM0061; LC Shelf Code NM, 28-RANTA, 2-.
2 ext. photos (1936).

The photos were taken by Frederick D. Nichols of the Washington office of HABS. In August 1936 and July–September 1937, Nichols took about 45 photos of structures in the counties of Santa Fe, Taos, Rio Arriba, San Miguel, Colfax, Doña Ana, and Otero. Each structure was documented with four or fewer photos. Nichols, an architecture graduate from Yale University, was a leading employee at the Washington office of HABS from 1933 until he joined the navy during World War II. He compiled the HABS 1941 catalog. In 1936 HABS documentation was funded by the Works Progress Administration.

RANCHOS DE TAOS
TAOS COUNTY
House (Recessed Portal) (NM-95)
Control Nr. NM0061; LC Shelf Code NM, 28-RANTA, 3-.
1 ext. photo (1936).
See Ranchos de Taos, *Caretaker's House* (NM-94).

RANCHOS DE TAOS
TAOS COUNTY
House, Adobe (Typical Roof Construction) (NM-42)
Control Nr. NM0063; LC Shelf Code NM, 28-RANTA, 5-.
1 ext. photo (n.d.).

This photo is undated and unattributed. It does not appear in the 1941 HABS catalog but is in the 1959 catalog. However, it is unlikely that it dates from between 1941 and 1959, a period during which HABS was inactive in New Mexico.

It is probable that the photo was taken by one of the three HABS administrators from the Washington, DC, office who photographed in New Mexico in the late 1930s: Frederick D. Nichols (1936, 1937), John P. O'Neill (1937), or Delos Hamilton Smith (1940). Of these, only Nichols is recorded as having photographed in Taos County. Between 1936 and 1941 HABS documentation was funded by the Works Progress Administration.

RANCHOS DE TAOS
TAOS COUNTY
House, Territorial Period (NM-96)
Control Nr. NM0062; LC Shelf Code NM, 28-RANTA, 4-.
1 ext. photo (1936).
See Ranchos de Taos, *Caretaker's House* (NM-94).

RANCHOS DE TAOS
TAOS COUNTY
Long, Horace G., House (NM-62)
Control Nr. NM0020; LC Shelf Code NM, 28-RANTA, 6-.
9 sheets (1963, including plans, elevations, sections, details). This project was prepared by the Fort Burgwin Research Center, Fred Wendorf, Director, in cooperation with the Museum of New Mexico. Charles S. Pope, Supervising Architect, Historic Structures, Western Office of Design and Construction, NPS, assisted in preparing the drawings for the HABS collection at the Library of Congress. The structure was measured and drawn in 1960–61 under the direction of Bainbridge Bunting, Associate Professor of Architectural History, University of New Mexico, by Jean Lee Booth and William R. Sims, Jr., students at the University of New Mexico. Presentation modifications of 1964 were by NPS student architect Mark Steele, University of Kentucky. The project was financed from funds of the "Mission 66" Program of NPS, Branch of Plans and Design, USDOI.

RANCHOS DE TAOS
TAOS COUNTY
Mission Church of Ranchos de Taos (NM-7)
Control Nr. NM0059; LC Shelf Code NM, 28-RANTA, 1-.

PROJECT 1:
32 sheets (1934, including plans, elevations, sections, details, color sheet; 10 int. photos (1934).

This project was undertaken by HABS, USDOI, Office of National Parks, Buildings, and Reservations [NPS], Branch of Plans and Design. It was approved of by the governor of Taos Pueblo and prepared under the direction of John Gaw Meem, HABS National Advisory Board member and A. Leicester Hyde, District Officer for District 36 (Utah, Colorado, New Mexico).

The delineators were Benjamin J. Bloser, William P. Cover, R. G. McComas, Karl Mertz, and John J. Thompson. The 1934 photos were taken by James M. Slack [M. James Slack?] and the 1936 photo by Frederick D. Nichols. The data pages were prepared by A. Leicester Hyde.

PROJECT 2:
1 ext. photo (1936); 3 data pages (1936).
The photo was taken by Frederick D. Nichols of the Washington office of HABS. The data pages were prepared by A. Leicester Hyde. Between 1936 and 1941 HABS documentation was funded by the Works Progress Administration.

In August 1936 and July–September 1937, Frederick D. Nichols took about 45 photos of structures in the counties of Santa Fe, Taos, Rio Arriba, San Miguel, Colfax, Doña Ana, and

Otero. Each structure was documented with four or fewer photos. Nichols, an architecture graduate from Yale University, was a leading employee at the Washington office of HABS from 1933 until he joined the navy during World War II. He compiled the HABS 1941 catalog.

PROJECT 3:

1 ext. photo (1980).

The photographer Walter Smalling, Jr., took 11 photos of structures at Taos, Chimayó, Las Trampas, Los Alamos, and Albuquerque for HABS in 1980.

RODEY
DOÑA ANA COUNTY
St. Francis de Sales Church (NM-43)
Control Nr. NM0076; LC Shelf Code NM.7-ROD.1-.
1 ext. photo (n.d.).

This photo is undated and unattributed. It does not appear in the 1941 HABS catalog but is in the 1959 catalog. However, it is unlikely that it dates from between 1941 and 1959, a period during which HABS was inactive in New Mexico.

It is probable that the photo was taken by one of the three HABS administrators from the Washington, DC, office who photographed in New Mexico in the late 1930s: Frederick D. Nichols (1936, 1937), John P. O'Neill (1937), or Delos Hamilton Smith (1940); or by photographer Donald W. Dickensheets (1940). Of these, only Nichols is recorded as having photographed in Doña Ana County. Between 1936 and 1941 HABS documentation was funded by the Works Progress Administration.

ROMEROVILLE
SAN MIGUEL COUNTY
Houses on Plaza (NM-87)
Control Nr. NM0039; LC Shelf Code NM.24-ROMVI.3-.
1 ext. photo (1936).

The photo was taken by Frederick D. Nichols of the Washington office of HABS. In August 1936 and July–September 1937, Nichols took about 45 photos of structures in the counties of Santa Fe, Taos, Rio Arriba, San Miguel, Colfax, Doña Ana, and Otero. Each structure was documented with four or fewer photos. Nichols, an architecture graduate from Yale University, was a leading employee at the Washington office of HABS from 1933 until he joined the navy during World War II. He compiled the HABS 1941 catalog. In 1936 HABS documentation was funded by the Works Progress Administration.

ROMEROVILLE
SAN MIGUEL COUNTY
Romero Barn (NM-44)
Control Nr. NM0045; LC Shelf Code NM.24-ROMVI.1-.
2 ext. photos (n.d.).

These photos are undated and unattributed. They do not appear in the 1941 HABS catalog but are in the 1959 catalog. However, it is unlikely that they date from between 1941 and 1959, a period during which HABS was inactive in New Mexico.

It is probable that the photos were taken by one of the three HABS administrators from the Washington, DC, office who photographed in New Mexico in the late 1930s: Frederick D. Nichols (1936, 1937), John P. O'Neill (1937), or Delos Hamilton Smith (1940); or by photographer Donald W. Dickensheets (1940). Of these, Nichols and Dickensheets are recorded as having photographed in San Miguel County. Between 1936 and 1941 HABS documentation was funded by the Works Progress Administration.

ROMEROVILLE
SAN MIGUEL COUNTY
Romeroville Church (NM-86)
Control Nr. NM0040; LC Shelf Code NM.24-ROMVI.2-.
1 ext. photo (1936).

See Romeroville, *Houses on Plaza* (NM-87).

SAN ILDEFONSO PUEBLO
SANTA FE COUNTY
Kiva (NM-90)
Control Nr. NM0051; LC Shelf Code NM.25-SAILFOP.2-.
1 ext. photo (1937).

The photo was taken by Frederick D. Nichols of the Washington office of HABS. In August 1936 and July–September 1937, Nichols took about 45 photos of structures in the counties of Santa Fe, Taos, Rio Arriba, San Miguel, Colfax, Doña Ana, and Otero. Each structure was documented with four or fewer photos. Nichols, an architecture graduate from Yale University, was a leading employee at the Washington office of HABS from 1933 until he joined the navy during World War II. He compiled the HABS 1941 catalog.

SAN ILDEFONSO PUEBLO
SANTA FE COUNTY
San Ildefonso, Pueblo of (NM-89)
Control Nr. NM0092; LC Shelf Code NM.25-SAILFOP.1-.

1937 PROJECT:

2 ext. photos (1937).

These photos were taken by Frederick D. Nichols. In August 1936 and July–September 1937, Nichols took about 45 photos of structures in the counties of Santa Fe, Taos, Rio Arriba, San Miguel, Colfax, Doña Ana, and Otero. Each structure was documented with four or fewer photos. Nichols, an architecture graduate from Yale University, was a leading employee at the Washington office of HABS from 1933 until he joined the navy during World War II. He compiled the HABS 1938 and 1941 catalogs.

1973 PROJECT:

2 sheets (1973, including plan, sections); 1 ext. photo (1973, copy photo of photogrammetric plate); 4 data pages (1985–86).

This project was undertaken by HABS, NPS, USDOI. It was approved by the San Ildefonso Pueblo governor and tribal council. The documentation was prepared at the School of Architecture, OSU, under the direction of Perry E. Borchers, Research Supervisor.

Aerial photography was by the New Mexico State Highway Department in 1973. Ground survey control was by Perry E. Borchers, Joe Kingsolver of the Bureau of Indian Affairs, and Tom Merlan, the New Mexico State historic preservation officer. Images were plotted on the Wild A7 Autograph at OSU by Borchers and drawn by OSU student Bruce Casterline in 1974.

The photo is a copy of a photogrammetric plate by Perry E. Borchers. The data pages are an inventory of photogrammetric images prepared by the Photogrammetric Images Project (1985–86). They consist of twenty-one 9.5 × 9.5-inch glass plate aerial diapositives produced by Borchers in 1973, with survey control information and survey control contact prints for each plate.

SAN JOSÉ
SAN MIGUEL COUNTY
San José del Vado, Village of (Spanish-American Villages of the Pecos River Valley) (NM-126)
Control Nr. NM0088; LC Shelf Code NM.24-SAJOS.1-, 3 sheets (1975, plans, sections); 1 ext. photo (1975, copy photo of photogrammetric plate); 2 data pages (1985–86).

This project was undertaken by HABS, under the direction of John C. Poppeliers, Chief, in cooperation with the New Mexico State Planning Office. It was prepared by the New Mexico State Historic Preservation Division and the Office of Archaeology and Historic Preservation, NPS, USDOI. The project was completed during the summer of 1975 at the HABS field office, Pecos, New Mexico, by Project Supervisor Perry E. Borchers, the School of Architecture, OSU.

Aerial photography was by Koogle & Pouls Engineering, Inc., Albuquerque in 1974. Survey control was by Gary Matlack, NPS. Images were plotted on the Wild A7 Autograph at OSU by graduate research assistant Muzzafir El-Ghazali and drawn by Project Foreman Jack W. Schafer (University of Cincinnati) and student assistant architects Joseph J. Bitello (Washington State University) and Michele F. Lewis (Rhode Island School of Design) in 1975. Plotting was supervised by Perry E. Borchers.

The data pages were written by project historian Nelson Arroyo-Ortiz (Cornell University). Susan McCowan, a HABS architectural historian in the Washington, DC, office, edited the report in 1983 for preparation of transmittal to the Library of Congress.

The photo is a copy of a photogrammetric plate by Perry E. Borchers. The data pages are an inventory of photogrammetric images prepared by the Photogrammetric Images Project (1985–86). They consist of three 9.5 × 9.5-inch glass plate aerial diapositives, with survey control information and survey control contact prints for each plate.

SAN JUAN PUEBLO
RIO ARRIBA COUNTY
Pueblo of San Juan (NM-101)
Control Nr. NM0129; LC Shelf Code NM.20-SAJUP.1-, 1 ext. photo (1974, copy photo of photogrammetric plate); 4 data pages (1985–86).

This project was undertaken by the New Mexico State Historic Preservation Division and NPS, USDOI. It was approved by the San Juan Pueblo governor and tribal council. The documentation was prepared under the direction of Perry E. Borchers, the School of Architecture, OSU. Aerial photography was by the New Mexico State Highway Department.

The photo is a copy of a photogrammetric plate by Perry E. Borchers. The data pages are an inventory of photogrammetric images prepared by the Photogrammetric Images Project (1985–86). They consist of twenty-one 9.5 × 9.5-inch glass plate aerial diapositives and survey control information and survey control contact prints for each plate.

SAN MIGUEL
SAN MIGUEL COUNTY
San Miguel del Vado, General View (Spanish-American Villages of the Pecos River Valley) (NM-139)

PECOS VALLEY PROJECT, 1975.
Control Nr. NM0036; LC Shelf Code NM.24-SAMIG.1-, 4 sheets (1975, including plans, sections); 1 ext. photo (1975, copy photo of photogrammetric plate); 2 data pages (1985–86).

This project was undertaken by HABS, under the direction of John C. Poppeliers, Chief, in cooperation with the New Mexico State Planning Office. It was sponsored by the New Mexico State Historic Preservation Division and the Office of Archaeology and Historic Preservation, NPS, USDOI. The project was completed during the summer of 1975 at the HABS field office, Pecos, New Mexico, by Project Supervisor Perry E. Borchers, the School of Architecture, OSU.

The aerial photography was by Koogle & Pouls Engineering, Inc., Albuquerque in 1974. The survey control was by Gary Matlack, NPS. Images were plotted on the Wild A7 Autograph at OSU by graduate research assistant Muzzafir El-Ghazali and drawn by student assistant architects Michele F. Lewis (Rhode Island School of Design) and Zeno A. Yeates (Tulane University) under the supervision of Perry E. Borchers in 1975.

SAN MIGUEL
SAN MIGUEL COUNTY
Warehouse and Stable (Spanish-American Villages of the Pecos River Valley) (NM-139-A)
Control Nr. NM0086; LC Shelf Code NM.24-SAMIG.2-, 1 sheet (1975, elevations).

This project was undertaken by HABS, under the direction of John C. Poppeliers, Chief, in cooperation with the New Mexico State Planning Office. It was sponsored by the New Mexico State Historic Preservation Division and the Office of Archaeology and Historic Preservation, NPS, USDOI. The project was completed during the summer of 1975 at the HABS field office, Pecos, New Mexico, by Project Supervisor Perry E. Borchers, the School of Architecture, OSU.

The drawing is by student assistant architects Michele F. Lewis (Rhode Island School of Design) and Joseph J. Bitello (Washington State University).

SAN MIGUEL
SAN MIGUEL COUNTY
Territorial House, San Miguel del Vado (Spanish-American Villages of the Pecos River Valley) (NM-139-B)
Control Nr. NM0079; LC Shelf Code NM.24-SAMIG.3-, 2 sheets (1975, including plan, elevations).

This project was undertaken by HABS, under the direction of John C. Poppeliers, Chief, in cooperation with the New Mexico State Planning Office. It was sponsored by the New Mexico State Historic Preservation Division and the Office of Archaeology and Historic Preservation, NPS, USDOI. The project was completed during the summer of 1975 at the HABS field office, Pecos, New Mexico, by Project Supervisor Perry E. Borchers, the School of Architecture, OSU. The delineator was student assistant architect Joseph J. Bitello (Washington

SANTA ANA PUEBLO
SANDOVAL COUNTY
Santa Ana Mission Church, Pueblo of (NM-125)
Control Nr. NM0037; LC Shelf Code NM.22-SANAP.2-.
4 sheets (1975, including plan, elevations).

Part of the Pecos River Valley Project of 1975, this recording was undertaken by HABS, under the direction of John C. Poppeliers, Chief, in cooperation with the New Mexico State Planning Office. It was sponsored by the New Mexico State Historic Preservation Division and the Office of Archaeology and Historic Preservation, NPS, USDOI. The documentation was prepared at the School of Architecture, OSU, by Project Supervisor Perry E. Borchers.

The aerial photography was by Koogle & Pouls Engineering, Inc., Albuquerque in 1976. The ground survey control and terrestrial photogrammetry were by Perry, Myra, Erik, Charlotte, and Christina Borchers. The images were oriented and plotted on the Wild A7 Autograph at OSU by graduate research assistant Muzzafir El-Ghazali and drawn by Jack W. Schafer (University of Cincinnati), Kun-Hyuck Ahn, and Sumonta Jarupan (OSU) in 1976.

SANTA ANA PUEBLO
SANDOVAL COUNTY
Santa Ana, Pueblo of (NM-106)
Control Nr. NM0082; LC Shelf Code NM.22-SANAP.1-.
1 sheet (1979, plan).

Part of the Pecos River Valley Project of 1975, this recording was undertaken by HABS, under the direction of John C. Poppeliers, Chief, in cooperation with the New Mexico State Planning Office. It was sponsored by the New Mexico State Historic Preservation Division and the Office of Archaeology and Historic Preservation, NPS, USDOI. The documentation was prepared at the School of Architecture, OSU, by Project Supervisor Perry E. Borchers.

The aerial photography was by Koogle & Pouls Engineering, Inc., Albuquerque in 1975. The ground survey control and terrestrial photogrammetry were by Perry, Myra, Erik, and Christina Borchers. The images were oriented and plotted on the Wild A7 Autograph at OSU by graduate research assistant Muzzafir El-Ghazali in 1975 and drawn by Project Foreman Jack W. Schafer (University of Cincinnati) and Kun-Hyuck Ahn (OSU) in 1979.

SANTA CLARA PUEBLO
RIO ARRIBA COUNTY
Pueblo of Santa Clara, Central Portion (NM-98)
Control Nr. NM0102; LC Shelf Code NM.20-SACLAP.1-.
4 sheets (1973, including plans, elevations, sections); 1 ext. photo (1972, copy photo of Photogrammetric plate); 6 data pages (1985–86, including 4 historic photos).

This project was undertaken by HABS, NPS, USDOI. It was approved by the Santa Clara Pueblo governor and tribal council and prepared at the School of Architecture, OSU, under the direction of Perry E. Borchers, Research Supervisor.

Aerial photography was by the New Mexico State Highway Department in 1972. Images were plotted by Perry E. Borchers on the Wild A7 Autograph at OSU and drawn by OSU students Joseph Kawecki and James Lamsam, Research Assistant, in 1973.

The photo is a copy of a photogrammetric plate by Perry E. Borchers. The data pages are an inventory of photogrammetric images prepared by the Photogrammetric Images Project (1985–86). They consist of twenty-four 9.5 × 9.5-inch glass plate aerial diapositives produced in 1972, with survey control information and survey control contact prints for each plate.

SANTA CRUZ
SANTA FE COUNTY
Santa Cruz Mission (NM-45)
Control Nr. NM0052; LC Shelf Code NM.25-SANCRU.1-.
2 ext. photos (n.d.).

These photos are undated and unattributed. They do not appear in the 1941 HABS catalog but are in the 1959 catalog. However, it is unlikely that they date from between 1941 and 1959, a period during which HABS was inactive in New Mexico.

It is probable that the photos were taken by one of the three HABS administrators from the Washington, DC, office who photographed in New Mexico in the late 1930s: Frederick D. Nichols (1936, 1937), John P. O'Neill (1937), or Delos Hamilton Smith (1940); or by photographer Donald W. Dickensheets (1940). Of these, Nichols and Dickensheets are recorded as having photographed in Santa Fe County. Between 1936 and 1941 HABS documentation was funded by the Works Progress Administration.

SANTA FE
SANTA FE COUNTY
Applegate, Frank, House (NM-113)
Control Nr. NM0098; LC Shelf Code NM.25-SANFE.6-.
3 ext. photos (1937), 1 int. photo (1937).

The photos were taken by Frederick D. Nichols of the Washington office of HABS. In August 1936 and July–September 1937, Nichols took about 45 photos of structures in the counties of Santa Fe, Taos, Rio Arriba, San Miguel, Colfax, Doña Ana, and Otero. Each structure was documented with four or fewer photos. Nichols, an architecture graduate from Yale University, was a leading employee at the Washington office of HABS from 1933 until he joined the navy during World War II. He compiled the HABS 1941 catalog. In 1937 HABS documentation was funded by the Works Progress Administration.

SANTA FE
SANTA FE COUNTY
Borrego House (McCormick Prize House) (NM-14)
Control Nr. NM0111; LC Shelf Code NM.25-SANFE.4-.
5 sheets (1940, including plan, elevations, details); 1 ext. photo (1936), 7 ext. photos (1940); 3 data pages (1940).

This was undertaken as a Public Works Administration Project, Federal Project 498-A, and prepared under the direction of NPS, Branch of Plans and Design, USDOI.

The delineator was R. P. McClung. The photos were taken by Frederick D. Nichols (1936) and Donald W. Dickensheets (1940). The data pages were prepared by Trent Thomas, Architect in Charge, HABS, Southwest Unit, and approved by John Gaw Meem, District Officer.

SANTA FE
SANTA FE COUNTY
García House (NM-13)
Control Nr. NM0110; LC Shelf Code NM.25-SANFE.3-.
5 sheets (1940, including plan, details, restoration drawings); 1 ext. photo (1940), 2 int. photos (1940).

This was undertaken as a Public Works Administration Project, Federal Project 498-A, and prepared under the direction of NPS, Branch of Plans and Design, USDOI.

The delineators were R. P. McClung and Raymond T. Lovelady. The photos were taken by Donald W. Dickensheets

(1940). The data pages were prepared by Trent Thomas, Architect in Charge, HABS, Southwest Unit, and approved by John Gaw Meem, District Officer.

SANTA FE
SANTA FE COUNTY
Grade School at Loretto Academy (NM-134)
Control Nr. M0032; C Shelf Code M.25-SANFE.9-.
7 sheets (1966–67), including plans, elevations, details).

This project was prepared under the direction of Bainbridge Bunting, Associate Professor of Art History, University of New Mexico Art History Department. The measured drawings are by architecture students L. P. Affholter, B. J. Cekosh, and D. E. Ferro and were submitted as a term project for Architecture 261–262. Due to insufficient information at the time of editing, they may not conform to HABS standards. The reproduction rights were acquired by HABS under the direction of James C. Massey, Chief, in 1971.

SANTA FE
SANTA FE COUNTY
Mignardot House (NM-91)
Control Nr. NM0054; LC Shelf Code NM.25-SANFE.7-.
1 ext. photo (1936).
See Santa Fe, Applegate, Frank, House (NM-113).

SANTA FE
SANTA FE COUNTY
Nuestra Señora de Guadalupe (NM-112)
Control Nr. NM0026; LC Shelf Code NM.25-SANFE.8-.
1 ext. photo (1936).
See Santa Fe, Applegate, Frank, House (NM-113).

SANTA FE
SANTA FE COUNTY
El Palacio Real de Santa Fe (*Palace of the Governors*) (NM-2)
Control Nr. NM0109; LC Shelf Code NM.25-SANFE.2-.
26 sheets (1934 and 1939, including plans, elevations, sections, details, restoration plan); 10 ext. photos (1934), 2 int. photos (1934); 8 data pages (1934).

This project was undertaken by HABS, Office of National Parks, Buildings, and Reservations [NPS], Branch of Plans and Design, USDOI. It was approved by the governor of Laguna Pueblo and prepared under the direction of John Gaw Meem, HABS National Advisory Board member and A. Leicester Hyde, District Officer for District 36 (Utah, Colorado, New Mexico).

The delineators were Charles A. Dieman, Frederick A. Eastman, and John J. Windsor. The photos were taken by M. James Slack; the data pages were prepared by A. Leicester Hyde.

SANTA FE
SANTA FE COUNTY
Rael House (NM-15)
Control Nr. M0112; C Shelf Code M.25-SANFE.5-.
4 sheets (1940, including plan, elevations, section, details); 1 ext. photo (1936), 6 ext. photos (1940); 2 data pages (1940).

This was undertaken as a Public Works Administration Project, Federal Project 498-A, and prepared under the direction of NPS, Branch of Plans and Design, USDOI.

The delineator was Raymond T. Lovelady. The photos were taken by Frederick D. Nichols (1936) and Donald W. Dickensheets (1940). The data pages were prepared by Trent Thomas, Architect in Charge, HABS, Southwest Unit, and approved by John Gaw Meem, District Officer.

SANTA FE
SANTA FE COUNTY
Reredos of Our Lady of Light (Church) (*Cristo Rey Church*) (NM-140)
Control Nr. M0125; C Shelf Code M.25-SANFE.10-.
1 photocopy of photo (ca. 1969).

The only record of this reredos is a photocopy of a photo taken by Fred Mang, Jr., of NPS (ca. 1969).

SANTA FE
SANTA FE COUNTY
San Miguel Church (NM-1)
Control Nr. M0053; C Shelf Code M.25-SANFE.1-.
18 sheets (1934, including plans, elevations, sections, details, restoration sheet); 4 ext. photos (1934), 7 int. photos (1934); 3 data pages (1934).

This project was undertaken by HABS, Office of National Parks, Buildings, and Reservations [NPS], Branch of Plans and Design, USDOI. It was prepared under the direction of John Gaw Meem, HABS National Advisory Board member and A. Leicester Hyde, District Officer for District 36 (Utah, Colorado, New Mexico).

The delineators were Neal W. Cash, Charles A. Dieman, Frederick A. Eastman, and John J. Windsor. The photos were taken by M. James Slack; the data pages were prepared by A. Leicester Hyde.

SILVER CITY
GRANT COUNTY
Commercial Buildings (*Western Stationers* [*Southern Union Gas Company*]) (NM-150)
Control Nr. M0158; C Shelf Code M.9-SILCI.2-.
1 ext. photo (1976, copy photo of photogrammetric plate); 1 data page (1985–86).

This project was undertaken by the New Mexico State Historic Preservation Division and the Office of Archaeology and Historic Preservation, NPS, USDOI. It was prepared under the direction of Perry E. Borchers of the School of Architecture, OSU.

The photos are copies of photogrammetric plates by Perry E. Borchers. The data pages are an inventory of photogrammetric images prepared by the Photogrammetric Images Project (1985–86). They consist of two 9.5 x 9.5-inch glass plate diapositives; enlargements for 2.5 x 2.5-inch negatives; survey control contact prints for each plate and survey control information for each plate.

SILVER CITY
GRANT COUNTY
Commercial Building (*Peddler's Square*) (NM-151)
Control Nr. M0159; C Shelf Code M.9-SILCI.3-.
1 ext. photo (1976, copy photo of photogrammetric plate); 1 data page (1985–86).

This project was undertaken by the New Mexico State Historic Preservation Division and the Office of Archaeology and Historic Preservation, NPS, USDOI. It was prepared under

RECORDING A VANISHING LEGACY

120

the direction of Perry E. Borchers of the School of Architecture, OSU.

The photo is a copy of a photogrammetric plate by Perry E. Borchers. The data page is an inventory of photogrammetric images prepared by the Photogrammetric Images Project (1985–86). It consists of terrestrial stereopairs.

SILVER CITY
GRANT COUNTY
Silver City Museum (NM-143)
Control Nr. M0135; C Shelf Code M.9-SILCI.1-.
2 ext. photos (1976, copy photos of photogrammetric plates); 2 data pages (1985–86).

This project was undertaken by the New Mexico State Historic Preservation Division and the Office of Archaeology and Historic Preservation, NPS, USDOI. It was prepared under the direction of Perry E. Borchers of the School of Architecture, OSU.

The photos are copies of photogrammetric plates by Perry E. Borchers. The data pages are an inventory of photogrammetric images prepared by the Photogrammetric Images Project (1985–86). They consist of four 9.5 x 9.5-inch glass plate diapositive enlargements for 2.5 x 2.5-inch negatives, with one survey control contact print for each plate and survey control information for each pair.

SOCORRO
SOCORRO COUNTY
Baca Store (NM-46)
Control Nr. M0055; C Shelf Code M, 27-SOCO, 1-.
2 ext. photos (n.d.).

These photos are undated and unattributed. They do not appear in the 1941 HABS catalog but are in the 1959 catalog. However, it is unlikely that they date from between 1941 and 1959, a period during which HABS was inactive in New Mexico. It is probable that the photos were taken by one of the three HABS administrators from the Washington, DC, office who photographed in New Mexico in the late 1930s: Frederick D. Nichols (1936, 1937), John P. O'Neill (1937), or Delos Hamilton Smith (1940); or by photographer Donald W. Dickensheets (1940). None of the three worked in Socorro County, but both O'Neill and Smith recorded in nearby Bernalillo and Valencia counties. Between 1936 and 1941 HABS documentation was funded by the Works Progress Administration.

SOCORRO
SOCORRO COUNTY
Opera House (NM-47)
Control Nr. M0056; LC Shelf Code NM, 27-SOCO, 2-.
1 ext. photo (n.d.).
See Socorro, *Baca Store* (NM-46).

SOCORRO
SOCORRO COUNTY
Park Hotel (NM-48)
Control Nr. NM0057; LC Shelf Code NM, 27-SOCO, 2-.
1 ext. photo (n.d.).
See Socorro, *Baca Store* (NM-46).

SOCORRO
SOCORRO COUNTY
San Miguel Mission (NM-49)
Control Nr. NM0058; LC Shelf Code NM, 27-SOCO, 4-.
2 ext. photos (n.d.).
See Socorro, *Baca Store* (NM-46).

TALPA
TAOS COUNTY
La Capilla de Nuestra Señora de Talpa (NM-10)
Control Nr. NM0064; LC Shelf Code NM, 28-TALP, 1-.
12 sheets (1934, including plan, copies of inscriptions, elevations, sections, details, color sheet); 4 ext. photos (1934); 1 ext. photo (n.d.), 1 int. photo (1934); 2 data pages (1936).

This project was undertaken by HABS, Office of National Parks, Buildings, and Reservations [NPS], Branch of Plans and Design, USDOI. It was prepared under the direction of John Gaw Meem, HABS National Advisory Board member and A. Leicester Hyde, District Officer for District 36 (Utah, Colorado, New Mexico).

The delineators were H. Paul Atchison, Alan B. Fisher, Arthur Hoyer, Bradley P. Kidder, and A. B. Willison. The 1934 photos were taken by M. James Slack; the data pages were prepared by A. Leicester Hyde.

TALPA
TAOS COUNTY
La Morada de Talpa (NM-130)
Control Nr. NM0087; LC Shelf Code NM, 28-TALP, 3-.
3 sheets (1965, including plan, elevations).

This project was prepared under the direction of Bainbridge Bunting, associate professor of art history, University of New Mexico Art History Department. The measured drawings are by architecture student S. Sosa, Jr., and were submitted as a term project for Architecture 261–262. Due to insufficient information at the time of editing, they may not conform to HABS standards. The reproduction rights were acquired by HABS under the direction of James C. Massey, Chief, in 1971.

TALPA
TAOS COUNTY
Trujillo House (NM-74)
Control Nr. NM0019; LC Shelf Code NM, 28-TALP, 2-.
5 sheets (1963, including plan, elevations).

This project was prepared by the Fort Burgwin Research Center, Fred Wendorf, Director, in cooperation with the Museum of New Mexico. Charles S. Pope, Supervising Architect, Historic Structures, Western Office of Design and Construction, NPS, assisted in preparing the drawings for the HABS collection at the Library of Congress.

The structure was measured and drawn in 1960–61 under the direction of Bainbridge Bunting, associate professor of architectural history, University of New Mexico, by Jean Lee Booth and William R. Sims, Jr., students at the University of New Mexico. Presentation modifications of 1964 were by NPS student architect Mark Steele, University of Kentucky. The project was financed from funds of the "Mission 66" Program, NPS, Branch of Plans and Design, USDOI.

HABS INVENTORY FOR NEW MEXICO

TAOS
TAOS COUNTY
Adair House (NM-50)
Control Nr. NM0113; LC Shelf Code NM, 28-TAO, 1-.
1 ext. photo (n.d.).

This photo is undated and unattributed. It does not appear in the 1941 HABS catalog but is in the 1959 catalog. However, it is unlikely that it dates from between 1941 and 1959, a period during which HABS was inactive in New Mexico.

It is probable that the photo was taken by one of the three HABS administrators from the Washington, DC, office who photographed in New Mexico in the late 1930s: Frederick D. Nichols (1936, 1937), John P. O'Neill (1937), or Delos Hamilton Smith (1940); or by photographer Donald W. Dickensheets (1940). Of these, only Nichols is recorded as having photographed in Taos County. Between 1936 and 1941 HABS documentation was funded by the Works Progress Administration.

TAOS
TAOS COUNTY
Carson, Kit, House (NM-11)
Control Nr. NM0097; LC Shelf Code NM, 28-TAO, 2-.
1 ext. photo (1936).

The photo was taken by Frederick D. Nichols of the Washington office of HABS. In August 1936 and July–September 1937, Nichols took about 45 photos of structures in the counties of Santa Fe, Taos, Rio Arriba, San Miguel, Colfax, Doña Ana, and Otero. Each structure was documented with four or fewer photos. Nichols, an architecture graduate from Yale University, was a leading employee at the Washington office of HABS from 1933 until he joined the navy during World War II. He compiled the HABS 1941 catalog. In 1936 HABS documentation was funded by the Works Progress Administration.

TAOS
TAOS COUNTY
Chapel of Padre Antonio José Martinez (NM-110)
Control Nr. NM0096; LC Shelf Code NM, 28-TAO, 3-.
2 ext. photos (1936).
See Taos, Carson, Kit, House (NM-11).

TAOS
TAOS COUNTY
Meyers, Ralph, House (Corbels) (NM-51)
Control Nr. NM0075; LC Shelf Code NM, 28-TAO, 4-.
1 ext. photo (n.d.).
See Taos, Adair House (NM-50).

TAOS
TAOS COUNTY
Romero, Santiago, House (NM-136)
Control Nr. NM0031; LC Shelf Code NM, 28-TAO, 5-.
3 sheets (1966–67, including plan, elevation, section, detail).

This project was prepared under the direction of Bainbridge Bunting, associate professor of art history, University of New Mexico Art History Department. The measured drawings are by architecture students Jack A. Miller and Trinidad Romero and were submitted as a term project for Architecture 261–262. Due to insufficient information at the time of editing, they may not conform to HABS standards. The reproduction rights were acquired by HABS under the direction of James C. Massey, Chief, in 1971.

TAOS
TAOS COUNTY
Valdez, Don Antonio José, House (NM-137)
Control Nr. NM0091; LC Shelf Code NM, 28-TAO, 6-.
4 sheets (ca. 1966–70, including plans, elevations).

This project was prepared under the direction of Bainbridge Bunting, associate professor of art history, University of New Mexico. The measured drawings are by architecture students Earnest, Kilmer, and Kneblick and were submitted as a term project for Architecture 261–262. Due to insufficient information at the time of editing, they may not conform to HABS standards. They were purchased by HABS under the direction of James C. Massey, Chief, in 1971.

TAOS PUEBLO
TAOS COUNTY
Taos, Central Portion, Pueblo of (NM-102)
Control Nr. NM0099; LC Shelf Code NM, 28-TAOP, 2-.
8 sheets (1973, including plans, sections, elevations; 1 ext. photo (1973, copy photo of photogrammetric plate); 4 data pages (1985–86).

This project was undertaken by HABS, NPS, USDOI. It was approved by Taos Pueblo Governor Quirino Romero and Secretary Frank Marcus and prepared at the School of Architecture, OSU, under the direction of Perry E. Borchers, Research Supervisor.

The aerial photography was by the New Mexico State Highway Department in 1973. Ground survey control was by Perry E. Borchers, Myra Borchers, and Joe Kingsolver of the Bureau of Indian Affairs in 1973. Images were plotted on the Wild A7 Autograph at OSU University by Perry E. Borchers and drawn by OSU students Julsing J. Lamsam and Bruce Casterline in 1974.

The photo is a copy of a photogrammetric plate by Perry E. Borchers. The data pages are an inventory of photogrammetric images prepared by the Photogrammetric Images Project (1985–86). They consist of twenty-one 9.5 × 9.5-inch glass plate aerial diapositives, with survey control information and survey control contact prints for each plate. There are also fifteen reduced-size Xerox copies of the plotted elevation.

TAOS PUEBLO
TAOS COUNTY
Taos Indian Health Center (HABS NO. NM-177)
Control Nr. NM0190
18 photos of the Taos Indian Health Center building and 1934 architectural plans.

This report was prepared by William A. Dodge of the Albuquerque Area Indian Health Service, Office of Environmental Health and Engineering. The HABS Level II survey was completed under the terms of a Memorandum of Agreement signed by the Indian Health Service, Pueblo of Taos, and the State Historic Preservation Officer, New Mexico Advisory Council on Historic Preservation to satisfy consultation requirements under Section 106 of the National Historic Preservation Act of 1966 (as amended) and 36 CFR Part 800. Building No. 788 was determined eligible for inclusion on the

6. RELATED PUBLICATIONS

A list of publications, including state and local catalogs, publications of HABS/HAER, and the useful reference work, *Historic American Buildings Survey/Historic American Engineering Record: An Annotated Bibliography*, compiled by James C. Massey, Nancy B. Schwartz, and Shirley Maxwell (1992) are available from:

HABS/HAER
P. O. Box 37127
Washington DC: 20013-7127

7. HABS ON THE WEB

Not all HABS drawings and materials are currently on the web, but numerous Web sites contain or are linked to some HABS drawings and lots of information. A few of the more useful and interesting Web sits include:

National Park Service (www.nps.gov)
Advisory Council on Historic Preservation (www.achp.gov)
Heritage Preservation Services (www2.cr.nps.gov)

This has a direct HABS link, use the "search" for HABS/HAER. This also connects to Tribal websites and Tribal Historic Preservation Offices.

Natiional Register of Histoic Places (www.cr.nps.gov/nr)
For a direct connection to HABS information, including the collections (http://www.cr.nps.gov/habshaerv)
National Historic Landmarks (www.cr.nps.gov/nhl)
Or, for a virtual visit to National Historic Landmarks, (www2.cr.nps.gov/nhl/virtvist.htm)
Library of Congress (http://memory.loc.gov/) HABS is under the American Memory Link

APPENDIX A: ADDITIONAL RESOURCES FOR HABS RESEARCH

JAN DODSON BARNHART AND CAROL JOINER

Contributors Jan Dodson Barnhart and Carol Joiner have a combined total of over forty years' experience at the University of New Mexico General Library. Barnhart is the Associate Director of the Department of Development and Public Affairs and former director of the John Gaw Meem Archive of Southwestern Architecture. She serves as Vice President of the Dennis Chavez Foundation, is Past President of the New Mexico Architectural Foundation, President of the Friends of the Libraries, UNM, Past President of the Southwest Oral History Association, and Vice President of the Albuquerque Historical Society. She is the co-editor of Hispanic Heroes: Portraits of New Mexicans Who Have Made A Difference, published in 1992.

Joiner is a reference librarian with master's degrees in history, anthropology, and library science. One of her recent publications is "The Boys and Girls of Summer: The University of New Mexico Archaeological Field School in Chaco Canyon" in The Journal of Anthropological Research (spring 1992). In 1999, she retired from the University of New Mexico General Library.

APPENDIX B: HABS COLLECTIONS IN NEW MEXICO

JAN DODSON BARNHART
AND
CAROL JOINER

In undertaking the project of surveying the holdings in New Mexico of HABS materials, the current edition of *The American Library Directory* was used. Any institution, agency, or museum indicating a library holding or a subject interest in the field of architecture was contacted and a survey sheet filled out. If they had HABS materials, the contact person was requested to forward a list of items to attach to the survey sheet. Several institutions do not have any index, abstract, or context list of their materials.

This guide includes the Bainbridge Bunting Collection at the John Gaw Meem Archive of Southwestern Architecture at the University of New Mexico. Although most of the student measured drawings and photographs in the collection have not been submitted to HABS at the national level, Professor Bunting's goal was to have his students in the 1960s and 1970s carry on the HABS work of the 1930s in New Mexico.

We hope the information contained herein will be of assistance to researchers interested in HABS and its rich history of the built environment of this area.

NEW MEXICO INSTITUTIONS WITH HABS HOLDINGS

Fine Arts Library
University of New Mexico
Albuquerque, NM

Center for Southwest Research
John Gaw Meem Archive of Southwestern Architecture
Zimmerman Library
University of New Mexico
Albuquerque NM

History Library
Palace of the Governors
Museum of New Mexico
110 Washington Avenue
Santa Fe, NM

Southwest Room
New Mexico State Library
Santa Fe, NM

Special Collections Department
University Library
New Mexico State University
Las Cruces, NM

National Park Service Intermountain Region
2968 Rodeo Park Drive West
Santa Fe, NM

Office of Cultural Affairs
Historic Preservation Division
La Villa Rivera Building
228 East Palace Avenue
Santa Fe, NM

HABS HOLDINGS

Fine Arts Library
University of New Mexico
Albuquerque, NM

Holdings are on microfiche and include New Mexico, California, Florida, Arizona, and Texas. There is no separate index for drawings.

The library also has Historic New Mexico Buildngs: A Collection of Measured Drawings (16 volumes), photographic reproductions of the Bainbridge Bunting student measured drawings organized in bound volumes. The call number is x NA 730 N6B8, and the reference librarian has a list of contents. The original drawings are at the University of New Mexico in the John Gaw Meem Archive of Southwestern Architecture.

APPENDIX B: HABS COLLECTIONS IN NEW MEXICO

Center for Southwest Research
John Gaw Meem Archive of Southwestern Architecture
Zimmerman Library
University of New Mexico
Albuquerque, NM

The John Gaw Meem Archive of Southwestern Architecture was established in 1975 with the donation of Meem's works. This material forms the basis of a continuously growing collection of architectural donations. The John Gaw Meem Collection holdings include HABS drawings between 1933 and 1981, and correspondence concerning HABS measured drawings in notebooks and on microfilm. HABS measured drawings in notebooks and on microfilm. HABS in New Mexico are listed below.

The late Bainbridge Bunting donated a wealth of material to the collection. The Bainbridge Bunting Collection includes student measured drawings, black and white photographs, historical data, and literature on the architecture of New Mexico. Research collections at the John Gaw Meem Archive related to HABS in New Mexico are listed below.

- **HABS Drawings**

The John Gaw Meem Archive is currently purchasing the set of 17 by 24 inch format HABS drawings for New Mexico completed through 1985.

- **HABS Correspondence Files**

These files cover the years 1933-1981 and include HABS bulletins and correspondence concerning HABS, the Society for Preservation and Restoration of Mission Churches, and the publication of a book on HABS in New Mexico.

- **HABS Drawings in Notebooks**

The three notebooks contain sheets of drawings of sites documented by HABS between 1933-1940. An inventory is available.

- **Microfilm**

This microfilm reel of HABS measured drawings for New Mexico as of 1974 was issued by the Library of Congress and is titled Historic American Buildings Survey, Microfilm and Electrostatic Prints of Measured Drawings in the Library of Congress.

- **Bainbridge Bunting HABS Notebooks**

The 16 notebooks include drawings, photographs, aerial photographs, and data pages. An inventory is available.

- **Bainbridge Bunting HABS Student Measured Drawings**

The measured drawings collection includes over 950 sheets of structures in New Mexico and additional sheets on sites in other states. An inventory is available.

NAME		COUNTY	COMMENTS
History Library			
Palace of the Governors			
Museum of New Mexico			
Santa Fe NM			
Acoma			
Acoma Pueblo		Valencia [now Cibola]	83 sheets
San Esteban del Rey		Valencia [now Cibola]	31 sheets
Chimayó			
El Santuario del Señor Esquipula		Santa Fe	31 sheets
Laguna Pueblo			
Meeting House		Valencia [now Cibola]	4 sheets
San José de Laguna Mission Church & Convento		Valencia [now Cibola]	21 sheets
Nambé Pueblo			
Kiva		Santa Fe	6 sheets
Ranchos de Taos			
Mission Church of Ranchos de Taos		Santa Fe	6 sheets
Santa Fe			
El Palacio Real de Santa Fe (Palace of the Governors)		Santa Fe	26 sheets
Santa Fe Vicinity			
San Miguel Church		Santa Fe	18 sheets
Talpa			
La Capilla de Nuestra Señora de Talpa		Santa Fe	12 sheets

New Mexico State Library
Southwest Room
Santa Fe, NM

Library holdings include a microfiche edition of 11 fiches of photographs and written data on sites in New Mexico in the collection of the Library of Congress as of January 1979, titled Historic American Buildings Survey: The Microfiche Edition (Teaneck, N.J.: Somerset House, 1981).

Special Collections Department
University Library
New Mexico State University
Las Cruces, NM

Library holdings include a microfiche edition of 11 fiches of photographs and written data on sites in New Mexico in the collection of the Library of Congress as of January 1979, titled Historic American Buildings Survey: The Microfiche Edition (Teaneck, N.J.: Somerset House, 1981).

National Park Service Intermountain Region
2926 Rodeo Park Drive West
Santa Fe, NM

The National Park Service maintains a complete New Mexico inventory of HABS and HAER microfiche at their Santa Fe Office. The HABS/HAER Coordinator also retains drawings and other information on current HABS projects in New Mexico not yet sent to Washington, DC.

Office of Cultural Affairs
Historic Preservation Division
Santa Fe, NM

These drawings are in the reference library of the Historic Preservation Division and are available by appointment. The comment "NMHPD only" indicates that the sheets of drawings may be found at the New Mexico Historic Preservation Division and are not part of the Library of Congress HABS collections.

NAME	COUNTY	COMMENTS
Acoma Pueblo		
Acoma, Pueblo of (Sky City) (NM-6)	Valencia [now Cibola]	(1934)/83 of 83 sheets NM-Vol. 18 (+TS) and NM-Bk. 3
Acoma, Pueblo of (Sky City) (NM-6)	Valencia [now Cibola]	3 of 3 sheets oversize/photogrammetric Ohio State University
San Esteban del Rey Mission (NM-5)	Valencia [now Cibola]	31 of 32 sheets NM-Vol. 18 (+TS) and NM-Bk. 3
Alamagordo Vicinity		
La Luz, Town of (NM-141)	Otero	1 of ? oversize/photogrammetric Ohio State University NMHD only
Alcalde		
Los Luceros Chapel (NM-54)	Rio Arriba	5 of 5 sheets top drawer
Los Luceros House (NM-53)	Rio Arriba	9 of 9 sheets top drawer
Arroyo Hondo		
Upper Penitente Morada Chapel (Penitente Morada)(NM-60)	Taos	6 of 6 sheets NM-2 and top drawer
Bland Vicinity		
Ceremonial Cave (Bandelier National Monument)(NM-17)	Sandoval	2 of 2 sheets NM-2 (+TS) and top drawer
Kiva, Large (Bandelier National Monument) (NM-16)	Sandoval	2 of 2 sheets NM-2 (+TS) and top drawer
El Cerrito		
El Cerrito, Village of (Spanish-American Villages of the Pecos River Valley) (NM-127)	San Miguel	5 of 5 sheets
Chaco Canyon		
Bonito, Pueblo (Chaco Canyon National Monument) (NM-30)	San Juan	9 of 9 sheets NM-2 (+TS) and top drawer
Chaco Canyon Vicinity		
Kin Klizhin (Chaco Canyon National Monument) (NM-31)	San Juan	5 of 5 sheets NM-2 (+TS)
Chimayó		
Plaza del Cerro (Plaza San Buenaventura) (NM-128)	Rio Arriba	2 of 2 sheets oversize/photogrammetric 1-28 and 30-32 of 32 sheets, NM-2 NM Bk-3 and top drawer (books do not have Sheets 30-32)
El Santuario del Señor Esquípula (NM-9)	Santa Fe	
Cochiti Pueblo		
Pueblo of Cochiti (no HABS number)	Sandoval	1 of ? sheets oversize/photogrammetric
Galisteo		
Lucero House (NM-129)	Santa Fe	6 of 6 sheet

APPENDIX B: HABS COLLECTIONS IN NEW MEXICO

NAME	COUNTY	COMMENTS
Gila		
L. C. Ranch Headquarters (NM-144)	Grant	3 of 3 sheets oversize/photogrammetric Ohio State University NMHPD only
Hillsboro		
Hillsboro, Town of (NM-142)	Sierra	1 of ? sheet oversize/photogrammetric NMHPD only
Isleta Pueblo		
Pueblo of Isleta (no HABS number)	Bernalillo	1 of ? sheets oversize/photogrammetric NMHPD only
Jemez Pueblo		
Jemez, Pueblo of (NM-145)	Sandoval	2 of 2 sheets oversize/photogrammetric Ohio State University NMHPD only
Laguna Pueblo		
Laguna, Pueblo of (NM-27)	Valencia [now Cibola]	2 of ? sheets oversize/photogrammetric Ohio State University NMHPD only
Meeting House (NM-4)	Valencia [now Cibola]	4 of 4 sheets NM-Vol. 18 (+TS), NM Bk. 3 and top drawer
San José de Laguna Mission Church & Convento (NM-3)	Valencia [now Cibola]	21 of 22 sheets NM-Vol. 18 (+TS) and NM Bk. 3
Las Vegas		
Castañeda Hotel (NM-29)	San Miguel	2 of ? sheets oversize/photogrammetric
Las Vegas Vicinity		
Baca, Don José Albino House (NM-12)	San Miguel	19 of 19 sheets NM-2 (+TS) and top drawer
Montezuma Hotel (NM-28)	San Miguel	3 of ? sheets oversize/photogrammetric NMHPD only
Llano Quemado		
Fernandez, Sofio, House (NM-67)	Taos	4 of 4 sheets NM-2 and top drawer
Lordsburg Vicinity		
Shakespeare, Town of (no HABS number)	Hidalgo	1 of ? sheets oversize/photogrammetric Ohio State University NMHPD only
Los Alamos Vicinity		
Romero Cabin (NM-148)	Sandoval	2 of 2 sheets oversize National Park Service
Manzano		
Torreón, The (NM-11)	Torrance	3 of 3 sheets NM-2 (+TS) and top drawer
Nambé Pueblo		
Kiva (NM-8)	Santa Fe	6 of 6 sheets NM-Vol. 18 (+TS), NM-2 and top drawer
Nambé, Pueblo of (NM-107)	Santa Fe	2 of 2 sheets oversize/photogrammetric Ohio State University
Pecos		
Pecos Church, Ruins (NM-85)	San Miguel	14 of 14 sheets
Peñasco		
Romero House (NM-73)	Taos	6 of 6 sheets NM-2 and top drawer
Peralta		
Our Lady of Guadalupe (Church at Peralta) (NM-40)	Valencia	11 of 11 sheets top drawer
Picurís		
Picurís, Pueblo of (San Lorenzo Pueblo) (NM-100)	Taos	3 of ? sheets oversize/photogrammetric Ohio State University NMHPD only

NAME	COUNTY	COMMENTS
Puerto de Luna		
House (NM-138)	Guadalupe	6 of 6 sheets top drawer
Ranchito		
Martinez, José Maria, House (NM-71)	Taos	8 of 8 sheets NM-2 and top drawer
Martinez, Leandro, House (NM-64)	Taos	7 of 7 sheets NM-2 and top drawer
Martinez, Pascual, House (NM-70)	Taos	8 of 8 sheets NM-2 and top drawer
Ranchos de Taos		
Long, Horace G., House (NM-94)	Taos	9 of 9 sheets NM-2 and top drawer
Ranchos de Taos		
Mission Church at Ranchos de Taos (NM-7)	Taos	31 of 32 sheets NM-Vol. 18 (+TS), NM Bk. 3 and top drawer
San Ildefonso Pueblo		
San Ildefonso, Pueblo of (NM-89)	Santa Fe	2 of 2 sheets oversize/photogrammetric
San José		
San José del Vado, Village of (NM-126)	San Miguel	2 of 2 sheets oversize/photogrammetric
(Spanish-American Villages of the Pecos River Valley)	San José	
San Miguel		
San Miguel del Vado, General View (Spanish-American	San Miguel	4 of 4 sheets oversize/photogrammetric
Villages of the Pecos River Valley) (NM-139)		
Territorial House, San Miguel del Vado	San Miguel	2 of 2 sheets oversize/photogrammetric
(Spanish-American Villages of the Pecos River Valley)		
(NM-139-B)		
Warehouse & Stable, San Miguel del Vado	San Miguel	1 of 1 Sheets oversize/photogrammetric
(Spanish-American Villages of the Pecos River Valley)		
(NM-139-A)		
Santa Ana Pueblo		
Santa Ana Mission Church, Pueblo of (NM-125)	Sandoval	4 of 4 sheets oversize/photogrammetric Ohio State University
Santa Ana, Pueblo of (NM-106)	Sandoval	1 of 1 sheets
Santa Clara Pueblo		
Pueblo of Santa Clara, Central Portion (NM-98)	Rio Arriba	4 of 4 sheets oversize/photogrammetric
Santa Fe		
Borrego House (McCormick Prize House) (NM-14)	Santa Fe	5 of 5 sheets NM-2 (+TS) and top drawer
Garcia House (NM-13)	Santa Fe	5 of 5 sheets NM-2 (+TS) and top drawer
El Palacio Real de Santa Fe (Palace of the Governors) (NM-2)	Santa Fe	26 of 26 sheets NM-Vol. 18, NM Bk. 3 and top drawer
Rael House (NM-15)	Santa Fe	4 of 4 sheets NM-2 (+TS) and top drawer
Santa Fe Vicinity		
San Miguel Church (NM-1)	Santa Fe	18 of 18 sheets NM-Vol. 18, NM Bk. 3 and top drawer
Shakespeare		
Shakespeare, mining town (J. Hill Ranch) (no HABS number)	Hidalgo	1 of ? sheets oversize/photogrammetric Ohio State University NMHPD only
Talpa		
La Capilla de Nuestra Señora de Talpa (NM-10)	Taos	11 of 12 sheets NM-2 (+TS), NM Bk. 3 and top drawer
La Morada de Talpa (NM-130)	Taos	4 of 4 sheets top drawer
Trujillo House (NM-74)	Taos	5 of 5 sheets NM-2 and top drawer

APPENDIX B: HABS COLLECTIONS IN NEW MEXICO

APPENDIX B: HABS COLLECTIONS IN NEW MEXICO

NAME	COUNTY	COMMENTS
Taos		
Romero, Santiago, House (NM-136)	Taos	7 of 7 sheets top drawer
Valdez, Don Antonio José, House (NM-137)	Taos	5 of 5 sheets top drawer
Taos Pueblo		
Taos, Central Portion, Pueblo of (NM-102)	Taos	8 of 8 sheets oversize/photogrammetric
Tesuque		
Tesuque, Central Portion, Pueblo of (NM-103)	Santa Fe	8 of 8 sheets oversize/photogrammetric Ohio State University
Tiptonville		
Tipton House & Barn (NM-19)	Mora	4 of 4 sheets NM-2 (+TS) and top drawer
Trampas		
Atencio House (NM-76)	Taos	7 of 7 sheets NM-2 and 2 Sets top drawer; loose sets vary
de Cruz, José, House (NM-75)	Taos	6 of 6 sheets NM-2 and 2 Sets top shelf; loose sets vary
San José de Gracia Church (NM-61)	Taos	5 of 5 sheets top drawer
Tucumcari		
Baca-Goodman House (NM-108)	Quay	4 of 4 sheets oversize drawer
Vadito		
Casita Martinez (NM-72)	Taos	3 of 3 sheets NM-2 and top drawer
Watrous Vicinity		
Watrous House (NM-18)	Mora	25 of 25 sheets NM-2 (+TS) and top drawer
Zia Pueblo		
Pueblo of Zia (NM-104)	Sandoval	1 of ? sheets oversize/photogrammetric NMHPD only
Zuni Pueblo		
Mission Nuestra Señora de Guadalupe de Zuni (NM-124)	McKinley	12 of 12 sheets top drawer
Pueblo of Zuni, Central & Original Portion (NM-78)	McKinley	1 of 6 sheets oversize/photogrammetric

NOTES

CHAPTER 1

1. The gender-neutral term "drafter" has been used throughout this book, although the composition of HABS teams from 1934 to today has been overwhelmingly male. – ED.
2. HABS, Historic American Buildings Survey Catalogue of Completed Records, December 15, 1933–December 31, 1935 (mimeographed ed.) (Washington, DC: HABS, Branch of Plans and Design, NPS, USDOI, 1935); John P. O'Neill, comp. and ed., Historic American Buildings Survey: Catalog of the Measured Drawings and Photographs of the Survey in the Library of Congress, January 1, 1938 (Washington, DC: HABS, NPS, USDOI).
3. Frederick D. Nichols, comp. and ed., Historic American Buildings Survey: Catalog of the Measured Drawings and Photographs of the Survey in the Library of Congress, March 1, 1941 (Washington, DC: HABS, NPS, USDOI, 1941); Worth Bailey, comp. and ed., Historic American Buildings Survey Catalog Supplement: Catalog of the Measured Drawings and Photographs of the Survey in the Library of Congress, Comprising Additions Since March 1, 1941 (Washington, DC: HABS, Division of Design and Construction, NPS, USDOI, 1959).
4. State and local catalogs that have been formally published include California (1988), Alabama (1987), Georgia (1983), Indiana (1983), Iowa (1979), New Jersey (1977), Philadelphia (1976), Virginia (1976), Texas (1975), Maine (1974), Washington, DC (1974), Utah (1969), Michigan (1967), Chicago (1966), Virgin Islands (1966), Wisconsin (1966), Massachusetts (1965), and New Hampshire (1963). – ED.

CHAPTER 2

1. "New Mexico Interlude, the Documentation of a Death Mask," a speech delivered by Alan Fisher to the annual meeting of the Colonial Dames of Colorado, 21 November 1969. JGMA, 5. Unless otherwise noted, this paper draws on documents in the John Gaw Meem Archive of Southwestern Architecture (JGMA), John Gaw Meem Collection (JGMC), (HABS Correspondence) and the Bainbridge Bunting Collection (BBC) in the Center for Southwest Research, University of New Mexico.
2. HABS analysis of coverage by states, 1933–1956, by Agnes A. Gilchrist, 22 January 1958. NA
3. Biographical information on John Gaw Meem is drawn from Bainbridge Bunting's *John Gaw Meem: Southwestern Architect* (Albuquerque: University of New Mexico Press, 1988) and Beatrice Chauvenet's *John Gaw Meem: Pioneer in Historic Preservation* (Museum of New Mexico Press, 1985).
4. Leicester Hyde File, AIA. The National Advisory Committee became the National Advisory Board after World War II.
5. This and the previous paragraph draw on AIA architects' files and personal correspondence with Victor Hornbein, 1993.
6. Letter, Vint to Hyde, 18 December 1933. NA.
7. In this book Spanish and Native American words are italicized on first occurrence; definitions may be found in the glossary. Although many of these words have entered standard English usage and may be found in a standard English dictionary, they are defined because New Mexican usage may differ from standard English, and words such as *jacal*, *bulto*, and *zaguán* may not be familiar to all readers. – ED.
8. Letter, Lambert to Hyde, 1 January 1934. NA.
9. Meem offered to obtain a similar letter from the Archbishop of Santa Fe. Hyde believed that the Pueblos granted approval for the survey mainly because of the extensive New Deal relief programs for Indians in effect under the Collier administration. (Letter, Hyde to Vint, 18 April 1934. NA.)
10. Letter, Hyde to HABS, 25 April 1934. NA.

11. The Spanish recorded by the 1934 teams has been retained in this book, although it rarely conforms to correct usage by today's standards. The architects transcribed the language as they heard it and often used phonetic spelling. They also recorded colloquial Spanish used in casual conversation.
12. Letter, Cammerer to Ickes, 27 April 1934. NA.
13. Robert Bruegmann, "Habs at an Awkward Age: The 1960s and 1970s," in C. Ford Peatross, ed., *Historic America: Buildings, Structures, and Sites* (Washington, DC: Library of Congress, 1983), 212–17.
14. Leicester B. Holland, "H.A.B.S. Redivivus," *The Octagon* (November 1934): 15–16.
15. John P. O'Neill, comp. and ed., *Historic American Buildings Survey: Catalog of the Measured Drawings and Photographs of the Survey in the Library of Congress, January 1, 1938* (Washington, DC: HABS, NPS, USDOI, IV.
16. Charles E. Peterson, "The Historic American Buildings Survey: Its Beginnings," in C. Ford Peatross, ed., *Historic America: Its Buildings, Structures, and Sites* (Washington, DC: Library of Congress, 1983), 8–9; Delos Hamilton Smith File, AIA.
17. Letter, Vint to Jones, 23 October 1940. NA; Letter, Dorman to Vint, 31 October 1940. NA.
18. Bruegmann, "HABS at an Awkward Age," 215–17; John A. Burns, "Measured Drawings," in *Recording Historic Structures*, John A. Burns and the staff of HABS/HAER, eds. (Washington, DC: The American Institute of Architects Press, 1989), 112–13.
19. Elise Vider, "The Historic American Buildings Survey in Philadelphia, 1950–1966: Shaping Postwar Preservation" (Master's thesis, University of Pennsylvania, 1991), 5.
20. Perry E. Borchers, "The Measure of the Future and the Past," *AIA Journal* (October 1957): 354.

CHAPTER 3

1. In fact, the Palace of the Governors was remodeled between 1909 and 1913, when an 1878 Territorial portal was replaced by one in a regional revival style designed to evoke the appearance of the building in the late 1700s. See Chris Wilson, "The Santa Fe, New Mexico Plaza" (Master's thesis, University of New Mexico, 1981), 105–58. – ED.
2. Like many other authors, Hornbein reports that the mesa's height is 365 feet. Only photogrammetric analysis, discussed in Perry E. Borcher's chapter in this section, catches this error, identifying the correct height as about 225 feet. – ED.

CHAPTER 4

1. The authors are indebted to the following individuals for information and assistance: Allison Abraham, John Azar, Jan Dodson Barnhart, Dorrie Bunting, John P. Conron, Barbara Daniels, Sheila Hanna, Susan Haycock, Laura Holt, Marcia Mazria, James C. Massey, George Clayton Pearl, Richard Polesi, Robert Retting, Bonnie Putnam Verrardo, and Chris Wilson.
2. Bainbridge Bunting, "Take a Trip with NMA: An Architectural Guide to Northern New Mexico," *New Mexico Architecture* 12, nos. 9 and 10 (September/October 1970): 13–51.
3. Bainbridge Bunting, *Early Architecture of New Mexico* (Albuquerque: University of New Mexico Press, 1976); *Taos Adobes: Spanish Colonial and Territorial Architecture of the Taos Valley* (Taos: Fort Burgwin Research Center and the Museum of New Mexico Press, 1964; reprint, Albuquerque: University of New Mexico Press, 1990); *Of Earth and Timbers Made: New Mexico Architecture* (Albuquerque: University of New Mexico Press, 1974; reprint, 1990).
4. Bunting, *Taos Adobes*, 2.
5. Photographic reproductions of the Bainbridge Bunting student measured drawings are bound in the 16-volume set *Historic New Mexico Buildings: A Collection of Measured Drawings*, in the rare book collection of the Fine Arts Library, University of New Mexico.
6. Letter, James C. Massey to Bainbridge Bunting, 1 June 1967, nmhpd.
7. Letter, Massey to Bunting, 21 April 1970, NMHPD.
8. Letter, Bunting to Massey, 6 February 1971, NMHPD.
9. Letter, Massey to Bunting, 4 October 1971, NMHPD.
10. No doubt stated in other words at other times, this description was given by Bunting in a class lecture, August 25, 1977.

CHAPTER 5

1. Stanley Stubbs, *Bird's-Eye View of the Pueblos* (Norman: University of Oklahoma Press, 1950).
2. The terms "Anglo-American" and "European-American" are both used in this book. In New Mexico, "Anglo," "Anglo-American" generally refer to people of non-New Mexican origin who began to enter the area from eastern states with the American occupation in 1846 and the coming of the railroad in 1879. The designations "European-American" or "Euro-American" refer to all people of European descent, including Spain. – ED.

CHAPTER 6

1. William R. Gafford, "Seventeenth-Century Mission Church Roof Beams: A Structural Analysis," in James E. Ivey, *In the Midst of a Loneliness: The Architectural History of the Salinas Missions: Salinas Pueblo Missions Historic Structures Report* (Santa Fe: Division of History, Southwest Cultural Resources Center Professional Papers No. 15, Southwest Region, NPS, USDOI, 1988), 389.
2. United States General Accounting Office, *Report to Congressional Requesters: Cultural Resources: Problems Protecting and Preserving Federal Archaeological Resources* (Washington, DC: U.S. General Accounting Office, 1987), 39.
3. Larry V. Nordby, "Modifications to Chetro Ketl and Talus Unit Drainage, Chaco Culture National Historic Park: Project Design and Recommendations" (internal report on file at the Southwest Cultural Resource Center, Santa Fe, NPS, 1984), 2.

CHAPTER 7

1. Frederick D. Nichols, comp. and ed., *Historic American Buildings Survey: Catalog of the Measured Drawings and Photographs of the Survey in the Library of Congress, March 1, 1941* (Washington, DC: HABS, NPS, USCOI, 1941), IV.
2. Peter Nabokov, *Architecture of Acoma Pueblo* (Santa Fe: Ancient City Press, 1986), 27.
3. Ibid., 10.
4. Ibid., 15.
5. Nichols, *HABS Catalog*, 1941, IV.
6. Nabokov, *Architecture of Acoma*, 10.
7. Ibid., 15.
8. Ibid.
9. Ibid., 17.
10. Perry E. Borchers, "Photogrammetric Recording of Communal Architecture," draft version, 1–2.

CHAPTER 8

1. Peter Nabokov and Robert Easton, *Native American Architecture* (New York: Oxford University Press, 1989), 387.
2. Tierra Amarilla has been studied by Chris Wilson and David Kammer in their book *La Tierra Amarilla: Its History, Architecture, and Cultural Landscape* (Santa Fe: New Mexico Historic Preservation Division, 1989); reprint, Santa Fe: Museum of New Mexico Press, 1992). –ED.
3. Beverly Spears, *American Adobes: Rural Houses of Northern New Mexico* (Albuquerque: University of New Mexico Press, 1986).

CHAPTER 10

1. Charles E. Peterson, "American Notes: The Historic American Buildings Survey Continued," *Journal of the Society of Architectural Historians* 16, no. 3 (OCTOBER 1957): 30.
2. Peter Nabokov, *Architecture of Acoma Pueblo: The 1934 Historic American Buildings Survey Project* (Santa Fe: Ancient City Press, 1986), 4–7.
3. Habs Correspondence Files. JGMA, JGMC.
4. Agnesa Lufkin Reeve, *From Hacienda to Bungalow: Northern New Mexico Houses* (Albuquerque: University of New Mexico Press, 1988).
5. Christopher M. Wilson, "The Santa Fe, New Mexico Plaza," (Master's thesis, University of New Mexico, 1981), 105–58.

CARLEEN LAZZELL AND BOYD C. PRATT

Architectural historians Carleen Lazzell and Boyd C. Pratt have written and lectured widely on the architectural history of New Mexico. Lazzell, who earned her Ph.D. in American Studies at the University of New Mexico in 1996, has served as associate editor of New Mexico Architecture, and on occasion she serves as adjunct professor at the University of New Mexico School of Architecture. She is presently on the Board of Directors of the Historical Society of New Mexico. Pratt, a graduate of the University of New Mexico's M.A. in Architecture Program, has conducted a series of regional overviews of the state's cultural resources and, with Lazzell and Chris Wilson, compiled a biographical dictionary of historic New Mexico architects. He is currently farming and writing on San Juan Island, Washington.

ARLEEN LAZZELL
AND
BOYD C. PRATT

GLOSSARY OF ARCHITECTURAL TERMS

This glossary provides the reader with definitions of common words descriptive of architecture and photogrammetric terminology. Standard architectural terms not defined are assumed to be common knowledge. Contributor Perry E. Borchers has supplied definitions of photogrammetric terms.

Acequia. Moorish-derived word referring to an irrigation canal; *acequia madre*, literally "mother ditch," was the principal supplier from which water was diverted into laterals (called *contra acequias* or *sangrías*).

Adobe. Moorish-derived word for sun-dried brick made of earth and straw; the mud used to make these bricks or plaster walls; a building constructed of adobe mud or bricks.

Anasazi. Navajo word meaning "the Ancient Ones"; refers to prehistoric Puebloan group inhabiting the Four Corners area.

Apse. Altar end of a church.

Arroyo. Dry river or streambed, subject to flooding after rainstorms.

Ashlar. Masonry having a face of square or rectangular stones; in the case of random ashlar, the arrangement is haphazard.

Atrio. Walled forecourt of a church.

Banco. Bench along a wall, usually constructed of adobe.

Baptistry. Portion of a church set aside for the rite of baptism.

Bulto. Three-dimensional statue of a saint.

Buttress. Abutting pier that strengthens a wall.

Calvario. Spanish term for Calvary, or Way of the Cross; the processional space used by the Penitentes to reenact the Passion of Christ.

Camposanto. Literally "holy ground," a cemetery usually located within a wall or fence in front of a church.

Canal(es). Roof drainspout projecting through a parapet wall.

Casas reales. Literally "royal houses," the official residence offices of the governor, although it can also refer to other government buildings; in Santa Fe the Palace of the Governors.

Chiflón. Flue.

Choir loft. Second-story space overlooking the nave of a church that is reserved for the choir.

Ciénega. Swamp or marsh.

Ciminterio. Cemetery.

Convento. Priest's residential courtyard, usually directly attached to the church.

139

GLOSSARY OF ARCHITECTURAL TERMS

Corbel. Bracket used to support a roof beam.

Cornice. Projecting section at the top of a wall.

Crenellation. Parapet with alternating indentations and raised portions.

Cupola. Dome rising above a roof.

Dispensa. Storage or tool shed.

Espadaña. Curvilinear parapet of a church facade with a cutout for the bell.

Fogón. Corner fireplace (often misnamed "kiva fireplace").

Hacienda. Large landed estate or property; also refers to large residences associated with these; in New Mexico, the term was sometimes applied to courtyard-centered houses, although *rancho* and *placita* were more common terms.

Horno. Outdoor beehive-shaped adobe oven, introduced by the Spanish.

Jacal. Structure made of logs set vertically in a trench and chinked or plastered with adobe mud; palisaded construction.

Keres. One of several Puebloan language groups; spoken by the inhabitants of Acoma, Laguna, Santo Domingo, Cochiti, San Felipe, Santa Ana, and Zia.

Kiva. Pueblo word for ceremonial room.

Latillas (*latias*). Wood saplings laid on top of room beams (*vigas*) to support an earthen roof covering; see also *savinos* and *tablas.*

Laws of the Indies (*Recopilación de Leyes de los Reynos de las Indias*). Comprehensive set of laws concerning the Spanish colonization of their New World possessions, including town planning ordinances, first promulgated by Philip II in 1573, and the whole codified in 1681.

Mission. Historic: church/*convento* complex; contemporary: a Catholic church without a resident priest.

Molino. Mill; Spanish mills were distinguished by the horizontal millstone that turned counterclockwise.

Morada. Meeting house for the Penitentes; often with associated features of a *Via Crucis* (Way of the Cross) and *calvario*, representing Calvary, where Christ was crucified.

Nan-sipu. (Tewa) see *sipapu.*

Narthex. Entrance vestibule of a church.

Nave. Main body of a church in front of the altar reserved for the lay worshipper.

Nicho. Recessed or hollowed-out space in a wall used to hold a statue.

Ogee arch. Pointed arch, the sides of which are each formed with a reverse curve, slightly convex on top.

Optical model. A three-dimensional model that is created by overlapping and merging a pair of images (a stereopair) in a photogrammetric plotting instrument. In an optical model, structures and topography become three-dimensional visual forms that can be measured and drawn in detail. (Even in viewing simple nonphotogrammetric stereoprints, it is appropriate to refer to what is seen as an optical model, not a three-dimensional image.)

Oratorio. Private chapel.

Parapet. Low retaining wall at the edge of a roof.

Parroquia. Parish church.

Penitentes (also *Los Hermanos Penitentes* or *Cofradía de Nuestro Padre Jesus Nazareno*). Lay Roman Catholic brotherhood of Indo-Hispanic origin that observes certain rites related to the Passion of Christ and performs various mutual aid services, burials, and so forth; their meeting house is called a *morada.*

Photogrammetric plotting instrument. In stereophotogrammetry, the optical model contained in glass-plate stereopairs (or, more recently, in stable film diapositive pairs) is viewed, oriented, measured, and drawn in a complex analogue plotting instrument such as the Wild A7 Autograph or in analytical and digital plotting instruments.

Photogrammetric stereocamera. A camera used in stereophotogrammetry. The photogrammetric stereocamera consists of two wide-angle cameras mounted on an adjustable bar that take simultaneous photographs with parallel camera axes and with a base distance between cameras varying between 40 cm. and 3 m.

Photogrammetry. The science of measuring by photography. Photogrammetry employs mathematical and mechanical procedures to determine and to print in digital tabulation or to plot in orthographic projection the form, the dimensions, and the location of objects from perspective views of those objects recorded photographically.

Phototheodolite. A camera used in stereophotogrammetry. Phototheodolites are precise cameras mounted upon surveying instruments for the taking of successive photographs from widely separated camera stations. The surveying instrument, or theodolite, is used to determine the precise location of camera stations, to turn camera axes and inclination, and to mark camera horizon within the "object space" recorded in the photographs as a means of survey control.

Pintle door. Door that swings upon two pins (pintles) mortised into the lintel and sill.

Pithouse. Full or semisubterranean structure consisting of one or several excavated rooms (the "pit") covered by a superstructure of logs, branches, and mud.

Placita. Small courtyard or plaza surrounded (usually on all four sides) by a complex of buildings or rooms.

Plaza. Public square; the term can also refer to a fortified community or simply a settlement.

Plazuela. Courtyard-centered house, usually with room blocks on two or three sides and walls enclosing the remainder.

Portal(es). Long porch or portico with roof supported by vertical posts, facing either a plaza, *placita*, or *plazuela*.

Portería. Entrance to a mission church *convento*.

Po-wa-ha. Tewa for "life force."

Presidio. Permanent garrison of soldiers, often with formal fortifications.

Pretil. Parapet wall.

Pueblito. Small, Anasazi clustered-room ruin.

Pueblo. Originally a Spanish term referring to a "people," or "settlement," in New Mexico this word refers to either the ethnic groups or their settlements, including the structures; in English generally reserved for Pueblo Indians.

Raja. Split poles.

Ramada. Arbor or covered shade.

Reconquista. In 1692, twelve years after the Pueblos expelled the Spanish, who fled to El Paso, they returned to occupy the Pueblo area during what is known as the "reconquest."

Reredos. Screen or wall facing set behind an altar.

Retablo. Two-dimensional representation of a saint or saints.

Sacristy. Space where church vestments and sacred vessels are kept and where the clergy robe.

Sagrario. Tabernacle.

Sala. Parlor; room used for entertaining visitors.

Sanctuary. Space in a church where the altar is located.

Savinos. Full saplings, often of juniper (from the word *sabino*, cedar or juniper), used for *latillas*.

Scissors truss. Form of truss without a bottom chord; so-named because of secured pivot point.

Sipapu. Puebloan word meaning earth navel, "belly root," symbolic center of world, point of emergence (*nan-sipu* in Tewa).

Stereopairs. Pairs of glass-plate photographic images used in stereophotogrammetry.

Stereophotogrammetry. A photogrammetric procedure that employs a pair of photographic images, or "stereopairs," taken from two camera stations displaced from each other to duplicate and exaggerate the normal horizontal parallaxes and stereobase of binocular vision. When these images are inserted in a stereoscopic viewing instrument, the observer will see a three-dimensional "optical model" of the object photographed. Exaggeration of stereobase exaggerates depth and, therefore, the accuracy of measurement of depth and, therefore, the accuracy of height and width as well.

Survey control. In stereophotogrammetry, survey control consists of measurements within the picture area that, together with control points recorded upon the camera horizon, are used to orient the plates within the plotting instrument, to level the optical model, and to establish scale and determine accuracy through calculation of standard error. Survey control notes, together with the photographic stereopair, make up the basic photogrammetric record.

Tablas. Adzed boards of short lengths, often used for ceiling boards.

Terrón(es). Bricks of cut sod, usually taken from marshy areas (*ciénagas*).

Tewa. One of three subgroups of the Tanoan language spoken by Pueblo Indians in north-central New Mexico: *Tewa* (Nambé, Pojoaque, San Ildefonso, San Juan, Santa Clara, and Tesuque); *Tiwa* (Isleta, Picurís, Sandia, and Taos); and *Towa* (Jémez).

GLOSSARY OF ARCHITECTURAL TERMS

Tierra bendita. Blessed or sacred earth.

Torreón. Round tower, often two stories, used for defensive purposes.

Transept. Lateral arms of a cruciform church.

Transverse clerestory window. Window formed by the difference in elevation between the nave and the transept or altar area, used for the purpose of illuminating the reredos, or altar screen.

Vara. Standard Spanish Colonial linear measurement, approximately a yard (33 inches); x varas of land refers to the width of long lot fields.

Via Crucis. In Latin, "Way of the Cross"; see *calvario*.

Viga. Horizontal roof beam, often projecting beyond the exterior wall surface.

Visita. Church or congregation without a resident priest, served by a *visitador*.

Zaguán. Covered hallway joining two separate buildings or rooms; often used to refer to a large double-door entrance to a fortified plaza or *placita*.

Zapata. Wooden double corbel capital; a bolster.

SELECTED BIBLIOGRAPHY

This bibliography lists all of the references given in the text, and it also includes selected sources that might be of use in further study of the architectural history of New Mexico and the history of the Historic American Buildings Survey.

A comprehensive list of resources for research on the Historic American Buildings Survey may be found in *Historic American Buildings Survey/Historic American Engineering Record: Annotated Bibliography*, compiled and annotated by James C. Massey, Nancy B. Schwartz, and Shirley Maxwell (Washington, DC: HABS/HAER, National Park Service, U.S. Department of the Interior, 1992).

Bailey, Worth
1959 (see Historic American Buildings Survey, 1959)

Beaty, Laura
1983 "The Historic American Buildings Survey." *National Parks and Conservation Magazine.* (March/April): 1–7.

Borchers, Perry E.
1989 "Photogrammetric Recording of Communal Architecture in New Mexico." Draft version.

1988 "Photogrammetry and Related Documentary Techniques for the National Park Service," 27–29, *Trends, Publication of the Park Practice Program.* Volume 26, No. 1, Washington, DC.

1982 "Photogrammetric Recording of Historic Architecture and Archeological Sites of the Indian and Spanish Cultures in the Southwestern United States," 1.23–1.52, *Compendio de las ponencias, II congreso panamericano, fotogrammetría, fotointerpretación y geodesia.* México, DF.

1977 *Photogrammetric Recording of Cultural Resources.* Publication No. 186, Technical Preservation Services Division, Office of Archaeology and Historic Preservation. Washington, DC: NPS.

1976 "Photogrammetry of Primitive Architecture and Archaeological Ruins in New Mexico and Arizona," 11–18, *Sonderdruck aus Architectur-Photogrammetrie II, LandesKonservator Rheinland.* CIPA International Symposium on Architectural Photogrammetry, Bonn, Federal Republic of Germany, 1976.

1957 "The Measure of the Future and the Past." *AIA Journal* (American Institute of Architects) (October): 352–55.

Boucher, Jack E., and Marion D. Ross
1972   "Jacksonville in HABS Color." *Historic Preservation* 24 (April–June): 26–28.

Bruegmann, Robert
1983   "HABS at an Awkward Age: The 1960s and 1970s." In *Historic America: Buildings, Structures, and Sites*, 211–24. Washington, DC: Library of Congress.

Bunting, Bainbridge
1990a *Of Earth and Timbers Made: New Mexico Architecture*. Albuquerque: University of New Mexico Press, 1974; reprint.

1990b *Taos Adobes: Spanish Colonial and Territorial Architecture of the Taos Valley*. Taos: Fort Burgwin Research Center and the Museum of New Mexico Press, 1964; reprint, Albuquerque: University of New Mexico Press.

1983   *John Gaw Meem: Southwestern Architect*. Albuquerque: University of New Mexico Press, A School of American Research Book, 1966; reprint.

1977   Class lecture, University of New Mexico, Albuquerque, 25 August. In collection of Agnesa Reeve.

1976   *Early Architecture in New Mexico*. Albuquerque: University of New Mexico Press.

1970   "Take a Trip with NMA: An Architectural Guide to Northern New Mexico." *New Mexico Architecture* 12, nos. 9 and 10 (September/October): 13–51.

n.d.   Bainbridge Bunting Slide Library. Fine Arts Building, University of New Mexico, Albuquerque.

n.d.   Bainbridge Bunting Student Measured Drawing Collection. 16 volumes. John Gaw Meem Collection, Center for Southwest Research, Zimmerman Library, University of New Mexico, Albuquerque.

n.d.   *Historic American Buildings: A Collection of Measured Drawings*. 16 volumes. Fine Arts Library, University of New Mexico, Albuquerque.

Bunting, Bainbridge, Thomas R. Lyons, and Margil Lyons
1983   "Penitente Brotherhood Moradas and Their Architecture." In Marta Weigle, ed. *Hispanic Arts and Ethnohistory: New Papers Inspired by the Work of E. Boyd*. Santa Fe: Ancient City Press.

Bureau of Labor Statistics
1992   *CPI-U, All Urban Consumers*. Washington, DC.: U.S. Government Printing Office.

Burns, John A.
1991   "CAD-Photogrammetry: A Powerful Documentation Tool: HABS/HAER Measured Drawings and CAD-Photogrammetry." *CRM (Cultural Resources Management)* 14, no. 3: 4–5.

1990   "Architects and the Historic American Buildings Survey, 1933–1990." In *The Role of the Architect in Historic Preservation: Past, Present, and Future*, 26–36. Washington, DC: AIA Press.

1989   *Recording Historic Structures: Historic American Buildings Survey/Historic American Engineering Record*. Burns, John A., ed., and the staff of HABS/HAER, National Park Service, U.S. Dept. of Interior. Washington, DC: AIA Press.

Chauvenet, Beatrice
1985   *John Gaw Meem: Pioneer in Historic Preservation*. Santa Fe: Museum of New Mexico Press.

Connally, Ernest Allen
1961   "Preserving the American Tradition: The National Park Service Program for Students." *AIA Journal* (May): 56–60.

Drexler, Arthur, ed.
1977   "Beaux Arts Buildings in France and America." In *The Architecture of the Ecole des Beaux-Arts*, 417–94. New York: The Museum of Modern Art.

Gatford, William R.
1988   "Seventeenth-Century Mission Church Roof Beams: A Structural Analysis." In *In the Midst of a Loneliness: The Architectural History of the Salinas Missions: Salinas Pueblo Missions Historic Structures Report*, by James E. Ivey. Santa Fe: Division of History, Southwest Cultural Resources Center Professional Papers No. 15, Southwest Region, NPS, USDOI.

Gamble, Robert
1987   *The Alabama Catalog, Historic American Buildings Survey: A Guide to the Early Architecture of the State*. Tuscaloosa: University of Alabama Press.

Harrington, John Peabody
1916   "The Ethnogeography of the Tewa Indians." *Twenty-Ninth Annual Report of the Bureau of American Ethnology, 1907–1908*. Washington, DC: U.S. Government Printing Office.

Hayes, Alden C.

1974 *The Four Churches of Pecos.* Albuquerque: University of New Mexico Press.

Hayes, Alden C., J. N. Young, and A. H. Warren

1981 *Excavation of Mound 7, Gran Quivira National Monument, New Mexico.* Washington, DC: Publications in Archaeology No. 16.

Historic American Buildings Survey

1983 *Historic America: Buildings, Structures, and Sites Recorded in the Historic American Buildings Survey and the Historic American Engineering Record.* Peatross, C. Ford, ed., and Alicia Stamm, comp. Washington, DC: published for the Library of Congress by the U.S. Government Printing Office.

1981 *Historic American Buildings Survey: The Microfiche Edition.* Teaneck, NJ: Somerset House.

1974 *Historic American Buildings Survey. Microfilm and Electrostatic Prints of Measured Drawings in the Library of Congress.* Washington, DC: Library of Congress.

1970 *Recording Historic Buildings.* Harley J. McKee, comp. Washington, DC: Historic American Buildings Survey, Office of Archaeology and Historic Preservation, National Park Service, U.S. Department of the Interior, 1968; 2nd edition, expanded, Washington, DC: NPS, USDOI.

1968 *Recording Historic Buildings.* Harley J. McKee, comp. Washington, DC: Historic American Buildings Survey, Office of Archaeology and Historic Preservation, National Park Service, U.S. Department of the Interior, 1968; Washington, DC: NPS, USDOI.

1959 *Historic American Buildings Survey Catalog Supplement: Catalog of the Measured Drawings and Photographs of the Survey in the Library of Congress, Comprising Additions since March 1, 1941.* Worth Bailey, comp. and ed. Washington, DC: HABS, Division of Design and Construction, NPS, USDOI.

1941 *Historic American Buildings Survey: Catalog of the Measured Drawings and Photographs of the Survey in the Library of Congress, March 1, 1941.* Frederick D. Nichols, comp. and ed. Washington, DC: HABS, NPS, USDOI.

1938 *Historic American Buildings Survey: Catalog of the Measured Drawings and Photographs of the Survey in the Library of Congress, January 1, 1938.* John P. O'Neill, comp. and ed. Washington, DC, NPS, USDOI.

1935 *Historic American Buildings Survey Cattalogue of Completed Records, December 15, 1933– December 31, 1935* (mimeographed ed.). Washington, DC: HABS Branch of Plans and Design, NPS, USDOI.

1933 HABS Circular No. 1. December 12.

Hosmer, Charles B.

1981 *Preservation Comes of Age: From Williamsburg to the National Trust, 1926–1949.* Charlottesville: University Press of Virginia for The Preservation Press.

Ivey, James E.

1988 *In the Midst of a Loneliness: The Architectural History of the Salinas Missions: Salinas Pueblo Missions Historic Structures Report.* Santa Fe: Division of History, Southwest Cultural Resources Center Professional Papers No. 15, Southwest Region, NPS, USDOI.

Jackson, J. B.

1985 *The Essential Landscape.* Albuquerque: University of New Mexico Press.

Johnson-Nestor/Architects-Planners

ca. 1986 Survey of Catholic Mission Churches of New Mexico. Survey forms and final report on file, Office of Cultural Affairs, Historic Preservation Division, State of New Mexico, Santa Fe.

Kessell, John L.

1980 *The Missions of New Mexico Since 1776.* Albuquerque: University of New Mexico Press.

Kubler, George

1992 *The Religious Architecture of New Mexico in the Colonial Period and Since the American Occupation.* Colorado Springs: Taylor Museum of the Colorado Springs Fine Arts Center, 1940; reprint, Albuquerque: University of New Mexico Press.

Linley, John

1983 *The Georgia Catalog, Historic American Buildings Survey: A Guide to the Architecture of the State.* Athens: University of Georgia Press.

Markovitch, Nicholas C., Wolfgang F. E. Preiser, and Fred G. Sturm, eds.

1990 *Pueblo Style and Regional Architecture.* New York: Van Nostrand Reinhold.

Massey, James C.

1966 "Preservation Through Documentation." *Historic Preservation* 18, no. 4 (July/August): 148–51.

SELECTED BIBLIOGRAPHY

Massey, James C., and Bainbridge Bunting
1967–71 Correspondence. Office of Cultural Affairs, Historic Preservation Division, State of New Mexico, Santa Fe.

McKee, Harley J.
1968–70 (See Historic American Buildings Survey, 1968, 1970).

Meem, John Gaw
1933–39 NPS Correspondence files. John Gaw Meem Collection, Center for Southwest Research, Zimmerman Library, University of New Mexico.

Mindeleff, Victor
1891 "A Study of Pueblo Architecture in Tusayan and Cibola." *Eighth Annual Report of the Bureau of American Ethnology, 1886–1887.* Washington, DC: U.S. Government Printing Office.

Nabokov, Peter
1986 *Architecture of Acoma Pueblo: The 1934 Historic American Buildings Survey Project.* Santa Fe: Ancient City Press.

Nabokov, Peter, and Robert Easton
1989 *Native American Architecture.* New York: Oxford University Press.

Nichols, Frederick D.
1941 (see Historic American Buildings Survey, 1941).

Nordby, Larry V.
1984 "Modifications to Chetro Ketl and Talus Unit Drainage, Chaco Culture National Historic Park: Project Design and Recommendations" (internal report on file at the Southwest Cultural Resource Center, Santa Fe). Santa Fe, NPS, 1984.

O'Neill, John P.
1938 (see Historic American Buildings Survey, 1941).

Peatross, C. Ford
1983 (see Historic American Buildings Survey, 1983).

Peterson, Charles E.
1983 "The Historic American Buildings Survey: Its Beginnings." In *Historic America: Buildings, Structures, and Sites,* 7–22, Washington, DC: Library of Congress.

1981 "NPS — In and Out of Philadelphia." In *Philadelphia Preserved: Catalog of the Historic American Buildings Survey.* Philadelphia: Temple University Press, 1976; 2nd edition, xxi–xlvi.

1963 "Thirty Years of NPS." *AIA Journal* (American Institute of Architects) 40, no. 5: 83–85.

1958 "American Notes: NPS News." *Journal of the Society of Architectural Historians* 17, no.1: 30.

1957 "American Notes: The Historic American Buildings Survey Continued." *Journal of the Society of Architectural Historians* 16 no. 3 (October): 29–31.

1936 "Our National Archives of Historic Architecture." *The Octagon* 8, no. 7: 12–16.

1933 "The Historic American Buildings Survey Continued." *Journal of the Society of Architectural Historians* 16, no. 3 (October): 29–31.

Poppeliers, John C.
1968 *Preservation Through Documentation.* Washington, DC: Government Printing Office.

Poppeliers, John C., et al.
1973 *Documenting a Legacy.* Washington, DC: U.S. Government Printing Office for the Library of Congress.

Reeve, Agnesa Lufkin
1988 *From Hacienda to Bungalow: Northern New Mexican Houses, 1850–1912.* Albuquerque: University of New Mexico Press.

Rusinow, Irving
1942 *A Camera Report on El Cerrito, A Typical Spanish-American Community in New Mexico.* Miscellaneous Publication No. 479 Bureau of Agricultural Economics, U.S. Department of Agriculture. Washington, DC: U.S. Government Printing Office.

Scholes, F. V., and L. P. Bloom
1944–45 Friar Personnel and Mission Chronology, 1598–1629. Vols. I and II, *New Mexico Historical Review* 19 (October) and 20 (January).

Scully, Vincent
1972 *Pueblo: Mountain, Village, Dance.* New York: The Viking Press.

Smith, Carol C.
1983 *Fifty Years of the Historic American Buildings Survey.* Alexandria: NPS Foundation.

Spears, Beverly
1986 *American Adobes: Rural Houses of Northern New Mexico.* Albuquerque: University of New Mexico Press.

Stubbs, Stanley A.

1950   *Bird's-Eye View of the Pueblos.* Norman: University of Oklahoma Press.

Swentzell, Rina

1985   "An Understated Sacredness." *Mass: Journal of the School of Architecture and Planning,* University of New Mexico 3: 24–25.

1976   "An Architectural History of Santa Clara Pueblo." Master's thesis, University of New Mexico.

Tompkins, Sally Kress, et al.

1986   "A Tradition of Excellence in Documentation." *CRM Bulletin* (Cultural Resources Management) 9, no. 3: 1–24.

Treib, Marc

1986   "The Sanctuaries of New Mexico." Manuscript. Office of Cultural Affairs, Historic Preservation Division, State of New Mexico, Santa Fe.

United States General Accounting Office

1987   *Report to Congressional Requesters: Cultural Resources: Problems Protecting and Preserving Federal Archaeological Resources.* Washington, DC: U.S. General Accounting Office.

Vider, Elise

1991   "The Historic American Buildings Survey in Philadelphia, 1950–1966: Shaping Postwar Preservation." Master's thesis, historic preservation, University of Pennsylvania (unpublished).

Wilson, Chris

1981   "The Santa Fe, New Mexico Plaza." Master's thesis, art history, University of New Mexico (unpublished).

Wilson, Chris, and David Kammer

1992   *La Tierra Amarilla: Its History, Architecture, and Cultural Landscape.* Santa Fe: New Mexico Historic Preservation Division, 1989; reprint, Santa Fe: Museum of New Mexico Press.

Wilson, J. P.

1985   "Before the Pueblo Revolt: Population Trends, Apache Relations and Pueblo Abandonments in Seventeenth-Century New Mexico." In *Prehistory and History in the Southwest: Papers of the Archaeological Society of New Mexico, No. 11.* Albuquerque: Archaeological Society of New Mexico.

Woodbridge, Sally B.

1988   *California Architecture: Historic American Buildings Survey.* San Francisco: Chronicle Books.

MANUSCRIPT COLLECTIONS

American Institute of Architects Library and Archives, Washington, DC

National Archives, Record Group 515, Historic American Buildings Survey, Washington, DC

New Mexico Historic Preservation Division Library, Santa Fe, NM

John Gaw Meem Archive of Southwestern Architecture, Center for Southwest Research, University of New Mexico, Albuquerque, NM. Holdings include the John Gaw Meem and Bainbridge Bunting collections, both of which have files of NPS correspondence.